Grafters and Goo Goos

GRAFTERS AND GOO GOOS

CORRUPTION AND REFORM IN CHICAGO, 1833–2003

James L. Merriner

Southern Illinois University Press
Carbondale

Copyright © 2004 by the Board of Trustees,
Southern Illinois University
All rights reserved
Printed in the United States of America
07 06 05 04   4 3 2 1

Library of Congress Cataloging-in-Publication Data
Merriner, James L., 1947–
Grafters and Goo Goos : corruption and reform in Chicago, 1833–2003 / James L. Merriner.
        p. cm.
Includes bibliographical references and index.
    1. Chicago (Ill.)—Politics and government. 2. Political corruption—Illinois—Chicago—History. I. Title.
F548.3 .M47 2004
977.3′11-dc22   2003015588
ISBN 0-8093-2571-3 (alk. paper)

Printed on recycled paper. ♻

The paper used in this publication meets the minimum requirements of American National Standard for Information Sciences—Permanence of Paper for Printed Library Materials, ANSI Z39.48-1992. ∞

This one is for Milanne

The unexpress[ible] she.
—Orlando in Shakespeare's *As You Like It*

Contents

Illustrations

Preface

More than twenty years ago when I started reporting for a Chicago newspaper, I thought the city's reputation for lurid political wickedness was overblown, that it was an indelible but mythical hangover from the time of Al Capone. Surely, after decades of reform and the emergence of a well-educated, professional political class, public corruption—while it still made headlines—was the exception and not the rule.

With more experience, I marveled at the regular procession to jail of Chicago aldermen, judges, and state legislators, joined by Illinois governors and congressmen. My perspective was journalistic, and I wondered at how often media exposés of their wrongdoings demand little exertion in what is called investigative reporting. Not to disparage the Chicago media's tradition of aggressive investigations, but the task at times was like strolling through a field of rocks and choosing at random which ones to turn over. In fact, some turned over by themselves as prosecutors leaked damaging information about public officials to the news media.

At this point, protocol requires one to stipulate that most public officials are honest and dedicated and that the media sensationalize the relatively few felons. I readily so stipulate. But that does not dispose of the issue. How is it that so many Chicago-area politicians are crooks, even after more than a century of good-government reform campaigns, with reformers among the city's most lauded citizens? Is this experience peculiar to Chicago, or does the city's history have something to say to the nation as a whole?

While doing research for a biography of former U.S. House Ways and Means Committee chairman Daniel D. Rostenkowski of Chicago, I was surprised to find no general history of Chicago corruption and reform. There are many biographies of Al Capone, Richard J. Daley, and other figures, along with studies of various reform and crime-fighting movements—but no overview of the entire dynamic. This omission is perplexing because Chicago's mythology of constant crookedness easily matches or surpasses that of the Barbary Coast era in San Francisco, Tammany Hall in New York City, or the Pendergast machine in Kansas City (to name just three), or of the historically corrupt state governments of Illinois, Maryland, Massachusetts, Missouri, and Texas (to name just five).

Further research turned up many analyses of the Progressive reform movement of a century ago and of big-city political bossism. Yet both of those phenomena are mostly gone with the wind. Thus the need for this book, aimed both at general readers and political, history, and urban studies specialists, seemed clear.

The topic is current because America is confused about what exactly constitutes public corruption nowadays. With local, state, and federal governments regulating and subsidizing nearly everything, the line between legal and illegal manipulations of the system is blurred. For example, when Dan Rostenkowski pleaded guilty to the misuse of public and campaign funds in 1995, his defenders saw him as the victim of overzealous prosecutors and media scandalmongers who condemned him for activities that used to be legal—indeed, almost encouraged. The indictment and plea left many unconvinced that Rostenkowski was crooked.

Such a viewpoint suggests another question about Chicago: despite its delightfully colorful history, is the city really all that corrupt? Perhaps mythology overtakes reality. The scanty comparative data are suggestive but inconclusive. An academic survey of newspaper articles stated that the eastern north-central region, which includes Chicago, compiled 120 public corruption cases from 1970 to 1976. The nearest competitor, the south Atlantic region, had fifty-eight. Similarly, a 1977 study by the Justice Department showed that the northern district of Illinois led the country with 135 convictions of public officials in the previous seven years, compared with 101 in New York City and sixty-six in New Jersey. By themselves, these figures prove nothing. They might reflect exceptionally ambitious prosecutors in Chicago or any of a number of other factors.

Still, when I described this book project to colleagues and friends, the response was almost always a joke to the effect that it would take multiple volumes. Chicago's reputation for corruption is, if nothing else, a basis of local and even national folklore and humor. Indeed, the history is so rich that one of the difficulties in writing this book was deciding what to leave out. At the least, the names of many indicted public officials have been omitted as redundant if not tiresome.

Any study of reform and corruption is problematic in that *corruption* is not a specific crime. Likewise, *reform* is a slippery term lacking a consensual definition. One person's reform is to another a deformity of the social and political system, as the example of Prohibition more than amply demonstrates.

Corruption is defined herein as the use of improper political influence for private gain. Reform is the effort to prevent that activity.

My viewpoint is that the politics of corruption and reform were outgrowths of class, ethnic, and religious conflicts. The real story lies less in the dramatic clashes between bosses and reformers than in the ways their cultural backgrounds drove their agendas. If there is a single theme, it is that politicians tended to abuse their power while reformers tended to abuse their own, all while pursuing their own conceptions of self-interest as well as of the common good.

The organization of such a narrative sprawl might daunt better writers than I. The first question was whether to structure the book thematically or chronologically. Chronology won out for reasons of simplicity. Second, I did not want to compile a mere summary of previous works but to perform original research. Toward that end I reviewed the internal history of reform groups in neglected manuscript collections in various depositories. These documents revealed the ambiguities of reform and nominated few people for sainthood.

The larger dilemma was whether to concentrate on personalities or institutions, specific incidents or societal trends. The upshot was a compromise that examines major reformers and politicians against a backdrop of social history—a blend of anecdotes and analysis. To whatever extent that the blend succeeds, this book does not claim to be more than a one-volume overview of a very big story.

A few more words about what this book is not. It is not a history of Chicago crime and vice, except insofar as those activities were abetted by the political system. Readers who desire accounts of the city's many episodes of high criminal melodrama are invited to peruse a shelf of books offering them.

Nor is this a history of the Chicago political machine. The city's municipal politics was chaotically factional during its first century, and a Chicago machine worthy of the name did not emerge until 1931, quite late in the national urban experience. Chicago invented the skyscraper, the zipper, mail-order shopping, the "smoke-filled room," the Hostess Twinkie, and modern organized crime, but it did not invent the political machine.

Instead, from Chicago's origins in the 1830s, the city welcomed businessmen and politicians who wished to get rich. They were swiftly followed by reformers who strived to clean up the attendant corruption. The tension between these groups writes a large chapter in the American experiment of democratic self-government. *Grafters and Goo Goos* endeavors to explore this tension and draw some conclusions.

Three arenas of reform and resistance to it are identified: structural reform of the political system to promote honesty and efficiency, social reform to provide justice to the lower classes, and moral reform to combat vice. The three strands are historically braided, although the braid often frays. Yet the persistence of the braid, even as it winds and unwinds, is a constant.

This book seeks to identify the constants in the fight between corruption and reform through seventeen decades of Chicago history, amid a welter of changing social circumstances and customs—decades of alternating war and peace, depression and prosperity. In the matter of corruption and reform, the constants might be stronger than the variables. The players, rules, and scorekeepers change, but not the essential game.

Reformers and politicians animated and defined each other by their opposition, an us-against-them hardening of attitudes. The scorn with which politicians beheld reformers is suggested by the local epithet *goo goos,* short for good-government types. (A glossary of Chicago political terms is appended to the text.) Nevertheless, reform and corruption were curiously interdependent. A reciprocal relationship developed between reformers and corrupt politicians who were sometimes, in their own way, equally public-spirited. The politics of corruption and the politics of reform somewhere merged into a conjoined politics of interdependency. One of my intentions was to honor rare displays of moral courage, but the story is not a simple one of heroes and villains.

Finally, this book is written as a popular history, not an academic study. I nonetheless tried to gain a layman's understanding of the contributions of social science in this field and bring them to bear on the narrative. Some commentary about academic anatomies of corruption and reform is offered in the conclusion.

Many books tell that corruption and reform occurred. I wished to explore how they were *lived.* If readers are impelled to think anew about the constant problem of public corruption, then I will have realized my ambition.

Acknowledgments

Authors writing acknowledgments must decide whether to try to thank everyone in sight or just to name the principal helpers. Either way, they risk leaving someone out. My task is complicated by the fact that many informants for this book overlapped those for my three other books about politics and history. Sorting out these sources is a project that defeats me.

First, many thanks to three political experts who reviewed a draft of this manuscript for Southern Illinois University Press. They saved me from more than a few bonehead blunders and even tried to rescue me, to the extent anyone can, from my worst writing habit of breezy generalizing. Richard C. Lindberg, the foremost expert on the history of Chicago police and crime, read a later version of the manuscript, found some more mistakes, and offered valuable suggestions. My brother, Charles M. Merriner, brought a lawyer's perspective to this work and corrected or clarified many legal points for me.

If this book makes a contribution to history, these reviewers deserve much of the credit. Any remaining errors of fact or interpretation are mine alone.

Professors Paul M. Green of Roosevelt University and Melvin G. Holli of the University of Illinois at Chicago were not directly involved in this project. Even so, their expertise and cheery willingness to help have guided me along the road for many years.

More directly, thanks go to public affairs consultants David Axelrod, Jay D. Doherty, Larry P. Horist, Norton Kay, Paul Lis, Tom Roeser, Don Rose, and Thom Serafin. Also, Dick Simpson, a political scientist and the personification of "lakefront reformer," was a fund of knowledge. Furthermore, I thank officers and staffers of the Better Government Association, Chicago Crime Commission, City Club of Chicago, and the Union League Club; former U.S. attorney Scott Lassar and other U.S. attorneys in Chicago and Washington, D.C., who might prefer to be unnamed;

Illinois Issues editor Peggy Boyer Long; and present and former reporters and editors of the *Chicago Sun-Times* and *Chicago Tribune*. This last group includes especially Mark Brown, Mary Dedinsky, Bernard Judge, Ray Long, Nancy Moffett, Steve Neal, Chuck Neubauer, Charles Nicodemus, Suzy Schultz, Fran Spielman, Lynn Sweet, Basil Talbott Jr., and Charles N. Wheeler III; also, the late Harry Golden Jr., Hugh Hough, Charles "Chip" or "The Penguin" Magnus, M. W. Newman, Art Petacque, Mike Royko, and Jerome H. Watson.

I have spent much of my career writing criticism of politicians but actually like most of them. They can charm you out of your lunch money: that is how they get elected. They have keen insights into human nature, often sharper than those of reformers or journalists. Of the hundreds of politicians I have known, I salute two deceased men, politicians in the best sense of the word: John J. Hoellen and James C. Kirie. Hoellen, a Republican reformer, died in 1999 at eighty-four. When he first ran for alderman in 1947, he was shot at, but the shotgun misfired and he survived. Kirie, the longtime Leyden Township Democratic committeeman, died in 2000 at eighty-nine. He testified before a U.S. Senate rackets committee in the 1950s and for his trouble saw his home and a restaurant he owned bombed. Both men treated me with courtesy and candor. I miss our laughing talks about the old days when politics was fun, before it was totally taken over by media technicians.

When Archie Motley retired as chief of the archives and manuscripts division of the Chicago Historical Society, I worried that nobody could write a worthwhile book about Chicago without his amazing expertise. Many times, opening dusty boxes of historical society collections, I wanted to seek him out. However, current staffers of the society were able, diligent, and helpful. In the same way, librarians—underpaid public servants—at the Harold Washington Central Public Library in Chicago, the Newberry Library, Northwestern University, the University of Chicago, the University of Illinois at its Chicago, Champaign-Urbana, and Springfield branches, and the Oak Park, Illinois, public library were efficient and helpful.

The director of Southern Illinois University Press, John F. Stetter, saw promise in this project from the start. Editors and other staffers of the press were consistently professional and cordial.

Finally, a tip of the hat to friends and family members who provided moral support. I hope to repay the favors somehow, someday.

Grafters and Goo Goos

INTRODUCTION

By the end of the twentieth century, Lawrence S. Bloom was just about the last of his breed. He was an upper-middle-class professional, nominally a Democrat but independent of the party's organization, a moral entrepreneur, a proud reformer who tilted against windmills in a quest for honesty, efficiency, and rationality in local government. Also, he was a crook.

How strenuously, how earnestly had Chicago reformers fought for honesty, efficiency, and rationality since 1833. Those goals implicitly were placed on ballots as early as the "People's Ticket" of 1869. After so much history, after the creation of the welfare state, reform as personified by Bloom, although still honored, had become antique and quaint. The celebrated "lakefront liberals" of the 1960s and 1970s had moved on to serve as consultants and campaign contributors to such as President Bill Clinton and Mayor Richard M. Daley or as isolated academics and writers or outright cranks. Politics was peopled by a new class of professionals whose esteem for traditional, good-government reformist meddlers was kept under control. Still, Bloom presented himself as traditionally, morally meddlesome.

In his latter-day endeavors, Bloom stood on the shoulders of a historical parade of Chicago reformers. Mayors Joseph Medill (who served from 1871 to 1873), Edward F. Dunne (1905–7), William Dever (1923–27), Martin Kennelly (1947–55), Jane M. Byrne (1979–83), and Harold Washington (1983–87) had done their part, however inadequately, to cleanse the city of corruption. Bloom also rode on the backs of civic reform groups, such as the Citizens' Association (founded in 1874), Civic Federation (1894), Municipal Voters' League (1896), City Club (1903), Chicago Crime Commission (1919), Better Government Association (1923), and others.

Their glory days were mostly long past. For all the good work of these people and institutions, Chicago remained corrupt. Even so, reformers could count on Larry Bloom to rise on the floor of the city council in the old, ugly gray fortress of the city-county building at LaSalle and Randolph streets to denounce boodle in the city budget.

Mayors under whom he served indulgently refrained from the Richard J. Daley technique of cutting the electricity to an enemy alderman's microphone. Let Bloom spout off—what did it matter? Mayor Richard M. Daley (the son of Richard J.) might smile patronizingly and leave the dais to confer with machine aldermen in the anteroom of the council chambers, sometimes in the adjoining men's room, to cut deals. To cut deals: to ensure that everybody gets something in the sweetness of compromise, the accommodation of competing interests, just as in a marriage. The resolution of these interests often was private, not democratic, just as it had been since Chicago's founding.

Chicago newspapers applauded Bloom for his reformist posture even as the same press consistently supported the politicians who brushed the coats of the status quo. During the regency of Richard J. Daley (1955–76), a small cadre of reform aldermen fought but almost never bested him. Bloom was not elected to the city council until 1979, after Daley's death. After reform mayor Harold Washington died in 1987, Bloom might well have felt sometimes alone and abandoned in the reform movement.

Reformers won many battles, but the war never ends. In 1999, two Chicago aldermen went to jail for financial misdeeds that were typically and depressingly petty. Twenty-seven incumbent or former aldermen had been indicted for official corruption within twenty-seven years. A felony conviction denies aldermen their pensions, a circumstance that much bothers them. An alderman (never indicted) backed a bill in 1999 to lower the aldermanic retirement age from sixty to fifty-five, explaining, "If you can survive 20 years without going to jail, then you need a pension and you should have it."[1]

Bloom was the "last" reform politician in the sense that he was popularly regarded as an unstained white hat. Nearly everybody else wore gray or black hats. Some ward political operations still were underwritten by vice rake-offs in a tradition dating to the 1830s. Many Chicagoans were dismayed by, yet took a furtive pride in, the city's history of insouciance toward public corruption. It was a staple of national folklore and humor.

Bloom was an heir of the intellectual and reformist legacy of the Hyde Park precincts of the University of Chicago on the city's South Side. The area, annexed to Chicago in 1889 and host of the world's fair in 1893, never really coupled with the city's politics. The Village of Hyde, with no officers, revenues, debt, or personnel, existed as an official governmental entity for decades after the annexation. The official designation of municipality provided continuing opportunities for boodle. In like manner, shells of Cook County township school offices endured into 2003.

Much of Hyde Park's history of reform was underwritten by WASP capitalists. John D. Rockefeller endowed the university in 1891. The intellectual community there produced reform aldermen Charles and Robert Merriam, Paul Douglas, and Leon Despres. There once was a notoriously crooked North Side alderman named Paddy Bauler, forever remembered for his 1955 statement, "Chicago ain't ready for reform." When Hyde Park's Douglas, fifty-one years old, resigned his aldermanic seat during World War II to volunteer for the marines as a private, Bauler hollered, "Good riddance to bad rubbish!"[2] Forty-seven years later, machine aldermen regarded Larry Bloom as bad rubbish. As a Jew fighting Catholic mayors supported by Protestant money, Bloom in his own person exemplified the city's history of religious, ethnic, and class conflicts and accommodations.

Bloom, born in 1943, took his bachelor's and law degrees from the University of Chicago. In 1979 he was elected Fifth Ward alderman to succeed Despres, who retired. Council district remapping after the 1980 census, which federal courts later ruled had discriminated illegally against minorities, split Hyde Park so that the Fifth Ward was three-quarters black. This change was an obvious machine ploy to defeat Bloom. He faced six black challengers in 1983, yet won 64 percent of the vote. Bloom joined Mayor Harold Washington's minority of twenty-one reformist aldermen.

Aldermen are less powerful than their party's ward committeemen unless they are aldermen and committeemen at once in a tradition more than a century old. Bloom's Fifth Ward Democratic committeeman in 1979 was—an odd occupation for a committeeman—a University of Chicago research chemist, Alan M. Dobry. Dobry was a veteran of the Independent Voters of Illinois-Independent Precinct Organization, a goo-goo amalgam dating to the 1940s. The IVI-IPO tore itself up with internal arguments and descended into irrelevancy in the 1980s. Anyway, Dobry advocated ending patronage, the machine's slating of candidates, and its funding of primary election favorites.

In 1984, after failing to unseat Bloom in 1983, the machine did not deign to field an opponent against Dobry for committeeman. This apparent forfeit actually was an insult, underlining Dobry's and Bloom's marginalization. The machine paid little mind to Hyde Park intellectuals—the Merriams, Douglas, Despres, Dobry, Bloom.

Bloom was an unusual reformer in that he was ambitious for high political office. Like many of his reformist ancestors, though, he was not unduly modest. He ran unsuccessfully for Cook County state's attorney, city treasurer, and mayor. As an alderman, he was an acerbic and maverick self-proclaimed conscience of the city council. "Which trucking firm got 2 percent of the contract? And it better not end with a vowel," he once blurted on the council floor about an alleged boodle.[3] Italian Americans demanded, and got, an apology.

On 8 July 1997, Bloom was indicted on fourteen counts of taking sixteen thousand dollars in bribes, misusing city funds, and helping a legal client evade $283,000 in property taxes. The charges expressed typical Chicago grittiness. Bloom allegedly had deployed city workers to clean up waste from a rock-crushing operation illegally dumped by a private contractor. Bloom was one of eighteen people, including six incumbent or former aldermen, convicted in Operation Silver Shovel. It was a federal sting using a villainous mole and more than eleven hundred secretly taped recordings, both audio and video. The feds had grown inordinately fond of moles and hidden technology. Over decades, the concept of reform had journeyed from general social uplift to a branch of law enforcement, featuring occasional prosecutorial excesses and the steady production of mass-mediated scandals.

The Operation Silver Shovel mole, Robert Christopher, paid a visit to Bloom. The scene would seem to have been invented by a heavy-handed satirist, but satirists are challenged to keep up with Chicago corruption. Here was Christopher, the low-life con man, trying to con Bloom, the Hyde Park intellectual. Bloom was no political naïf, newly arrived in office from mean streets and lusting after silk suits and Italian shoes, but an experienced and successful lawyer. Yet Bloom agreed to help Christopher obtain city waste-dumping contracts. In time the pile of construction debris became five stories high on an entire city block and required two years and $5 million to remove. The debris would not have been there but for the federal sting.

The U.S. attorney in Chicago, Scott R. Lassar, was sensitive to criticism that he targeted African American and Hispanic aldermen and threw in merely for public relations purposes a white liberal, Bloom. Like the indicted blacks and Hispanics, cynics noted, Bloom happened to be a foe of Mayor Richard M. Daley. If Daley indeed was superintending the prosecutions of his opponents (for which there is no evidence), it would have been in keeping with Chicago mayoral history. Chicago, Cook County, and even federal prosecutors frequently have been faulted for not striking at the heart of corruption. Moreover, some critics hold that corruption cannot be prosecuted away, however vigorous the prosecutors.

Corruption in our democracy seems to be institutional, systemic, whatever number of small fish are ushered to jail by the Justice Department or local prosecutors. Bloom was the biggest fish netted in Operation Silver Shovel.

In an interview with the author, former U.S. attorney Lassar insisted he had not singled out minorities or Bloom. Waste dumping required vacant lots, and Lassar maintained that he could not help it that such lots were concentrated in poor areas represented by members of minorities. As for Bloom, Lassar said he was shocked while listening to one of the mole's secret tapes. "Practically the first word out of [Bloom's] mouth was his sense of disappointment that he was not getting his own like [prominent white machine aldermen.]"[4]

Other sources disclosed that the mole told Bloom his bribes would be disguised as campaign contributions, some from dead persons, to which Bloom quipped, "The more dead the better." This after wise commentators had pronounced the machine dead, despite the ongoing potency of the Chicago phrase, "getting your own." Newspaper columnist Mike Royko, perhaps the wisest commentator, had suggested decades earlier that the city's official motto, *Urbs in Hortis* (city in a garden) should be replaced with *Ubi est Mea?* (where's mine?).

Bloom's response to the indictment was typical. He complained that he "was mugged, not by a petty thief or street tough, but by agents of my own government."[5] Also customary was editorial hand-wringing: How could a reformer do this? Why do so many aldermen keep getting indicted? Will they never learn? Haven't modern ethics laws and regulations sufficed? Is Chicago singularly cursed?

Typically as well, Bloom had to sell his house and move into an apartment to meet his legal defense bills. On 5 December 1998, he pleaded guilty to a single count of misreporting on tax forms a bribe of six thousand dollars. As part of the deal, he signed an addendum admitting he had actually pocketed fourteen thousand dollars (not the sixteen thousand cited in the indictment). The sentencing judge was moved to quote F. Scott Fitzgerald: "Show me a hero and I'll write you a tragedy."[6]

The goo-goo community was crestfallen. Leon Despres, one of Chicago's quasi-official grand old men of reform, said, "I really had confidence in him and I believed him when he told me to keep my mind open." Bloom's rabbi said, "He is not an evil man but maybe a foolish man, trusting and sometimes careless."[7] Nearly identical words had been voiced by the priest of St. Stanislaus Kostka Roman Catholic Church, across the street from the Northwest Side home of U.S. Representative Dan Rostenkowski, when that politician was indicted in 1994. BLOOM JOINS LONG, SAD LIST, the *Chicago Tribune* headlined, with a subhead reading, "Larry Bloom, Hyde Park liberal and independent voice on the City Council for 16 years, pleads guilty to tax fraud and enters the local hall of shame."[8]

Bloom served six months in federal prison in 1999 at a "Club Fed" in Oxford, Wisconsin. There he would pass former Chicago public officials in the halls (three other aldermen, a water reclamation commissioner, and a state representative), whereupon they jokingly cried out, "quorum call!" Jailed Chicago political crooks tend to retain a sense of humor. Rostenkowski, on the lecture circuit, tells audiences about his "Oxford education." Bloom, upon his release, called Oxford "an absurd place. Most of the people there may have committed crimes, but the harm being done to their families because of their absence far outweighs any benefit to society."[9] This was another common comment from Chicago politicians put behind bars.

In fairness, questions about what constitutes public corruption and how to punish it remain open. A case can be made that the government really did "mug" Bloom. The methods of reformers, especially reformers in the cloak of prosecutors, tend toward impurity, much as those of corrupt politicians do.

On 2 January 2000, Bloom published an apologia in the *Chicago Tribune,* POLITICAL CORRUPTION CAN BEGIN AT HOME. Bloom cogitated (with the author's interpolations):

> But is it any wonder that politicians occasionally make the choices that benefit themselves when we routinely make political choices that benefit only ourselves without considering the impact on others? [Or: How dare you voters judge me?] . . . Yes, power corrupts. But so do selfishness and complacency. . . . I admit that I may have been blinded to the implications of giving minor political assistance to a client and [campaign] contributor [the mole Robert Christopher] by the fact that it happens so regularly on all levels of government. [Or: Fourteen thousand dollars in bribes is small-time corruption—true enough, in point of fact.] . . . Personally, I will be satisfied if the public failure of hokey political corruption stings, locally and nationally, deters future prosecutors from such escapades. If there is evidence of political corruption, by all means investigate it and prosecute to the fullest extension of the law. But it cheapens our sense of justice, and is an abuse of power, when prosecutors are

seen to be creating the opportunities for political crime rather than tracking those crimes down where they actually may be occurring in seats of power. [Or: Why didn't the U.S. attorney go after bigger fish than I?] . . . Behind the formal organization of government is the underlying principle that we cannot expect more from government than we are willing to give. We can demand that those in positions of power set an example. But we should also be honest enough to recognize that the attitudes of the governors will quite likely reflect the behavior of the governed. [Or: Guilt is collective, not mine personally.]

This passage, with its kitchen-blender puree of self-justification and sharp political and moral commentary, is difficult to analyze. Apart from posing the question of Bloom's degree of venality, it summarizes the conundrums of corruption and reform in Chicago. Bloom abused his powers as a public official, but prosecutors may well have transgressed their own ethics. Aside from the issue of possible (although not, courts mostly ruled, legally actual) entrapment into crimes, Silver Shovel visited real harm on neighborhoods with its waste dumps.

The public, reformers, and prosecutors were not sure about what defines public corruption. Nor is there certainty about what "the behavior of the governed" communicates about their expectations of elected officials. Nor is it clear whether Bloom was not, on balance, a real reformer or whether his enemies really were corrupt. All that can be said for sure is that yet another Chicago politician was imprisoned for violating the normative standards of his time. Many other local politicians likewise entered jail while expressing mystification over their prosecution.

Chicago's first reformer, the Reverend Jeremiah Porter, sailed into town in 1833 on fire to remove vice and sin. He was an intolerant Protestant. Bloom was a tolerant Jew. Yet somewhere there might be a nexus between the first reformer, Porter, and the last, Bloom, some membrane between the vexing interdependency of corruption and reform. The following narrative seeks to find it. Through the intervening years, the trio of public money, private money, and vice often linked arms and strolled up neighborhood streets to city hall. However strewn the streets were with rubble and potholes, traps and menaces, the three usually found their way and were greeted warmly. Reformers for the trio of structural governmental change, social justice, and moral uplift looked on with disapproval and exchanged expressions of self-regard.

1

Frontier, Finances, and Fire

1833–71

If the Angel Gabriel came to Chicago, he would surely lose his character within a week.

—Chicago evangelist Dwight L. Moody

Chicago's first reformer appeared three months before the place was even incorporated as a town. A boat carrying the Reverend Jeremiah Porter moored at the mouth of the Chicago River on 11 May 1833. He saw "a wide, wet prairie, as far as the eye could reach, on a muddy river winding south over a sand-bar to the Lake with a few scattered dwellings."[1] The settlement had forty-seven houses and about three hundred people.

Porter (1804–93) was a Yankee Presbyterian evangelist whose venture into the frontier must have been as daring for its time as an astronaut's launch into space. Born in Hadley, Massachusetts, to an old New England family, Porter was ordained a pastor at Princeton Theological Seminary in New Jersey. There he answered a call to preach at Sault Ste. Marie in the Upper Peninsula of Michigan. So he took a stage to Albany, New York, a flatboat on the Erie Canal to Buffalo, a steamer to Cleveland and Detroit, and then a schooner to Mackinac, Michigan.

On deck during his voyage, Porter "found a man on his way to Chicago, and heard from him that the United States Government was about to build a light-house there, and he was going to open a boarding-house, and believed it—Chicago—would become a fine place for business."[2] That unidentified shipmate of Porter was a prophet.

Fur agents at Sault Ste. Marie sent a canoe paddled by Native Americans to fetch Porter from Mackinac, but it had to return in a snowstorm. Soon came three French voyageurs and a black man in a small bark canoe. After three days and nights of paddling across Lake Huron and up the St. Mary's River, Porter had to break ice on shore to land the boat at Sault Ste. Marie.

Upon taking his first pulpit, the clergyman persuaded town residents and Fort Brady soldiers to forgo the sins of dancing and drinking. Emboldened by this success, he accompanied the Fort Brady garrison when it was dispatched to relieve troops at Fort Dearborn in Chicago. At the time, the entire south bank of the main branch of the Chicago River was reserved for the U.S. military as a redoubt for Indian wars.

On their journey to Chicago along the western shore of Lake Michigan, Porter's party saw no human habitation except for a fur post at Milwaukee. Thus he was disappointed in fulfilling an assignment from church superiors in New England to find settlements of whites or Native Americans ripe for missionary visits.

After rough winds and seasickness kept Porter on board for a day at Chicago, he rowed upriver to meet local businessmen at a tavern on shore at Goose Island. The village had not been shepherded by clergy except for a few itinerant Baptist and French Jesuit missionaries and Methodist country circuit riders.

Even at that early date, the cultures of Jesuits and Protestants clashed. The first Catholic priest permanently assigned to Chicago, John M. I. St. Cyr, arrived just ten days before Porter. Later, Porter openly spoke about kneeling outside St. Cyr's church late at night to pray that it not prosper.

An old woodcut shows Porter looking as smug as any anticlerical cartoonist might wish. Behind round frameless spectacles, his eyes had the hint of a twinkle. Thin lips curved at the corners in a wraith of a smile, an expression conveying the benevolence of a Christian pastor. It also suggested the self-satisfaction of bourgeois respectability that many others found annoying. A fashionable beard in the shape of a shovel blade adorned his chin, while the upper lip was clean-shaven. Porter was fully a man of his times, as were his enemies.

He organized the first permanent Protestant church and, for his pre-
miere sermon, took a text from John 6:8–9: "One of his disciples, Andrew, Simon Peter's brother, saith unto him, 'There is a lad here, which
hath five barley loaves, and two small fishes: but what are they among so
many?'" Porter was frustrated, for he inscribed in his journal that evening,
"The first dreadful spectacle that met my eyes on going to church was a
group of Indians sitting on the ground before a miserable French dram
house, playing cards, and as many trifling white men standing around to
witness the game."[3]

When obstacles arose to building a new church on a nearly inacces-
sible mud hole at Clark and Lake streets, now a north node of the Loop,
Porter's flock did not turn the other cheek. Land-grabbers started nailing
up a store on the Lake Street frontage of a lot that the parishioners had
bought. Under darkness of night, members of the congregation yoked
oxen to chains and pulled down the trespassing structure. Dragging it two
hundred yards away, they demolished it with hammers, axes, and saws.
This was not the last time that reformers employed dubious means. The
First Presbyterian Church, thirty by forty feet and built for six hundred
dollars, was dedicated on 4 January 1834 in weather recorded at twenty-
nine degrees below zero—wintry conditions that figuratively greeted many
later reformers.

By October, Porter called a town meeting, which mobilized a committee of nine to eliminate gambling in that wide-open frontier outpost. Ever
after, reformers were prone to setting up enumerated committees to pass
judgment and high-minded resolutions while deliberating at anguished
length over proper ends and means. "But what are they among so many?"
Porter saw no miracle of loaves and fishes or even a town ordinance against
gambling. Still, the next summer, he declaimed a "season of prayer" that
yielded vows of conversion from young men, the destruction of two "gam-
bling-nests," and the jailing of two gambling operators. The reverend
would be dismayed to learn that Illinois now avidly encourages gambling
in a state lottery and on franchised floating casinos.

Chicago's first social and moral reformer was driven by religious conviction. Although many later reformers were wholly secular, the religious

impulse to clean up government and society propelled much of the city's history. Religious people walked all three avenues of reform—moral, social, political—with degrees of zeal that varied over time. The results when ecclesiastical and secular reform forces combined often were unsatisfactory to both sides, but in sum, religious history is a major stream of the corruption-and-reform current.

Porter's career followed America's first two Great Awakenings. Like the tides of corruption and reform, these events had no distinct beginning or end, no formal canon of beliefs, no easily quantified data. Yet they undeniably happened. Their sectarian, doctrinal disputes fill many volumes.[4] The first Awakening, roughly 1734–40, saw frontier settlers writhe in the ecstasy of being saved. Visibly ecstatic conversion experiences are common across times and cultures. However, this Awakening was a specifically American, Protestant, and counter-Enlightenment rebellion against the staid, established urban eastern churches. It split the Protestant hierarchy over questions of its seemliness, authenticity, and Biblical sanction. At the same time, it laid the bedrock for a later revolt against authority in the form of the anticolonialism of the American Revolution.

The second Awakening occurred from the 1790s to about 1820 and likewise included frenzied enthusiasms whipped up by itinerant evangelists in reaction against scientific rationalism. The second Awakening differed from the first in that it galvanized a specific political agenda, mainly the abolition of slavery—a sin against both God and a proper worldly state—along with the suppression of drinking, gambling, and disallowed sex. When Porter revisited Chicago to give a speech to the historical society in 1859, he implored his audience to stand fast against slavery and alcohol. Reformers were dismayed and puzzled that Christian citizens tolerated and even fomented so much wickedness. They felt driven to challenge corrupt authority. Authority usually rose to the challenge.

Just two days after Porter's first Chicago sermon, St. Cyr performed the town's first Catholic baptism. J. Baptiste Beaubien, an original settler who ran a fur trading post, and his family (twenty-three children by two wives) were Catholics. This church affiliation inspired Porter's flock to pray for their souls. Porter conducted the first Presbyterian communion on 7

July 1833. On 19 October, the first Baptist church was organized by the Reverend Allen B. Freeman.

As early as August 1835, Protestant clergy combined to form the Chicago Bible Society. By 1851 there were enough Jews in Chicago to found the first synagogue. The home Catholic church of Chicago Poles, St. Stanislaus Kostka, was founded in 1867 and that of the Chicago Irish, the Church of the Nativity, in 1868. These dates are not cited for the sake of historical punctilio. Religious antagonisms were a wellspring of Chicago history.

However strenuous his labors against gambling, Porter left Chicago in September 1835 for a pastorate in the farm country of Peoria, Illinois, with a Chicago bride he had married in Yankee territory, Rochester, New York. Although he failed in Chicago, Porter certainly had courage and faith. Not to place too heavy a burden of historical anticipation on Porter, but he personified a nativist romanticism for the virtuous country over the evil city and an antidemocratic impulse that despised the recreations favored by the urban working class. Such viewpoints characterized some of Porter's later epigones who lacked his moral stamina. Porter's long career, including distinguished service in frontier Texas and the Civil War, also posed the still vexing problem of the proper role of a democratic state in upholding personal virtue and social order.

The advent of Chicago's first crooked politician, in contrast to Porter's reformist priority, is undocumented and open to interpretation. Perhaps some members of the town's first elected board of five trustees in 1833 were corrupt. That is, they were land speculators who did not operate entirely aboveboard. They were mostly bereft of explicit regulations of the kind forever favored by reformers in the belief that written restrictions produce moral behavior. In the ensuing 170 years, many such restrictions were imposed, often without the intended results.

Land speculators came by canoe, wagon, horseback, or on foot to the muddy marshes along the Chicago River. They were drawn by government promises to build a harbor and a canal there. The frontier idea of Jacksonian democracy, with its naked system of political spoils, inspired them.

A Hollywood producer planning a film about the early days of Chicago might hesitate to show it as squalid and ramshackle as it really was. It was home to log hovels, the fast buck, vice, and the lawless use of knife and gun. The hovels long since have been replaced by one of the world's most grandiose skylines of tall buildings, but the other features draw the disapproval of clergy and clerisy to this day.

Chicago originally was an accident of geography. A low ridge west of the town was a midcontinental divide separating waters draining east to the Great Lakes and thence to the North Atlantic Ocean from those flowing west to the Mississippi River and the Gulf of Mexico. The first European explorer in the area, the Frenchman Louis Jolliet, had foreseen the potential of a canal through that ridge back in 1673.

In 1814 President James Madison asked Congress to underwrite a canal from Chicago to the Illinois River to connect the Great Lakes and the Mississippi. Public affairs moved more slowly in those days, and Madison's idea was put aside as fanciful. Then, before Chicago was platted in 1830, Congress gave Illinois a strip of land in which to build such a canal. "Internal improvements," as the idea was known then, transfixed the federal government much as social welfare entitlements do now. Public works still continue to excite politicians and reformers, as in, for instance, plans to spend billions of dollars to expand Chicago's O'Hare International Airport.

Congress in 1833 appropriated twenty-five thousand dollars to construct a harbor at Chicago. This project was urged by Jefferson Davis, a young army engineer who became president of the Confederacy. The sandbar at the mouth of the Chicago River was dredged, and two five-hundred-foot wooden piers were erected.

In 1835 the Illinois legislature approved state subsidies for the canal, which in time cemented Chicago's place as a national trade center, even though the canal soon was superseded by railroads. The critical swing vote on public subvention of the canal was cast by a young and ambitious downstate politician named Abraham Lincoln.

The historian Donald L. Miller has recognized that Chicago as a commercial center did not, free-market mythology to the contrary, evolve organically from its origins as a frontier outpost of fur traders and artisans engaged in a barter economy.[5] Instead, government intervention in

the economy practically invented the place. For a time, buying and selling plots set aside to finance the canal was not just the city's leading but
nearly its only business. For at least the next thirty years, Chicago was a
concentration of young men seeking their fortune. This is the demo-
graphic group most given to gambling—in both its legal (speculating in
lands and commodities) and illegal forms—and violence.

Their coming had been delayed by the Black Hawk Indian War of 1832.
Many Chicago residents greeted by the Reverend Porter had gathered there
for the protection afforded by Fort Dearborn. Indian resistance was eliminated with an 1833 treaty under which three tribes of Native Americans
agreed to move west of the Mississippi by 1835. In the interim, they would
receive two annuities of goods to be distributed in Chicago. Many of those
goods were stolen by government agents. Town residents also "distinguished themselves by their dexterity in basely stealing blankets from the
ignorant and besotted Indians," twenty-five-year-old Chicago lawyer Joseph N. Balestier recalled in 1840.[6] Porter spoke approvingly of the Christian liberality of the Treaty of Chicago, noting that it gave the Indians five
million acres west of the Mississippi in exchange for four million east of
it. Whether a good deal or not, the displacement of Chippewa, Ottawa,
and Potawatomi opened up Chicago to whites, creating its first land boom.

It was the biggest land boom the young United States had seen. Congress had granted to Illinois for public auction every alternate section in
a six-by-one-hundred-mile zone of canal land. "The mechanic laid aside
his tools and resolved to grow rich without labor. . . . Even the day-la-
borer became learned in the mysteries of quit-claim and warranty [deeds],
and calculated his fortune by thousands," Balestier observed.[7] Meanwhile,
the city's criminals, unburdened by the middle-class values of efficiency
and rectitude, thrived. Many residents gambled, drank, whored, and tolerated corrupt local government. At the same time, they created something new under the sun: from mud hole to metropolis in one lifetime.

Mindful of its reputation as a moral snake pit, the town in September
1834 passed an ordinance against Sunday alcohol sales. It was ignored, as
state and local Sunday closing laws were flouted ever after. Gleefully an-
ticipating the canal project, saloons, as distinct from bars in hostels,

sprouted up in Chicago by 1835. They "were miserable in the extreme. The Sauganash was esteemed the best; but the crowd of strangers and the scarcity of provisions rendered every tavern in the place an abode of misery. The luxury of a single bed was almost unknown and the table had no charms for the epicure," to quote Balestier again.[8] A chapter of the American Temperance Society opened as early as 1833. Some hotels were advertised as temperance houses serving no alcohol, yet the city directory of 1844 listed one man's occupation as bartender at the American Temperance House.

Taking further action against vice, trustees in 1835 hired the first town constable and passed ordinances against discharging firearms within town limits or running a gaming house. A "house" but not gambling itself was prohibited, just as keeping a "house of ill fame" or "disorderly house" was made illegal in 1838—but not prostitution. Reformers spent many decades fighting drinking, gambling, and prostitution, often meeting indifference at best from city hall.

Ground was broken for the Illinois and Michigan Canal on the Fourth of July, 1836. By opening eastern markets to Illinois farmers via the Great Lakes, the waterway promised to raise the price of corn from twelve and a half to fifty cents a bushel. The freewheeling, get-rich-quick nature of the time might be conveyed by analogy in Mark Twain's account in *Roughing It* (1872) of the silver rush in Nevada City. Twain noted the procession of civilization to the frontier—first whiskey, then churches. The pattern already had been cut in Chicago: drinking, gambling, sharp dealing, pastoral struggling for moral reform, and spending on public works.

The canal groundbreaking ceremonies also manifested an early outbreak of ethnic enmities in Chicago. Uptown swells took a steamboat christened *Chicago* down the South Branch of the Chicago River to witness the flag-waving pageantry and oratory. The vessel drifted by Irish immigrants huddled along the banks of a settlement called Hardscrabble (later renamed Bridgeport), the terminus of the planned canal. These Irish lived in shanties that, with those in Boston, produced the American epithet "shanty Irish." These conditions existed before the influx of Irish caused by the potato famine of 1845 inflamed nativists in Boston, New

York, Chicago, and elsewhere. Still, the riverbank appearance of the Irish who did the backbreaking work of excavating the canal disturbed the beau monde on that steamboat.

The South Branch banks already had been quarried and some Irishmen picked up stones from the debris, hurling them at men and women on the promenade deck of the *Chicago*. This attack was an adumbration of the violence by labor against capital that colored much of the rest of the century. The boat nosed up to the bank there so that its male excursionists might disembark to do their manly duty. The *Chicago American* reported, "Some fifty passengers leaped ashore, some with bludgeons, and the assailants were soon led, covered with blood and wounds, captive to the boat . . . though the capture of a dozen Irishmen is no great feat," the newspaper went on to sneer.[9] Irish grievance against such nativist contempt vivified Chicago politics for the next 150 years and more. So did the city's practice of segregating ethnic groups by neighborhood.

Conflict between Yankee migrants from New England on the deck of the *Chicago* and Catholics from Ireland along the river was an ominous harbinger. A Catholic newspaper in Cincinnati already had described the efforts of the likes of Jeremiah Porter in the Northwest frontier: "Here we see the grinning teeth, and bristling mane of this Presbyterian wolf, as he prickles up his predestinating ears."[10]

Historians have defined the relationship of nativist Protestants and immigrant Catholics as a contest between different values of rectitude. Catholics were *ritualists*, depending on formal liturgy, sacraments, and hierarchy. Protestants were *pietists*, holding that salvation was gained not by institutionalized ritual but by a personal conversion experience of accepting Christ as savior.[11] Protestants tended to oppose drinking and gambling, especially on Sunday. Saved people should not do these things, if for no other reason than to honor the scriptural proscription against being a "stumbling block" to the salvation of your fellow man. Catholics took a more relaxed view. The late Chicago novelist Nelson Algren expressed the split more colloquially as the "live-and-let-livers" against the "do-as-I-sayers."[12] The difference was not just a theological one but a determinant of how different groups cast their votes.

In our secular age, an effort is needed to appreciate the extent to which religious disputes drove nineteenth-century history. That 1836 incident of rock throwing and bludgeoning produced many offspring.

Chicago, newly chartered as a city instead of a town, in March 1837 elected William Ogden its first mayor. The Jacksonian Democratic candidate, he defeated Whig challenger John Kinzie, an original settler, 489 votes to 217. Ogden (1805–77) might be labeled Chicago's first unethical politician in the sense that he backed legislation to enhance the value of his real estate holdings. However, the notion of conflict of interest bothered few people at the time.

Ogden was a transplanted Yankee Protestant and an enthusiastic canal-lands speculator and railroad builder. He deserves to be numbered among the great Americans of his generation or at least regarded as the major founder of Chicago. Contemplating a portrait of Ogden, a contemporary French historian remarked, "That is the representative American, who is a benefactor of his country, especially the mighty West: he built and owns Chicago."[13] Of course, he did not own all of it, but close enough.

As a New York state legislator, Ogden had helped build the Erie Canal, which opened in 1825 and connected the Hudson River to Lake Ontario. In 1830 Illinois canal commissioners started selling lots for just fifty or one hundred dollars. By 1834 an Ogden brother-in-law bought a Chicago parcel for one hundred thousand dollars, sight unseen. Ogden, a thirty-year-old lawyer from upstate New York, went to the frontier Northwest in the spring of 1835 to eyeball and professionally survey his relative's land. Ogden waded through bogs with water over the ankles of his boots and wrote back, "You have been guilty of the grossest folly. There is no such value in the land and won't be for a generation."[14] Ogden waited until the summer sun baked the mud dry, then started selling it off. When speculators bought a third of it for more than his kinsman had paid for the entire acreage, Ogden decided to stay in Chicago. Washington, D.C., already had removed the Native Americans and built a harbor, and moreover both the national and Illinois capitals were subsidizing the Illinois canal.

As mayor, Ogden superintended a settlement of 4,170 people, four hundred dwellings, ten taverns, and five churches. Ogden was its first esteemed booster politician in the same way that Porter was the original respectable reformer.

Just three months after Ogden's mayoral inauguration, a national depression (a banking *panic*) visited ruin on the speculators. The state of Illinois went all but bankrupt. Chicago fared better only because of the ministrations of Ogden. He pledged personal funds to support the city's debt and jawboned creditors not to foreclose (the relationship between city hall and municipal bond holders influenced much of the remainder of Chicago's history). Ogden and local bankers and businessmen induced the city council to issue unsecured scrip to pay bills (a practice repeated by the board of education in the Depression of the 1930s.)

Thus the equivocal moral nature of Chicago's public officials was established from the start. They might take graft, condone vice, pad the payroll, commit vote fraud, and give away civic utility franchises to private businesses. Nevertheless, they consistently intended to expand the city's economy. This defense against charges of malfeasance has lasted. Indicted politicians even now protest that they merely endeavored to bring more dollars into their ward, city, legislative district, or state. Boosterism as a civic virtue is permanent in Chicago history.

Ogden served only one year as mayor but continued to collaborate with city officials to build hundreds of miles of streets and two bridges over the river. He even designed and constructed the city's first swinging drawbridge. When canal digging stopped for lack of public funds, he organized the sale of private bonds. In 1848, the same year the canal opened, Ogden laid the first ten miles of railroad track. As a member of the city council, railroad president Ogden sponsored an ordinance to grant his railroad a right of way from the west, an obvious conflict of interest.

Amid this exercise in delineating Chicago "firsts"—a corrupt treaty to remove Native Americans, first reformer, first prominent businessman-politician with conflicts of interest, first collective ethnic violence, and so forth—the first recorded incident of polling-place mayhem should be cited. Again, this episode had many successors.

The legend that Chicago's first election of town trustees in 1833 produced a larger number of votes than of registered voters is charming but untrue. Still, the city's founders were sons of Jacksonian democracy, believing that to the victor belongs the spoils. Originally there were six wards, meaning that the system of ward-level politics was the genesis and still the underpinning of Chicago government.

The 1836 presidential contest between Jackson's designated Democratic heir Martin Van Buren and Whig challenger William Henry Harrison prompted Harrison partisans to assign a "vigilance committee" of nine poll watchers, lest Democrats try to steal the election (Harrison carried Chicago by six votes but lost the nation). This attempt to suppress vote fraud originated a long and frustrated civic effort. Soon enough, suspicions of vote fraud yielded to actual violence. Harrison ran again in the "Log Cabin and Hard Cider" race of 1840. Actually, he was no poor log-cabin pioneer but a member of the upper middle class.

Chicago's tradition of bare-knuckled, high-spirited politics as public entertainment might date from that 1840 campaign. Seventy Chicago men decided to go to midstate Springfield for a Whig convention:

> Great preparations were made. We secured fourteen of the best teams in town, got new canvas covers made for the wagons, and bought four tents. We also borrowed the Government yawl—the largest in the City—had it rigged up as a two-masted ship, set it up on the strongest wagon we could find, and had it drawn by six splendid gray horses. Thus equipped, with four sailors onboard, a good band, and a six-pound cannon to fire occasional salutes, we went off with flying colors, amid the cheers and well-wishes of the numerous friends that accompanied us a few miles out. . . . The prairie was covered with water, and the wagons would often sink up to the axles in mud, making it a most tedious and fatiguing journey. But on reaching the tavern, and finding an old [rac]coon there, with a barrel of cider on the stoop—emblems of the Whig party—we soon made ourselves jovial around the camp-fire.

When this procession reached Joliet on the second night, it was warned that Irish canal workers plotted to burn the boat. That scheme was thwarted, but a riot appeared at hand when the pilgrims tried to ford a river the next morning. By loading and displaying their "shot-guns and old horse pistols," they intimidated a "howling mob" of "200 or 300 men and boys." The rest of the seven-day trek was uneventful, but the Whig partisans avoided Joliet on the return trip.[15]

When election day came in Chicago, brawls broke out. "Violence at the point of rifles, brandished about at will, added to the general disorder and to the discomfort of some," a historian primly recorded.[16] The sheriff arrested an agitator, whereupon the mob—led by a state Supreme Court justice—marched to the jail to demand the release of the prisoner. The sheriff unholstered his gun and threatened to shoot any man who tried to storm the lockup, just as in scenes from a hundred western movies.

Moderate prosperity returned by the mid-1840s. In 1847 the city hosted a Rivers and Harbors Convention, launching its career as a national convention center. Boosters billed it as the largest deliberative body ever assembled. Its purpose was to press for more federal subsidies for transportation. Among the twenty thousand convention delegates and hangers-on was a newly elected Whig congressman, Abraham Lincoln from Springfield, who attracted admiring notice from the Chicago and New York press.

Also attending was Cyrus H. McCormick of rural Virginia, who had visited Chicago two years earlier. The convention persuaded him to stay and build a factory to produce his revolutionary mechanical reapers. McCormick was aided by a twenty-five-thousand-dollar investment from the ever at-hand William Ogden. The machines reduced the labor required to gather a bushel of wheat from three hours to ten minutes. Accordingly, wheat supplemented corn as an Illinois cash crop for the national and world markets. McCormick, pressing many patent-infringement suits, was represented at times, opposed at another, by lawyer Lincoln.

Along with burgeoning industrialism, vice and poverty paraded into Chicago. A study of 1848–49 tax records showed that three-fourths of heads of families owned no land or commercial property. Indeed, the richest 1 percent held 52 percent of the city's wealth, a proportion much exceeding that in Boston or New York.[17] Whatever else might be inferred from these data, Chicago was a unique frontier development, always seeming to mirror while exaggerating national trends.

The year 1848 was epochal for Chicago, which witnessed its first telegraph line, strung to Milwaukee, on 11 January, the founding of the Board of Trade to transact speculative contracts on commodities on 13 March, the opening of the Illinois and Michigan Canal on 10 April, and the inaugural run of the Galena and Chicago Union Railway on 20 November. Within nine years, Chicago was the center of the largest railroad network in the world. Original settlers such as Kinzie and Ogden could scarcely believe their eyes at the cyclonic growth. "Old Settlers" met regularly for the rest of the century for mutual self-congratulations.

Meanwhile, animosity between Yankee pietists and immigrant ritualists attained the pitch of violence in the "Lager Beer Riot" of 21 April 1855. Protestant prejudice had resulted that year in the election of the Native American, or "Know-Nothing," party mayor Levi D. Boone, a grand-nephew of the frontiersman Daniel Boone. In his inaugural address, Boone denounced aldermen for spending public funds for their suppers and silver-handled canes. In addition,

> I should feel it beneath me as a *man,* much more so as a public officer, to make any distinction either in my personal or official treatment of my fellow-citizens, on the single ground of their nationality [emphasis in original]. . . .
>
> When, however, I come to count the true friends of my country, and those to whom our institutions may be safely committed, I am frank to confess, gentlemen, and I know many, both of native and foreign birth, who think with me, I cannot be blind to the existence in our midst of a powerful politico-religious organization, all its members owning, and its chief officers bound under an oath of allegiance to the temporal, as well as the spiritual supremacy of a foreign despot. . . . [T]o their defeat I cheerfully consecrate my talents, my property, and if need be my life.[18]

After this attack on popery, the mayor ordered that all policemen must be native-born Americans, angering the Irish and doing nothing to abet the city's notoriously flimsy law enforcement. Boone also undertook to enforce a state law closing saloons on Sundays, passed in 1843 but ignored, and to raise liquor license fees from fifty to three hundred dollars, valid only for three months instead of a full year. The high fees, respectable citizens reasoned, would drive the worst dives out of business while reducing the total amount of drunkenness (a scheme revived with similar lack of success in 1882 and 1906). Sixty percent of the population at the time was foreign-born, including many Germans and Irish apt to drink on Sunday, their one day of leisure.

Police closed North Side German beer gardens on Sundays but looked the other way when "American" saloons serving whiskey south of the river opened their back and side doors. About two hundred Germans were arrested for refusing to close or to pay the higher fees. A test case went to court. Before testimony could be taken, a mob of five hundred Germans and Irish, encouraged by a fife and drum, stormed the courthouse. In the ensuing riot, a policeman lost an arm from gunfire and his assailant was hunted down and fatally shot in the back. Mayor Boone invoked martial law. A judge freed all the saloonkeeper defendants. (Chicagoans suffered no more serious restrictions on drinking, despite many attempts to impose them, until Prohibition in the 1920s.) Only fourteen men were indicted for mob violence, of whom just two were convicted. Later they were granted new trials, which never convened—a typical ratio of indictment to conviction in early judicial efforts to clean up Chicago criminality.

All the same, there was relatively little public corruption then—but only in the sense that city hall was too small to provide much boodle over which to fight. The city's politics remained fractionalized and government frail, run by capitalists who prospered with public works while ward leaders administered vice. Both of these groups shared an interest in the status quo. However tense the social friction between nativists and immigrants, the absence of an ethnic political machine meant that the Protestant business oligarchy did not feel its status threatened. The conjunction of business and political leadership was, so to speak, the machine, as the doings of another Chicago mayor will illustrate.

Mayor Boone was replaced in 1856 by Thomas Dyer, a hard-drinking Irishman, though not a Catholic. He celebrated his inauguration with a parade featuring a float of what were decorously called "female convivials," scandalizing the *Tribune*. Dyer in turn was unseated in 1857 by "Long John" Wentworth (1815–88), another of those ambulatory Chicago caricatures who seem to have been invented by a novelist with an overexcited imagination. Unexceptionally, violence at the polls during Wentworth's election killed one man and wounded several others.

A six-foot-six man who did not regard humility as a virtue, Wentworth, of Sandwich, New Hampshire, legendarily walked into Chicago barefoot in 1836, carrying his boots, so as not to cake them with mud, and a jug of whiskey, to bathe his sore feet. Immediately he started buying land. His first letter home, characteristically for a Yankee, concerned money and morals: "Land is worth $40 a square foot. The young men are mostly those who have made a fortune out of nothing and are consequently quite dissipated. . . . [A]rdent spirit is always put upon the table for dinner and most all take their drink."[19] For twenty-five years he owned and edited the *Chicago Democrat,* from which perch, along with a seat in Congress, Wentworth had brought the Rivers and Harbors Convention to town in 1847.

He owned a large suburban farm but mostly lived at a downtown hotel. There he daily checked off items on the restaurant menu in his room, then proceeded to dine there without having wasted any time ordering at table: a telltale of the energy of those who built Chicago. A photograph shows Wentworth standing with a frock coat, walking stick, and silk top hat, the nineteenth-century gentleman to the millimeter, altogether sobersided as photographic convention then required. He was independent and honest, and was the city's first strong mayor despite the weak formal powers of the part-time office. He endeavored to crack down on prostitution and wipe out the vice district.

The north riverbank was called the Sands—now the start of the "Magnificent Mile" of Michigan Avenue upscale retailing, anchored by the Tribune Tower—then an assembly of shanties of gambling, prostitution, and violence. The Sands included a fifty-cent brothel boasting "Gentle Annie" Stafford, who, escorted by pimps, assaulted a rival whorehouse in

April 1857. They broke down the front door and beat its residents with clubs. Respectable Chicagoans paid little mind to this incident, for they found it expedient to confine low-level vice to a small area, thus protecting middle-class neighborhoods and travelers from its threats. This practice was followed for many decades, and when finally it was overturned in 1910–14, the results were not what reformers might have wished.

On 20 April 1857, Wentworth, with a posse including his fire department and thirty police, descended on the Sands. Pimps and gamblers who might have fought the posse with gunfire craftily had been removed in advance by the attraction of a distant, fifty-dollar dogfight. Wentworth told the prostitutes to move their furniture to the street, then hitched teams of horses to chains and pulled down nine shanties.

Why did Wentworth do this? True, he was a Yankee pietist (though a heavy drinker) and an anti-Catholic bigot. But the essential fact was that Sands property titles were in litigation in federal court. Early in April 1857, William Ogden bought the interests of a major litigant as he wished to build a pier for his warehousing and shipping businesses. Ogden told the affected Sands residents to vacate their premises, offering to buy them out for a fair price. Many refused to sell. Ogden reported this misfortune to Wentworth.

Thus by Wentworth's raid, Ogden gained a purchase on the lucrative north bank of the river. The pimps, prostitutes, gamblers, and thieves of the Sands merely crossed the river after Wentworth's assault and regrouped on the south bank. Staged, official raids against gambling and prostitution became a fixture of the Chicago story, notably the politically motivated, large-scale raids of 1893, 1911, 1914, 1916, 1932, 1938, 1941, 1943, 1951, and 1964. As for Ogden, his Sands beachhead was a short-lived triumph because soon the nation entered another panic.

Aside from vice and poverty, Chicago also suffered from abysmal public health. Cholera epidemics traumatized the city in 1848–49 and 1854 because raw sewage was dumped in the river and lake, the sources of drinking water. Capitalists paused from building railroads and buying and selling land and commodities to consider how to sanitize the water with sewers and water intake cribs far out in the lake—and indeed how to rescue the city itself.

It was sinking into the eternal mud. The streets were barely higher than the level of the lake. On 31 December 1855, there began a twenty-year project to raise sidewalks and streets and jack up buildings four to ten feet out of the muck, still regarded as a major engineering feat. As usual, business leaders and not city government drove the effort. There was a ramification of corruption in that elevating buildings and streets created a network of underground passages and earthen rooms. Indeed, this subterranean habitat might have been the origin of the term *underworld* for organized crime. It was peopled by pickpockets, muggers, and thieves loosely directed by Roger Plant, the city's first crime boss. Plant ran the Barracks, a one-stop-shopping saloon, brothel, and gambling parlor at Monroe and Wells streets. Like the Sands, Plant's underground vice district was isolated and grudgingly tolerated by the city's commercial leadership.

Meanwhile, the 1850s also witnessed the coming to Chicago of Protestant men who became rich capitalists of great national influence. They were Potter Palmer, who more or less invented the idea of shopping as recreation, from Lockport, New York, in 1852; Joseph Medill, a Canadian by way of Cleveland, who in 1855 with some partners bought the *Chicago Tribune,* and railroad sleeping-car inventor George M. Pullman in 1859. He was a cabinetmaker and house mover from Albany, New York, who engineered key parts of the building-raising project. These tycoons contributed chapters to the history of nineteenth-century corruption and reform.

Medill, embodying a paradox common to the time, was both an abolitionist on the slavery issue and an open racist. He was a founder of the Republican party, having bought a newspaper in Coshocton, Ohio, and renamed it the *Republican* as early as 1850. Then he orchestrated the presidential nomination of Abraham Lincoln in Chicago's new "Wigwam" on 15 May 1860. The city laid off some police to release five thousand dollars in public funds to build the Wigwam. Oddly, despite pervasive crime, the city seemed cavalier about its police force. (In 1860 the police numbered sixty-seven in a population of 109,206.) Lincoln's nomination was won by hard-edged political dealing—backers included Democrat-turned-

Republican Ogden. Their tactics included the distribution of fake convention tickets, an expedient revived by Mayor Richard J. Daley in 1968.

For his political payoff, Medill at first asked only a modest favor from President Lincoln, the appointment of a *Tribune* partner as local postmaster. This official would strive to increase the newspaper's circulation throughout the Northwest, thereby spreading the blanket of abolitionist, pro-Union thought and building up the Republican party as well as the centrality of Chicago in the region. It was good for the paper, good for the city, good for the party, and good for the country! Such has been the booster attitude of some Chicago public officials to the present day.

The Civil War multiplied Chicago's industrial base. On the eve of the war, there were 469 manufacturers employing 5,593 people. As wartime industry boomed, Lincoln told Cyrus McCormick, a pro-Confederate, that his reaper plant was worth a Union army division because it freed farm labor for military service. In December 1865, eight months after peace was declared, the stockyards that have entered national mythology were opened. During the 1860s, the city's population nearly tripled from 109,206 to 298,977. The number of manufacturers by 1870 was 1,176 with a payroll of 27,076.[20]

No Civil War actions were fought in or near Chicago, but the city remained familiar with violence. A hotbed of pro-Union, antislavery sentiment, it also was a locale for "copperheads," northerners who backed the Confederacy. These included lower Mississippi River gamblers who had fled the South for the Sands and its descendants, establishing the Chicago tradition of the gentleman gambler. McCormick bought the antiwar *Chicago Times* in 1859. In 1863 a Union general ordered the closing of that copperhead newspaper. A mob vowed in reprisal to shut down the Republican *Tribune* as well, prompting Medill to call out armed guards to protect his newspaper. The crisis was mediated by Ogden, who persuaded leaders of both parties to telegraph Lincoln with a plea to rescind the general's order. Lincoln did so. The incident highlighted not only the growing importance of the press but the ways in which the commercial elite resolved political conflicts.

The next year, Medill led a delegation to Washington to implore Lincoln to ease Chicago's draft call, considering that the city already had sent so many volunteers into battle. The city feared a local ignition of the 1863 draft riots that had seared New York. According to Medill, the president scolded him, "Medill, you are acting like a coward. You and your Tribune have had more influence than any paper in the Northwest in making this war. You can influence great masses, and yet you cry to be spared at the moment when our cause is suffering. Go home and send us those men."[21] Sheepishly, Medill's group did so. Medill probably inflated his closeness to Lincoln, but his importance in establishing the mass-circulation press during a period of expanding literacy is undeniable. The role of the press in "influenc[ing] great masses" will be a theme of this narrative.

Another tradition laid down in Chicago's early decades was the public investigative committee. In 1868 Alderman "Honest John" Comisky, father of the later owner of the Chicago White Sox (whose spelling of the family name had changed to Comiskey), chaired such a committee. These panels need villains, so Comisky's blamed corruption on the civilian Chicago Police Commission. It had been established by the state legislature in 1861 over local objections (and not disbanded until 1875). The state takeover so enraged Mayor Wentworth that he spitefully fired the entire police force on 27 March 1861, an often cited but overnight and trivial incident. Police detested civilian review, and the state commission's history was commonly scandalous. A member caught in adultery was forced to resign, shifting the panel's partisan balance. Partisan newspapers reacted as expected.

Alderman Comisky summoned to testify before his committee Carrie Watson, a famous madam who followed local custom by marrying a gambling lord. She had begun a prostitution career as an eighteen-year-old virgin, later opened her own house on South Clark Street, and became a liberal benefactor of churches and synagogues. Watson went to city hall in a white carriage with yellow wheels, teamed by four black horses, and entered council chambers in a bejeweled white dress. Perhaps Comisky's exercise served the purpose, and placed a precedent, of scandal as civic entertainment. Scandal as a driver of reform is another theme of this narrative.

As the Comisky committee's bashing of the state suggests, a primary element in the generation of Chicago corruption was enmity between the industrial city and the rural and small-town downstate. New Englanders settled Chicago by overland and Great Lakes transit; southerners followed rivers upstream to inhabit downstate. The legislature, convening bienni- ally in Springfield, jealously denied Chicago adequate revenues, represen- tation according to its population, or a strong city government. As far back as 1839, the legislature abolished Chicago's office of high constable but took two months to inform the city. City fathers then sardonically asked to be notified sooner when the legislature should decide "to remove Chicago from the shore of Lake Michigan."[22] Besides the police board in 1869, the state also created three Chicago park boards. Members were appointed by the governor (or, later, local judges). Not until 1934 was a unified Chicago Park District created to consolidate no fewer than twenty-two park entities. (Now reformers are saying the centralized park district should be decentralized.)

Units of Chicago, Cook County, and Illinois governments were so numerous and overlapping that only full-time politicians could keep track of them all. This typically American system of eager localism not only upheld inefficiency but made secret handshake deals and private payoffs inviting—indeed, almost necessary. A matrix of favors and coercions de- veloped, nearly impenetrable to reformers even now.

Antagonism between the state and city, along with almost satirically manifold rosters of public jurisdictions, are seminal in the provenance of corruption. These were not matters of merely formal institutional struc- tures but wide-armed welcomes for sharp insider dealing. When the Pro- gressive Era crested decades later, reformers strived to consolidate and rationalize competing jurisdictions with some but, as always, unsatisfac- tory success.

During the 1860s, Chicago was growing so fast, so haphazardly, and with so much disorder that opportunities for public corruption dilated exponentially. Actual thievery, as distinct from insider deals and boodling, began to trouble moralistic citizens. An example: the tax on a gallon of whiskey was two dollars. A whiskey ring not only escaped the tax but suborned police to seize liquor shipments from other cities that tried to undersell the ring. In a separate matter, the state legislature, anti-Chicago and controlled by railroad money, in 1869 authorized railroads to pay eight hundred thousand dollars for Chicago lakefront land valued at more than three times that amount. The governor vetoed the bill. Despite that seeming reprieve, the combination of liquor and railroad trusts generated a reaction in the form of the city's first serious political reform movement.

Businessmen, the press, and even the nascent labor movement in its opposition to the abuses of industrialism united behind a reform People's Ticket in November 1869. It elected as mayor Roswell B. Mason, a civil engineer, builder of the Illinois Central Railroad, and no politician. The Mason campaign was among the earliest of middle-class efforts to place businessmen instead of politicians in public office to sweep government clean. Indeed, it happened two years before New York, led by the then-Republican *New York Times,* upset the Tammany Hall machine. Chicago's venture into honest government, like New York's, was temporary.

A city council ring known as McCauley's Nineteen, after Alderman James McCauley, allocated the boodle. Seven incumbent and seven former aldermen were indicted on corruption charges. Four were convicted and sentenced to six months in jail and fines of one hundred dollars. Three defendants were acquitted by a judge's directed verdict. Other charges were dismissed or ignored. Four convictions out of fourteen indictments are at least an improvement on the score of two convictions among fourteen defendants from the Lager Beer Riot. Other corrupt aldermen were ousted in the 1871 election but not enough to prevent thirteen Republicans and eight Democrats from organizing a new ring. The persistence of political venality continued to frustrate reformers for the next 130 years.

Aside from actions in city hall, those of retailer Potter Palmer and former mayors John Wentworth and William Ogden exemplified the culture of insider deals. Palmer made a fortune in dry goods before and during the war, forming a partnership with Marshall Field and another businessman in 1863. In 1865 Palmer retired to Europe at age thirty-nine for health reasons. Leisure did not suit him, being a Chicagoan, and he returned in 1868 to launch a second career in real estate development. Single-handedly, he contrived to displace the city's retail strip from the east-west axis of Lake

Street to the then-undistinguished State Street running north and south. He achieved his goal, the best historian of nineteenth-century Chicago noted in some wonderment, "without resort, apparently, to threats or bribery."[23] City fathers had no inkling of his scheme until he approached them to seek a widening of State Street, seeing as how he had bought nearly a mile of its frontage. Soon was established Marshall Field's department store and eventually the mail-order giants of Montgomery Ward and Sears, Roebuck. Merchandise joined industry and transportation as the bases of the astonishing Chicago economy.

Wentworth and Ogden now reappear in this story because their business practices impeded efforts to purify the water supply. Ground was broken in 1864 for a two-mile tunnel out under the lake to draw in fresh water. Still, sewage continued to pollute the river and lake. It might have been halted by passage and enforcement of strict sanitation laws. The capitalist oligarchy did not take this option seriously, lest it drive business away. Instead, they embraced a radical idea to make the Chicago River run backward. Downstream towns were unhappy at the notion of greeting Chicago's sewage but the city assured them that the offal would be diluted and deodorized. Bond sales enabled engineers, without property tax increases, to deepen the old Illinois and Michigan Canal so that the river backed into it with the help of large pumps at Bridgeport. Ideally, the water would have been diverted to leaching beds at irrigation farms but politically powerful property owners prevented condemnation of valuable land for this purpose.

On 18 July 1871, a temporary dam across the river was demolished but onlookers at opening-day ceremonies—always a favorite Chicago ritual—could not discern a current downstream from the river into the canal. Inspired by ingenuity, they tossed straws onto the surface and, sure enough, they floated lazily southwest to hurrahs. Among its many feats, Chicago had conquered nature by making water flow upstream. However, the drift was so slow that people as far away as La Salle, Illinois, complained of sewage stench during the summer heat.

Earlier that year, Ogden and Wentworth perceived that the river project would increase the value of swampland they owned—"Mud Lake," west of the city—so they built a ditch from the Des Plaines to the Chicago rivers to drain their swamp. Spring rains caused the Ogden-Wentworth Ditch to channel Des Plaines floodwater into the South Branch of the Chicago River, in turn making the river backwash into the lake despite the deepened canal. That ditch also deposited sediment in the canal so that it remained too shallow. Not until 1877 did the Ogden interests, after years of pleas from city officials, complete a dam at the Des Plaines River end of the ditch. This structure also proved ineffective in keeping Des Plaines waters out of the Chicago River. That river never really ran backward until 1900.

The July 1871 dam-breaking ceremony at the canal preceded by twelve weeks the Chicago Fire of 8–10 October. The story of the Fire has been told often and well. Merely noted here are the points that an incendiary cow probably did not spark it and that the holocaust killed about three hundred people (the exact number cannot be known), left ninety thousand homeless, and destroyed 17,450 buildings. Four-fifths of the central city burned, roughly four square miles.

A long drought, high prairie winds, and tumbledown wooden structures made the Fire so destructive, but its ultimate cause—as with so much of Chicago history—was political. The city council would not tax property owners enough to fund an adequate building code or fire and police protection. Respectable citizens preferred lax enforcement, no matter the hazard of fire or the proliferation of vice. An official inquiry concluded that the square-mile central business district at least tried to meet fire codes but the rest of the city, comprising immigrants' shanties, was culpable.[24] Immediately after the Fire, the press, spreading the cow-kicking-over-the-kerosene-lamp legend, called Catherine O'Leary a hag and a crone. She was thirty-five years old. Irish immigrants had yet another reason to hate the bigotry of the Protestant middle class. Not surprising is that one of Mrs. O'Leary's sons became a gambling lord.

The allegedly fireproof limestone building of the *Tribune* burned down. Medill quickly found a surviving print shop to bring out a paper. The first post-Fire edition, with embers still burning, carried an editorial with the amazing headline, CHEER UP!, under which Medill exhorted, "In the midst of a calamity without parallel in the world's history [more Chicago brag-gadocio], looking upon the ashes of 30 years' accumulations, the people of this once-beautiful city have resolved that CHICAGO SHALL RISE AGAIN."[25]

Medill's partner William Bross caught the first available train to New York to incite investors, "Go to Chicago now. Young men, hurry there! Old men, send your sons! Women, send your husbands. You will never again have such a chance to make money. The fire has leveled nearly all distinctions."[26] History has validated the positive attitude of Medill and Bross, although the Fire did not level "nearly all [class] distinctions."

Another telling detail is that city hall offices were moved temporarily to a Yankee Protestant bastion, the First Congregational Church. Even more significant is that the pietists' Relief and Aid Society, founded dur-ing the panic of 1857, took over the distribution of money and goods that poured in from cities all over the world for Chicago's succor. A contem-porary historian noted favorably that Mayor Mason would not even dream of letting the city council handle this wealth: "Before he went out of of-fice he had the courage to intrust [sic] all moneys, and supplies received by him on behalf of the people of Chicago, to the Relief and Aid Society, instead of to the city council."[27] Low-life politicians could hardly be trusted with such beneficence—only respectable Protestants.

Cartons of books arrived to restock the presumably destroyed central library, but in fact Chicago had no library and city fathers puzzled over where to put all the books. At length they selected an empty water tower. More to the point, the Relief and Aid Society sat in judgment of applicants for relief. It rejected those deemed unworthy, who might become dependent on public charity. Early the next year, the society dropped from its relief rolls eight hundred families who had shown insufficient diligence in get-ting on in the world. The city council reasserted itself and took over the society's aid distribution job—and $1 million of its money—in May 1872.

Defenders of political machines have described them as self-policing welfare systems. The decidedly nonmachine Relief and Aid Society not only was self-policing but engaged in what conservatives later would con-demn as the welfare state's social engineering. Two decades after the Fire, during the depression of 1893–97, the society operated two wood yards, advertising: "The object of the yards is to give employment to such distressed able-bodied men as are known, through investigation, to be worthy of help. Last year we gave work at our North and West side yards to 4931 men, who fully appreciated the chance to earn a dollar when all other sources of employment were closed to them."[28] No less an authority than Jane Addams later would come to weigh carefully whether civilian reformers or government politicians were better judges of who was "worthy of help." Still later, the New Deal more or less settled the question.

The city recovered from the Fire with astounding swiftness, inventing modern architecture in the process. The Fire also resulted in Medill's election in November 1871 as a reform mayor. The rudiments of Chicago corruption and reform had been established: first, a concentration of young men in a wide-open, lawless frontier town; second, campaigns against vice and crime led by Protestant evangelists; third, a class division of Yankee Protestant businessmen and immigrant Catholic laborers; and fourth, a complex of political favors and coercions. This scaffolding of government was erected on, fifth, a bewildering multiplicity of governmental bodies. Sixth was a notion of politics as public entertainment and its spoils not attended by high ethical standards, and seventh was an assumption that government should intervene in the economy with public works and business subsidies.

Medill's two-year term (1871–73, extended from one year in 1863) was not a happy one for him or his city. Its social dynamo continued to be steered by the conflict between reform and corruption, pietists and ritualists, such as former mayor Roswell Mason and city council boodler James McCauley, or Mayor Medill and the city and state lawmakers who opposed him. Before finishing his term, Medill fled the city in despair.

2

Businessmen Rebels

1872–93

In every American age, there has been a group that has sounded the cry of corruption: the cry that political values are being debased, the political system subverted, public officials bought out. This group is the American gentility.
—Abraham S. Eisenstadt, "Political Corruption in American History"

Graft is what he calls it when the fellows do it who don't know which fork to use.
—Willie Stark in Robert Penn Warren's novel, *All the King's Men*

A wave of fires in the summer of 1874 had more to do with reform in Chicago than did the great Fire of 1871. The worst one started in a rag peddler's shack on 14 July and spread to destroy 812 buildings on forty-seven acres and to kill about twenty people. It burned down the slums between State and Clark streets south of Harrison Street, later the locale of the Levee vice district. "For the second time Chicago was like Louvain. Its heart had been consumed by fire. . . . [L]eading citizens walked around contemplating desolation and destruction."[1]

After more fires on 16 and 17 July, fire insurance companies had had enough. The Chicago Board of Underwriters refused to write policies unless the city modernized its fire department, a patronage playground—"the engine houses are little better than places of resort for lewd women, the fire-men use the horses to go off buggy-riding, and the whole thing is managed in the interests of a political clique," the *Tribune* scolded.[2]

Franklin MacVeagh (a wholesale grocer and later U.S. treasury secretary), Marshall Field, and others called a mass meeting. A resultant committee of one hundred pressed the underwriters' demands before the city council: extend the city's "fire limits" requiring construction of brick or stone, provide an adequate water supply, increase the size of the water mains, and gradually move lumberyards to the outskirts of the city. Naturally, reform did not happen at once. On 20 July, aldermen agreed to extend the fire limits but balked at other changes.

Accordingly, businessmen combined to achieve them. Thus was born on 24 July the Citizens' Association, the first urban reform group in the nation. Chicago then had no counterpart to New York's Tammany Hall and cannot claim to have invented political reform. However, the Citizens' Association may boast of its priority in the tradition of businessmen's civic reform organizations.

On 1 October, the National Board of Underwriters invited fire insurers to boycott Chicago. In the resulting embargo, city merchants found not only that they could not insure their stocks but that wholesalers refused to ship uninsurable wares. The Citizens' Association proposed hiring a former New York City fire commissioner to revamp the local fire department. The city council refused unless his fee was privately paid. So the association put up sixty-five hundred dollars and the city underwriters' board thirty-five hundred. The council thereafter enacted most of that New York civil engineer's recommendations. Two years later, the National Board of Underwriters called Chicago's fire department the best in the country. However, a baleful precedent had been set: private funding of a public job, which segued into the private funding of prosecuting people.

There had been numerous local businessmen's clubs for purposes of social networking. The first important one, the Chicago Club, was set up back in 1869 by banker (and later U.S. treasury secretary) Lyman J. Gage. The Citizens' Association was something new. Its explicit aim was to improve the urban environment. After fire protection was achieved, the group turned to other projects, such as a new city charter. That prototype spawned many offspring around the nation. In Chicago, business reform groups operated in various forms and degrees throughout the twentieth century. Their story is as much a part of Chicago history as the more familiar record of grafters and gangsters. Their belief was that regulated, rational public administration by itself would remove vulnerabilities for corruption.

MacVeagh, who was elected the Citizens' Association's first president, said that "while immediate fire protection is its most absorbing thought, the association assumes a larger field," explaining,

> Its business is with the whole question of our municipal government. Perhaps the most important business in America that is the most poorly done is the business of government, and of all the manifestations of government in this country by far the worst is large city government. . . .
>
> This city is governed for the most part by unfit and unworthy men, in an undignified, uncultured and demoralizing manner. Our system of city government is bad and produces bad rulers.[3]

Here was the viewpoint of the Protestant business class: get rid of undignified and uncultured "bad rulers," and all would be well. In that same year, 1874, the Women's Christian Temperance Union was founded in north suburban Evanston. Two years later, the Chicago Woman's Club was organized, as a new class of educated women strived for general social uplift. Additional men's clubs included the Citizens' Law and Order League in 1877 and the Union League Club in 1879. Middle-class reform was building up steam behind industrialism's own.

The breadth of Citizens' Association activities is suggested by the fact that, to alleviate intolerable stench from the stockyards, it forced the passage of the first ordinances regulating slaughterhouses (by the end of the 1870s, there were seventy meatpacking plants). That the founders of such associations were tycoons has invited the criticism that they were motivated by self-interest. They needed to protect their assets against, first, fire, then labor demands and predations by political grafters. Be that as it may, they also wanted to fashion a better city by their own lights. Reformist conflicts between pragmatists and visionaries, incrementalists and ideologues, never have been settled. In any case, within twenty years, a new generation of the middle and professional classes built on the Citizens' Association example to create more militant reform groups at the dawn of Progressivism.

In 1877, with fire insurance secured, the association debated whether it had achieved its goal and therefore should disband. "The trouble with reform," association president Murry Nelson complained, "is that reformers won't stay mad for more than six months."[4] *More than six months.* Nelson proposed "that, should an honest Board of County Commissioners be elected, then possibly the association would be of no more service to the city."[5] The group went on to remove, with dubious means, many crooked commissioners, but by and large, Nelson's ambition remained unfulfilled. To this date, an honest Cook County board is elusive.

Reformers could expect little cooperation from city hall after the truncated tenure of reform mayor Joseph Medill. The first thing Medill, elected on the "Union Fire-Proof Ticket," did in office was to close the gambling houses. For all the heroism of Chicago's recovery from the Fire, much of the populace was demoralized by the destruction of its worldly goods and in no mood to quit drinking and gambling. Meanwhile, the need to rebuild a city from scratch meant that work at good wages was plentiful. At the same time, the charred, skull-like frames of buildings amid the rubble offered hideouts for criminals, much like Roger Plant's original underworld. Under these conditions, Medill's police department—450 men in a city of three hundred thousand—stood little chance. Oddly, capitalists did not regard an adequate police force as a civic priority.

Goo goos led by the clergy got behind Medill's antivice drive but were ineffective. A civic committee of seventy broke apart in a struggle between those who could and those who could not countenance any legal drinking. The temperance—which meant prohibition—movement then devised a committee of twenty-five, which stumbled into futility. The liquor and gambling interests, not about to be outorganized, held a mass meeting in September 1873 and soon succeeded in electing their own mayor. By that time, Medill had abdicated.

Though a newspaperman, Medill would not have made a modern, media-savvy politician. He seemed comfortable only while spouting commands from his *Tribune* editor's desk. Political give-and-take was foreign to him. As a Republican boss, he did get the legislature to enact a Mayor's Bill in 1872, much expanding his powers as a temporary, emergency post-Fire measure. He also won rebuilding funds in the form of a $2.9 million repayment for the city's costs in digging the state-owned Illinois and Michigan Canal.

By mid-1873, the city council was fed up with Medill's dictatorial ways. Aldermen blocked the authority granted by the Mayor's Bill, which a council resolution called "pestiferous," to revoke saloon licenses. Medill, a teetotaler and nonsmoker, had tried to crack down on the worst dives and even dared to attempt to enforce the Sunday closing law. Under council opposition, Medill was overcome by physical and mental ailments and fled to Europe in August, not returning until 1874. In the interim, the city council elected an alderman to complete his remaining term as acting mayor.

Once back in Chicago, Medill bought a controlling interest in the *Tribune* with a loan from Marshall Field. Medill reinforced the paper's recent Civil War voice for Republican and nativist interests and for moral and political reform, spending thirteen years fighting private monopoly ownership of public transit. However, the *Tribune* did not hesitate to make its own sweetheart deals with the board of education to lease property for its newspaper offices.[6] The school board held eleven prime square miles under original land grants to fund schools.

Medill served at a critical juncture of Chicago history, becoming the first mayor to challenge the power of ward organizations supported by saloons, gambling, and prostitution. Neither he nor the committees of seventy and twenty-five were schooled in ward politics, though. Medill in sum was a transitional figure to generations of control of city government by Irish and other Catholic immigrant groups. Some Protestants, but no pietists or Puritans, later were elected mayor. Those mayors understood decentralized ward politics. Reformers generally did not, even though they were able to create a fire department separated from corrupt police control, to secure public works funds, and to keep local government favorable to business with boosterism and low tax rates. All the while, members of such groups as the Citizens' Association were planting the idea that civic government should be run by a businesslike centralized administration, not decentralized ward politics.

Republicans and Democrats—at the time, Chicago had a two-party polity—selected members of their party's Cook County Central Committee from each ward and suburban township. The ward or township committeeman was a potent and respected man, not the oafish stereotype of reformist derision. He could provide a constituent a job, give away turkeys or ducks at Thanksgiving and Christmas, write a rent check for a jobless tenant, gain a relative's admission to the county hospital, and sponsor local social and athletic outings. Voting for the committeeman's designated alderman, tax assessor, judges, state's attorney, and mayor when election days rolled around must have seemed to constituents a small price for these boons.

The committeeman controlled his alderman and provided for his ward's social needs, while his alderman took care of official business in the city council. The most powerful politicians were committeemen and aldermen at the same time, which remains the case to this day, however much eroded is the political machine.

The committeeman's treasure chest was filled by payoffs from local gambling houses, saloons, and brothels. This state of affairs has not entirely disappeared. In the nineteenth century and later, corruption was a matter not of a few bad apples but the whole bunch. Committeemen in effect appointed police commanders in their districts, who permitted vice operations as long as they and their patrolmen got their rake-offs and the ward political organization received its percentage. Especially notorious were the First Ward, encompassing both the central business district and the vice district, and the adjoining "Bloody Twentieth" Ward of the Near West Side, an area that has housed successively Irish, Italians, Jews, and African Americans.

Chicago was, in fact as well as cliché, a city of neighborhoods—an amalgamation of small towns as ethnically homogeneous and close-knit as any coal-mining county in Appalachia. Some historians hold that rigidly ethnic neighborhoods did not fully develop until the 1920s, but reconstruction after the Fire at least molded them. Street gangs or social and athletic clubs that were barely a step above gangs patrolled their neighborhoods against incursions by outsiders. Eventually, neighborhoods turned over ethnically in assembly-line fashion, driven by cheap housing prices as inner-city areas became disreputable. Still, stability was salient while it lasted. Ethnic families that occupied a neighborhood for a generation or so had put aside enough money, even just a dime or quarter or two a week, to buy housing in more desirable precincts farther from downtown. (After World War II, this process occurred with alarming, race-driven speed.)[7]

Little noted is how neighborhood unity and crooked politics dropped a kind of civic complacency over Chicago. However thin that blanket, it is still another element in the city's toleration and promotion of corruption. As long as the neighborhood offered ethnic cohesion and anyone could get a patronage job or other governmental benefit or gamble while taking a Sunday drink, nobody outside some clergy and their high-society allies got too upset. Both the working and capitalist classes were invested in the status quo. Even now, reformers can be astonished to learn the stability of the status quo.

Only some of the (then) eighteen to thirty-five wards were concentrations of vice and graft. That was sufficient to maintain systemic corruption. There were enough crooked wards to make mayors, prosecutors, tax assessors, and judges dependent on their votes. Thus the city elected in 1873 an ordinary pol, Harvey Colvin, on a People's Ticket to succeed Medill. Colvin's city treasurer, David A. Gage, came up $507,704 short in his accounts. He was indicted, beat the rap, but gave the city 254 acres to compensate—this land became Gage Park. Further, when Colvin's successor Monroe Heath took office, he discovered that uncollected taxes amounted to $5.5 million. Such was the nature of a city hall with which the Citizens' Association and its confederates had to deal.

The association gained some ground against vote fraud. It patrolled polling places to aid Heath's election. At Heath's request, the association arranged a million-dollar loan to the city, much as William Ogden had bailed out city finances in the 1830s and canal bonds in the 1840s. In later decades, reformers donated private funds to prosecute criminals, sometimes landing the reformers in trouble.

The nemesis of reformers was no mere mayor but Michael Cassius "Sure Thing Mike" (or "King") McDonald. An immigrant from the Irish Famine, McDonald (1839–1907) came to Chicago in 1862 and grew rich as a gambling kingpin, pimp, bail bondsman, and boxing promoter. When the police chief barred McDonald from police headquarters, the gambler countered by prevailing on state-appointed police commissioners to fire the chief. Medill then ousted the commissioners and defiantly rehired the chief. Nothing that Medill did as mayor seemed to come out right. McDonald ran the campaign to elect Colvin, who was friendlier to him.

McDonald had taken over a setup founded by Colonel Jack H. Haverly, who formed horse-race betting pools on the analogy of Board of Trade speculation in corn, wheat, and pork contracts. In time, Al Capone, like McDonald, also inherited a crime organization built by a student of capitalism, in his case, the gangster Johnny Torrio.

McDonald's achievement was to remove gambling from dives and alleys and make it a quasi-respectable, middle-class pastime run by gentleman gamblers such as those who came upriver from the South during the Civil War. In 1873 McDonald opened a luxurious parlor called the Store in a four-story building at Clark and Monroe streets, also his residence. It was the biggest of about thirty gambling parlors in the central business district. According to an unwritten agreement, the Store was raided now and again but McDonald always shook off the raids. The Store became in effect an auxiliary city hall, wherein McDonald secured a $128,500 contract to paint the courthouse. He did so with a worthless mixture of chalk and water.

In March 1882, McDonald, a restaurateur, and, of all people, the Quaker developer Potter Palmer were indicted for keeping gambling houses. Potter had a small parlor two doors south of the Store. Coincident with the charges was a revived Republican drive to clean up vice. Democratic Mayor Carter Harrison I testified for the defense. Early in his tenure, Harrison was accosted by a committee of clergy who asked whether he knew about the open "gambling hells" along Clark Street. Harrison reflected a moment before replying impishly that the divines were correct, for he had patronized the parlors just the night before. At McDonald's trial, the mayor said he had visited the Store often to caution McDonald against harboring too many idle men there. The defendant, though, had assured the mayor that he was out of the gambling racket. Cross-examined about a Kentucky boy who had lost his entire stake at the Store, Harrison answered to the effect that if a fellow Kentuckian had no more wits than that, it was just too bad. The boy himself suffered a curious loss of memory when called to the stand. All defendants were acquitted.

Next came a prosecution for vote fraud in 1884. Reformers, newspapers, and business interests had combined in 1883 for a Citizens' Ticket with Judge Eugene Cary as the Republican nominee for mayor. After Harrison won with 57 percent of the vote, the Union League Club hired private detectives to investigate a typical precinct. The sleuths found that George Washington, Thomas Jefferson, John Hancock, and similar notables had registered and voted. (Parallel ruses were discovered in a 1969 investigation of vote fraud.) Of 1,112 votes cast in the precinct, 907 were fraudulent. In the end, only seven of 171 precincts did *not* evince irregularities.

State's Attorney Luther Laflin Mills, a Union League Club member, indicted three election judges and two clerks. A judge ruled that under the lax state election code, he had to acquit them. However, in an ominous portent, federal prosecutors also were on the case. Even today, the U.S. Justice Department takes out many more Cook County politicians than local courts do. Washington was looking into bogus Illinois legislative elections because the legislature elected U.S. senators at that time.

The techniques were routine. Ballots were lifted from a box in the county clerk's office, fake ballots substituted, and a forged tally sheet drawn up. The ballot stuffers, though, absentmindedly forgot to remove the string that bundled the counterfeit ballots. A McDonald associate, Joseph C. "Chesterfield Joe" (or "Oyster Joe") Mackin, was indicted. Mackin had two claims to fame. He had sponsored crooked alderman "Bathhouse" John Coughlin in a political career and originated the saloon "free lunch" by giving away oysters with beer. Convicted along with two ward heelers, Mackin was sentenced to two years in prison for vote fraud. Emboldened, a Cook County grand jury then indicted him for perjury and he was sentenced to five years on that charge.

By 1885 the city council was fed up with the smearing of Chicago by reformers, newspapers, and prosecutors. It adopted a resolution expressing outrage:

> The fair name of the city has been traduced and vilified, and the impression has spread around that Chicago is not only a sinkhole of iniquity and corruption, but infested with thieves, bummers and ballot-box stuffers and disreputable characters generally. . . . The tendency of all this misrepresentation has been, not only to injure the fair credit and standing of the city, but drive away trade that has its natural market here.[8]

Many previous and subsequent official statements of this type could be cited. Their common theme is that muckraking interferes with commerce.

Whatever the importance of gambling and vote-fraud prosecutions, the Citizens' Association and other business groups were more alarmed by the thorns of organized labor amid the flowering of industrialism. The first major labor uprising came in 1877 during the fourth year of a national depression. The city council appropriated five hundred thousand dollars to build a new courthouse in the hope that some public-works jobs would appease the labor revolt.

The mythical melting pot boiled over as labor agitators fought for gains such as an eight-hour day. Some agitators were socialists; a few, anarchists. Unfortunately for them, they had foreign-sounding surnames (especially German Jewish) and published foreign-language newspapers, inciting respectable classes to impugn their Americanism. Industrialists maintained that ten- to twelve-hour days and six-day weeks did workingmen a favor by limiting their leisure opportunities for idleness and vice. Rhetoric was extreme on both sides in 1877 as mobs of trade unionists walked off their jobs, burned buildings, and attacked strikebreakers.

In July a railroad strike broke out in West Virginia, lighting fuses that burned quickly to Baltimore, Pittsburgh, and Chicago. The last city, harboring perhaps the most radical underclass in the country, was the seat of the Socialist Labor party. Chicago seriously prepared for civil war. Field armed his employees and dispatched his delivery wagons and horses to shuttle police riot squads. Mayor Heath deputized and armed thousands of "good and experienced citizens" to suppress "the ragged Commune wretches."[9] Heath also closed the saloons—many locked their front doors but obligingly opened side and back entrances—rang the fire bells, ordered "all idlers and curious people" off the streets, and telegraphed Washington for federal troops.[10]

Chicago's strike began on 23 July 1877, and a mass rally was held that night. At another rally the next day, police beat workers and fired gunshots over their heads. The next morning's *Tribune* declared that the city was in a "Red War." On the following day, police stormed a peaceful meeting of workers at Turner Hall and opened fire. One man was shot in the head, and others were wounded; as the panicked group ran to the exits, police clubbed them out the doors.

In three days of riots, thirty civilians but no police were killed. Nationally, another seventy workers died in the Great Uprising. Violence in Chicago ended when President Rutherford B. Hayes diverted six infantry companies to the city from guarding Sioux in the Dakotas.

The revolt of 1877 shocked the country much as did the urban and antiwar riots of the 1960s. It sparked many years of labor-versus-capital violence. America, "land of opportunity," had believed itself inoculated against the class warfare that was shaking Europe.

Chicago capitalists saw the city council's proposed new courthouse fund for the sop it was and instantly rallied the Citizens' Association to keep order. It collected $27,515 from businesses to give weaponry to the police and militia, the money spent as follows:

599 Breach [*sic*] Loading Springfield Muskets, costs, including freight, ...$5,904 30

400 Gun Slings and Belts, ...164 48

166 Cartridge Boxes, ...86 55
50000 Rounds Ammunition, ...1000 ...
Full equipment for Battalion of Cavalry, including saddles, bridles,
jackets, sabers, and two revolvers for each man.
Total cost, ...5,025 57
450 fatigue caps, ... 462 50
Battery, consisting of four twelve-pounder brass Napoleon Guns,
with limbers and caissons, and field harness complete, and assorted
lot of ammunition for same. Total cost, delivered in Chicago, ...
5,380
One Gatling gun, 10 long barrels, with limber and caisson, harness and
full complement of feed cases, and 20000 rounds of ammunition.
Cost, delivered in Chicago, ...5,483 08
Miscellaneous bills, including supplies for and cost of guard at the
several Armories, to date, ...423 85[11]

Fearing for the adequacy of even these measures, the association also
lobbied for a permanent U.S. Army presence. By 1887, Fort Highwood
(later renamed Fort Sheridan) was open for business in Lake County north
of the city. Wealthy citizens had donated 632 acres for it.

Unfortunately, in the viewpoint of those citizens, the fort was not established in time for the Haymarket Riot of 1886. Two men who belong
in the front rank of any parade of Chicago personalities, Mayor Carter
H. Harrison I and Governor John Peter Altgeld, dominate, if Haymarket
is considered as an episode of Chicago corruption and reform. The naming of Haymarket heroes and villains never has been settled by historians
of labor. It remains a touchstone for labor and capital alike.

Harrison (1825–93; mayor, 1879–87 and 1893), like "Long John" Wentworth in the 1850s, seems to have studied at the Chicago school of flam-
boyance. Born in a log house, an up-from-poverty status symbol of the
times, he nonetheless was a son of the Kentucky bluegrass plantation class
whose transplanted members formed a kind of aristocracy in exile in early
Chicago. Cantering a white mare around the city while waving a black
slouch hat, Harrison made Medill, for one, rather weak in the knees: "a

magnetic man . . . among all the Mayors ever produced in the United States there never was a man equal to him in . . . power over the masses, at the same time maintaining a strong personal popularity across party lines."[12] And Medill was a hard-rock Republican, Harrison a Democrat.

Dismissing alarms sounded by police brass and newspapers, Harrison issued a permit for a labor march and rally on 4 May 1886. It was called to support the eight-hour day and to protest the killing of two McCormick strikers and the wounding of four others by factory guards the day before. A police inspector—"Black Jack" Bonfield—expected a citywide riot and defied Harrison by calling out six hundred police reserves. Astride his white horse, Harrison visited Haymarket Square near Randolph and Des Plaines streets after speechmaking began at about 8:30 P.M. Seeing a calm, rainy scene of fewer than two thousand people, he ordered the reserves sent home. When the mayor rode home himself, Bonfield countermanded him again, pulling up some of his reserves. At 10:20 P.M., police ordered the crowd, by now small, to disperse. Somebody, never identified, tossed a bomb at the ranks of two hundred officers. Harrison heard the distant blast while pulling up his bedcovers. Within moments, panicked police began shooting into the panicked crowd. Seven police died. Civilian fatalities are minimally estimated at four to six. Regardless of whether the seven killed and sixty injured policemen were martyrs or provocateurs, something akin to a police state followed Haymarket.[13]

Field privately told Harrison to suppress free speech in the name of law and order, but Harrison refused. It hardly mattered. The Citizens' Association named a committee to meet daily to deal with the crisis. Among the members were Field, Murry Nelson, George M. Pullman, meatpacker Philip D. Armour, and Cyrus H. McCormick, son of the reaper inventor.

Young McCormick had demanded the appointment of Harrison's rebellious Inspector Bonfield. During a streetcar strike the previous year, McCormick locked out his workers sympathetic to the strike, gave pistols to strikebreakers, and called on Bonfield for help. In a precedent for defying Harrison, Bonfield had issued a shoot-to-kill order against rioting strikers. The earlier Turner Hall incident of 1877 had moved a judge to rule in a lawsuit that police had been guilty then of a criminal riot. (In

1968 the city would reprise the precedents of shoot to kill and an officially designated police riot.)

In the Haymarket aftermath, as Harrison appealed for calm, Bonfield and his men brutally interrogated hundreds of Haymarket suspects and strong-armed confessions. In its venom, the Haymarket fallout foreshadowed the national Red Scares of the 1920s and 1950s. Hundreds of radicals were jailed and physically abused without proper charges.

Trial and appellate judges railroaded Haymarket defendants to the gallows. Seven received death sentences. Another drew fifteen years in prison. Four of the seven were hanged—one had committed suicide on death row—on 11 November 1887. Probably none knew anything about a bomb plot, if there was one. The hangings were heavily guarded because police feared the event could ignite a citywide revolution.

Governor Altgeld pardoned the remaining defendants (two on death row and the fifteen-year convict) on 26 June 1893. The Chicago and New York press, which had not restrained its jubilation over the four executions, now roared for Altgeld's head. Among other sins, he had been born in Germany—the cradle of socialism and anarchism—and thus was not, the newspapers said, a real American. Aside from his strongly worded pardon statement, Altgeld kept a dignified silence. As a reformer, he was among the most courageous of the clan. At the same time, he kept a jealous hold on Democratic party patronage and became involved in the Ogden Gas franchise scam in Chicago. The roster of reformers offers few candidates for sainthood.

The journalist Henry Demarest Lloyd was, typically for the new breed of middle-class reformers, the son of a Protestant pastor. The literary and financial editor of the *Tribune,* Lloyd married a daughter of one of the paper's owners, William Bross, exhorter of New York investors after the Fire and later an Illinois lieutenant governor. In 1881 the *Atlantic Monthly* published "The Story of a Great Monopoly," Lloyd's article about the collusion of railroad financiers. It might be judged the first muckraking story, twenty years before muckraking became notorious. Soon Lloyd had an emotional breakdown. Later, he implored Altgeld to pardon the Haymarket defendants. As a consequence, Bross disinherited Lloyd and his wife from acquiring Bross's *Tribune* stock. Both Haymarket and muck-raking continued to rattle down the halls of American history with pin-ball-machine bounces still not wholly diagrammed.

In the context of social justice during the expansion of industrialism, George M. Pullman must be listed as a reformer, though a most peculiar one. A charter member of the Citizens' Association, he built an epony-mous model town south of Chicago to build his railroad sleeping cars. It was planned as a workers' paradise. Like all calculated utopias, it degen-erated. To keep his workers "clean, contented, sober, educated, and happy," Pullman forbade from his domain gambling dens, taverns, and brothels.[14] Also kept out were political bosses, union organizers, and—an astonish-ing step for the times—priests and all but one pastor. Pullman erected a church for his families, appointed the Presbyterian minister, and expected dutiful attendance at services.

Naturally, as soon as the town of Pullman was completed in 1881, work-ers crossed railroad tracks south to the village of Kensington, where beer foamed, cigars glowed, and dice rattled. In the year of Haymarket, Pullman's workers joined a national strike, calling for an eight-hour day. Pullman's re-pression of the action was ruthless. Even fiercer antilabor reprisals in the next decade would cause other capitalist reformers to turn against him.

During that era of labor trauma, the "Great Boodle Trial" of 1887 re-sulted from business reformers seeking cleaner, better-organized local government, in itself part of the fallout from Haymarket. Newspapers and civic groups were aflame to eliminate boodling. The trial was the most successful assault on public crooks to that date.

It required of reformers the use of impure methods, containing ele-ments of farce and illegality, as did previous and later prosecutorial en-thusiasms. Two county vendors were kidnapped, private funds were paid for public prosecutions, and a county official fled from his bathroom for Canada while the sheriff waited in the parlor. Satirists might have thrown away their pens against reality.

Three reformers on the Cook County board of commissioners and the press were probing a county government suppurating with corruption. The publicity inspired members of the county ring to cover their tracks. Some officials mysteriously quitted Chicago. County records were inexplicably lost or destroyed by fires somehow not reported to the fire department.

The ring had joined hands in 1883. In 1886 it was expanded after some commissioners, conspiring in a janitor's room of the county building, pressed the grievance that committee chairmen were hogging the boodle. Reformer J. Frank Aldrich of the Union League Club observed, "Commissioners would grow eloquent in depicting the sufferings of the poor and the hardships of the sick, and at the same time mentally calculate the 'divide' in the schemes that they were advocating for the alleviation of this distress."[15] As a trivial example, a commissioner's silk underwear costing eighty-five dollars was charged to the county poor house as a bale of muslin.

An aroused Citizens' Association reported, "We brought an injunction suit to restrain the county commission from entering into a contract to sink an artesian well at the poor farm. . . . From this case the reform movement in county affairs began." The statement added blandly, "A fund was raised for a prosecution."[16] Historians have pegged the fund at $150,000, but the association recorded only sixty thousand dollars. (A fund of that type would be raised in time against Al Capone.)

Nic Schneider, a plumber, and Fred W. Bipper, a butcher, were ordinary tradesmen who suddenly became wealthy on county contracts won through kickbacks and bribes for the ring. Citizens' Association president Murry Nelson had been elected a reform commissioner, an anomaly—reformers then mostly disdained seeking public office. Nelson and Aldrich were curious to note that Schneider's invoices were not itemized. Reformers purloined fraudulent invoices from a county safe to photograph them to build a case. An umbrella committee of business groups hired a private detective agency to tail Schneider. The Citizens' Association paid detective agency bills of thirty thousand dollars.

In Greenough's Saloon at Mike McDonald's Store, plumber Schneider toasted "county contracts" with the comment, "I am rich and by gracious in two years I shall be as rich as anybody. Bring us some more wine."[17] Soon after, Schneider was drinking there with a county commissioner. Both were startled when two faces peered in the window. They exited the tavern. The two strangers, private detectives, followed Schneider, who vanished.

The ring discovered that not only had Schneider disappeared but his papers were missing. Alarmed, they hired their own private detectives to find him. Through bribery, it was learned that he was in reformist captivity. Soon Schneider's brother swore out a warrant to arrest him for stealing money from a drunken friend. Nine cops tried to serve the warrant but were ejected by reformist detectives. Schneider, the reformers' involuntary and muffled guest, could overhear the ruckus from the second floor of the building. He elected to become a prosecution witness, shaved off his moustache and goatee, and fled to eastern states in disguise with two private-eye chaperons, staying one jump ahead of the ring's detectives.

Meanwhile, *Chicago Daily News* editor Melville E. Stone persuaded butcher Bipper to surrender his books to the paper. Hinting that the ring might kill him for this betrayal, Stone placed Bipper in the custody of a reporter who escorted him on a similar out-of-state tour.

So reformers had two key witnesses, Schneider and Bipper, but they did not have a grand jury. County commissioners selected not only grand jurors but trial jurors. Thus they controlled investigations and prosecutions of public corruption. State's Attorney Julius S. Grinnell, though a reformer, understandably was not eager to bring charges.

The Citizens' Association, Union League Club, and other groups were lobbying for grand jury reform bills in the legislature, meeting the usual resistance. Commissioner Aldrich came to the rescue.

Routinely, each of fifteen commissioners wrote two names of prospective grand jurors on blank cards to be drawn from a hat. Aldrich happened to hold the hat and noticed that all the cards that were drawn by a crooked commissioner had been bent or creased by his confederates. Aldrich reported this subterfuge to State's Attorney Grinnell, who then persuaded a judge to call a special grand jury. Officers raided county board offices, seizing all documents. The wardens and engineer of the county hospital, the warden of the insane asylum, the custodian of criminal court, many county contractors, twelve commissioners who had served in 1886, and seven incumbent commissioners were indicted on a total of 106 counts.

Defendants pleaded for a change of venue on the ground, accurate but unavailing, that private citizens improperly had financed their prosecution. Schneider and Bipper testified for the state. On 5 August 1887, all defendants were found guilty. The verdict thrilled the city; "the ball game at White Stocking Park was interrupted while the people cheered."[18] In contrast to previous stabs at governmental reform by the judiciary, sentences were serious. They ranged from fines of up to a thousand dollars to three years in prison.

Defendants included Ed McDonald, brother of Mike and engineer of the county hospital, and former police superintendent William J. McGarigle. College-educated, McGarigle had been touted as a reform chief. Actually, Mayor Harrison had appointed him at McDonald's behest. Later, McGarigle joined the county board and served as warden of the hospital. After his conviction, the county sheriff kindly drove him home to see his family before going to state prison. McGarigle asked for time to take a bath, then climbed out his bathroom window and ran down the street. A rowboat and schooner awaited to take him to Canada.

Daily News editor Stone got wind of McGarigle's expatriation and chartered a boat to overtake him. Hoping to intercept the fugitive, Stone was foiled when a competing newspaper publicized the attempt. Two years later, McGarigle cut a deal to return to Chicago from Banff, British Columbia, and clear the books by paying a thousand-dollar fine. He then ran a saloon in the Clark Street vice district.

Meanwhile, the legislature passed laws to reform the Cook County jury system. The Union League Club and the Citizens' Association rejoiced in the outcome of the Great Boodle Trial. "An epidemic of fraud has been followed by the corrective antidote of punishment," the association reported.[19] Jeremiah Porter's congregation had destroyed a claim-jumping building in 1833. Reformist techniques now included kidnapping, secreting of documents, and private funding of criminal indictments. Corruption persisted regardless of its opposition's techniques.

To the elements of corruption and reform catalogued at the end of the previous chapter, the development of ward-committee politics, the ethos of working-class neighborhood communities, and the countervailing rise of businessmen rebels may be added. Further, the growth of a mass-circulation press was critical. Circulation had been driven up by the Civil War and the steady climb of national literacy levels.

The *Tribune*, for example, was an invention of the modern public appetite for news. It was launched in 1847, enabled by the marvel of the telegraph, as a news offshoot of a literary paper, *Gem of the Prairie*. John Wentworth's *Democrat* merged with the *Tribune* in 1861, foretelling the role of the mainstream press in shaping public opinion as a mostly middle-class, probusiness, and antilabor organ. To be sure, there were Democratic and prolabor papers also. Partisan exuberance galvanized many publications. By 1896 Chicago was publishing thirty-eight dailies (eleven of them in foreign languages), 287 weeklies, 319 monthlies, and forty-two quarterlies.[20]

Carter Harrison declared that "the good name of Chicago has been shamelessly attacked for partisan purposes by a part of its press, which has grown fat with its prosperity. . . . As the Mayor of Chicago, proud of its good name, I cannot silently permit the good name to be tarnished by the slanders of men who, had they lived eighteen hundred and odd years ago, would have sold their master for thirty pieces of silver."[21] Harrison had a point in that the *Tribune, Daily News,* and others tended to preen over their exposés, such as those resulting in the Great Boodle Trial. This behavior fueled the romantic mythology of the Chicago press, which survives. The *Tribune* was rhapsodic: "Nowhere else do travelers find the calm repose, the insouciance, the neatness and elegance of attire, the quiet, unassuming manner, the soft, smooth voice, the graceful, languid gait that conspire in the construction of the Chicago reporter."[22] The comment referred to the paper's coverage of high society, not its investigations, which in itself told more than the *Tribune* realized. The Protestant Mayor Harrison and immigrant Catholics took care of the gritty business of politics while millionaires ran the essential functions of the city.

What critics now deplore as media arrogance, the media's assumption of entitlement as sanctioned by the First Amendment, was laid down in those days. The *Traveler* griped: "The Commercial Club is a very worthy and highly respectable body. But it has its weaknesses. One of these is an overweening notion of the importance of keeping its skirts clean from the contamination of the press. What holy water is understood to be to Satan, the ubiquitous reporter is to this august assemblage."[23] In other words, the media would not abide their exclusion from the formation of governmental and business policy. Reformers were just a bit tardy in perceiving the utility of media publicity. By the beginning of the twentieth century, national monthly magazines were powerful enough to create the volcanic eruption called muckraking.

The shaky joint venture between businessmen rebels and newspapers was suggested by a Citizens' Association debate about whether to raise money to pursue city council grafters in 1892:

> Much as we would like to, we have not sufficient evidence to convict anyone, nor to safely proceed. Our experience with gamblers in 1890 was not a favorable one: after great expense and trouble we gave the authorities sufficient evidence for conviction, when it turned out that the indictment was defective, and the principal offenders were let go with a fine. . . . [I]f the newspapers which first took [aldermanic corruption] up had believed it to be a feasible project to pursue to the end its managers would not have let the opportunity slip by: but they evidently thought the case hopeless or nearly so.[24]

Or, if the newspapers don't care, how can we? However, that same year, the association did try to break up the bail-bonding racket. Police would arrest prostitutes and gamblers without warrants, merely to assign them to justices of the peace who gave kickbacks from their fines to police and bondsmen. The association hired a friendly cop as its witness at a particular "justice shop": "For some two or three days before our policeman was taken away from the court, the defiant and insolent attitude of professional bailers, and other court loungers, even of the justices themselves— warned us that something was about to drop. It did. There were 128 arrests of street walkers in one night, and professional bonding again became very profitable."[25]

The association further recorded that "Bucket-shops are pursuing their unlawful methods as openly as the Board of Trade. [In fact, that form of gambling was invented on the analogy of the board.] No less than five are in operation within hailing distance of City Hall and one of them has a policeman there to keep order—One of these places has two Aldermen proprietors. To call them bucket-shops dignifies their methods—plainer language is: low, swindling, gambling concerns."[26]

The association also took up arms against ghost payrolling (then called "payroll stuffing"), a reform project that lasted through the 1990s. Aldermen nakedly made public their fees for job appointments: in the police and fire departments, fifty dollars; in the public works department, ten to fifty dollars depending on the salary; bridge tenders, who had no winter work when the river was frozen, seventy-five dollars. The association hired three detectives to buy jobs in public works. One went to the city yards at 1441 State Street and reported,

> The pay wagon arrived at 7:15 A.M. and stopped in front of Gus Berg's saloon. The city employes fell in line and prepared to receive their pay. Foreman Bracker stood on the steps of the pay wagon and handed the men their money which was in small envelopes. They do not go by names but by numbers. When numner [*sic*] 3 was called, saloon keeper, Gus Berg, stepped up and the envelope was given to him. He fell out of line and returned to the rear and entered the line again. When number 24 was called, saloon keeper Gus Berg handed it to him. There were 25 men in line and there were 42 numbers called and Foreman Bracker put in his pocket any unclaimed envelopes.[27]

In the 1990s, ghost payrolling had changed little in techniques or magnitude except that the pay was automated on computers.

Businessmen and the "construction of the Chicago reporter" conspired anew in a campaign to host a world's fair to commemorate the four hundredth anniversary of Christopher Columbus's voyage to America. In part this project was still another way to scour the stain of Haymarket from the city's reputation. *New York Sun* editor Charles A. Dana (who popularized the term *goo goos*) was the first to call Chicago the Windy City, not for its weather but for its blowhard solicitation of hosting the fair. Chicago's commercial elite and its press fretted that the city's reputation for wickedness would hinder its competition with New York for the fair. To do something about it, they strived mightily to keep the vice-tolerant Carter Harrison from regaining the mayor's office in 1893.

Much has been written about the magnificent World's Columbian Exposition of 1893, the "White City" that prefigured twentieth-century art and science. Our concern is with its attendant vice and reform. Secular reformist businessmen and newspaper editors, along with revivalist clergy, were joined by another type, the evangelical businessman. The prototype was Arthur Burrage Farwell (1852–1936). His Hyde Park Protective Association worked hard to keep the neighborhood near the fair dry. Against liquor money interests, the association had no chance. For one thing, Harrison was mayor once again.

Farwell's ancestors arrived in Boston as early as 1636. Farwell was saved in the primary pietistic conversion experience at age eleven. His uncle, known as the "Christian storekeeper," was a close friend of Chicago evangelist Dwight L. Moody and served as treasurer of the Citizens' Association fund for the Great Boodle Trial. Farwell's father was a U.S. senator. The young Farwell's faith caused a rift with his father. In 1880 a political poison-pen tactic known as a "midnight flier" accused the elder Farwell of secretly owning sixty acres nominally held by a notorious gambler and pimp. Farwell even was named the inventor of the secret land trust, a device still in use in Illinois to conceal the ownership of real estate. Shocked by the flier, the devout young Farwell believed that as a Christian, his father should not consort, socially or in business, with a gambler and pimp.

While working for his uncle's sales firm, Farwell led the 1884 campaign that convicted Joseph Mackin of vote fraud. Having "taken the pledge" against alcohol at a meeting of the Women's Christian Temperance Union, he closed unlicensed saloons, called "blind pigs," in Hyde Park. His activism against alcohol and prostitution lasted well into the next century, when he said, "The greatest power in the world is the power of love. With the application of a little love all the world's difficulties can be settled. . . . If bootleggers [during Prohibition] loved their brothers as they should there would be no more wood alcohol deaths, and the county jail could be used as a museum."[28] This professed faith was remarkable in light of his many disappointments. Like many other reformers, Farwell suffered the fate of outliving his reforms.

Harrison had stepped down in 1887 and left for a world tour. For his posttour 1893 reelection, he had to defeat the major newspapers, religious reformers, and the inchoate Irish-Democratic machine. Fisticuffs punctuated the Democratic nominating convention, out of which the Irish-favored candidate, a wealthy publisher, stormed. The mob then chose Harrison by forfeit. Republicans ran a dull stockyards millionaire, Samuel W. Allerton. If Allerton lost, preachers prophesied, the wrath of God would befall the city.

Harrison campaigned against, among others, transit pirate Charles T. Yerkes, whom the city taxed on only four thousand dollars of his assets. (This scandalous circumstance and others like it were in small part by-products of anti-Chicago state laws constricting municipal taxation.[29]) Harrison said, "There are men in this city who pose as reformers who regularly permit the assessors to value their whole property for less than they paid for the pictures on their walls [a dig at art collector Yerkes]; who cheat the city, then thank God they are not thieves, like the aldermen."[30] He perceived that Allerton's campaign was not just a matter of elitist hypocrisy but a struggle to keep Catholic immigrants from controlling city politics.

Harrison accepted fifteen thousand dollars from gambling lords and put the money in his private safe. He called on a friend to ask, "Please return this money if anything happens to me before the election. I will return it afterwards." Understandably confused, the friend asked, "Why did you take it then?" Harrison explained, "Well, if I did not take their money they would not trust me, and go against me."[31] Many Chicago politicians, then and now, would have understood and approved of such pragmatism.

To cast his own vote, Harrison went to a barn owned by gambling boss Mike McDonald, walking past a gauntlet of thugs. Voters passing ballots through a slot in the door were in jeopardy of having their gold rings lifted by thugs inside. Newly elected, Mayor Harrison promptly launched gambling raids in the First Ward, not a gesture toward his defeated reformist opponents but a feint to cement an alliance with ward bosses once the raids were called off.

On 1 May, fourteen days after Harrison's election, the world's fair opened in Jackson Park. The fair's board of directors already had voted to sell beer there, and liquor was sold covertly.

Any of the estimated twenty-seven million fairgoers could easily find alcohol and vice near the Midway in the Levee of Chicago legend. It was the heir of the Sands vice district wrecked by Mayor Wentworth in 1857. The name "Levee" apparently derived from southern riverfront levees where steamboat passengers would disembark for gambling and prostitution. The expression for visiting the fair's Levee was "going down the line." Many rubes were mulcted, going down the line. While the fringes of the Levee were murderously dangerous, police pairs patrolled its gaslit heart diligently, as too many robberies and killings would be poor public relations for the fair.

Underground guidebooks directed tourists explicitly to the safer bagnios and gaming parlors. Dwight Moody drew tens of thousands to revivalist camp meetings outside the fair. Moody was a grandson of the Great Awakenings, joining the legacy of the Reverend Porter and business evangelists such as Farwell. Pietism did not sleep while Harrison merrily winked at the Levee. At Moody's camp meetings, members of the Women's Christian Temperance Union in black bonnets distributed pamphlets warning people away from the Levee. Unwittingly, they informed many of them how to get there. In its rudiments, the Levee anticipated the crime syndicate of the 1920s.

Upon the conclusion of the fair, an English writer, publisher, and reformer named William T. Stead paid a visit. He stunned Chicago—wracked by labor violence, economic depression, and the eternal conflict between corruption and reform—more than Citizens' Association types, Moody, or Farwell ever did. Stead published a book speculating on what would happen if Christ came to Chicago. From his comfortable quarters in the Commerce Club, Stead did not think the Lord would be pleased. In this conviction he was joined by business leaders who thanked God they were not thieves like the aldermen.

3

Progressives and Muckrakers

1894–1909

Unlike other large cities, Chicago in the Progressive era never experienced the reforms that consolidated overlapping and wasteful governmental bodies, encouraged government by experts, and diminished the influence of local party politics.
—Maureen A. Flanagan, "The Ethnic Entry into Chicago Politics"

One reason that the shortfalls of reformers are puzzling is the formidable assets on their side—wealth, prestige, and moral and spiritual zeal. William T. Stead's *If Christ Came to Chicago!* exemplified and excited all of these like a symbol of that industrial age, an electric dynamo. Stead spoke of urban reform in ecclesiastical terms, calling for a "City Church." He had inherited fervor from the traditions of the Great Awakenings and abolition. At the same time, he expressed a new wave of Protestant thought known as the social gospel.

Aside from piety, the outstanding feature of Stead's book is its empiricism. He named names and cited figures. He published a detailed, color-coded map of the Levee, identified its owners, and furthermore listed the paltry tax assessments on streetcar king Charles Yerkes and other millionaires.[1] These revelations were accomplished with a scrutiny of public records in a foretaste of what is known now as investigative reporting. Stead merged piety with the scientific rationalism of the Enlightenment in a slippery combination that we still strain to define.

Like other visitors, Stead (1849–1912) found the city at once fascinating and repellent. "The building of the city, and still more its [post-Fire] rebuilding, are one of the romances which light up the somewhat monotonous materialism of Modern America."[2] He could not understand how its Christian builders tolerated so much crime and poverty.

Mayor Carter Harrison I, killed by a deranged job seeker as the fair closed, did not live to see the nation enter a four-year depression late in 1893—paradoxically, the same year that the United States became the world's biggest industrial power. That winter's depression was so severe in Chicago that poor children, their parents unable to buy coal, sometimes spent all day in bed as their only defense against freezing to death. A typical Irish immigrant who survived infancy had a life expectancy of thirty-seven years. One person in fifteen went beyond elementary school.

Just eleven days after his arrival, Stead convened afternoon and evening mass meetings at his own expense in the Central Music Hall (at the site of the present Marshall Field's department store). He managed to place on stage at the same time capitalists and labor leaders, including even one of the recently pardoned Haymarket defendants. One wishes that modern technology had been available to record Stead's remarks. The son of a Congregationalist preacher, he had talked with Levee lowlifes that morning until 3 A.M. and said he found them preferable in some ways to hypocritical churchgoers. He further dismayed his audiences by stating that respectable women, by doing nothing against social evils, were more culpable than Levee whores. We do not know whether cheers or jeers held sway in the resulting audience uproar. If Stead was not inflammatory enough, a socialist speaker urged the use of dynamite if necessary to wreck the established order. Stead promptly reclaimed the stage to denounce this notion.

In the end, Stead impaneled a committee of five, including settlement-house founder Jane Addams and millionaire "dry" crusader Turlington W. Harvey. This group became the nucleus of the Civic Federation. Stead charged it to be as well organized as New York's Tammany Hall. Although it did not meet that standard, it was a reform group different from the Citizens' Association. It was morally charged for social justice.

Stead completed his 460-page indictment in February 1894. The cover lithograph showed an angry Jesus driving money changers from the temple with the faces of the money changers clearly recognizable as Yerkes, Bathhouse John, and others. The book was an instant sensation. Seventy thousand copies sold out in one day. The New York press applauded; Chicago's tended to label Stead a foreign demagogue. "He has meddled in a gratuitous, offensive, and . . . insulting manner. . . . [H]is methods and intemperate gabble do not commend him to Chicago," the *Tribune* harrumphed.[3]

An unnoticed facet of the book is its enthusiasm for public works. Stead foretold the St. Lawrence Seaway, which he said would make Chicago the world's premier seaport, and predicted that hydroelectric turbines, publicly owned, would power the city. Progressives twinned public works with social reform as means of urban uplift, but the ways in which public works fuel political corruption eluded them. Reformers often overlook the institutional frameworks of corruption, however ardent their moral energy.

Also, in the utopian vision of Stead's final chapter, only the best citizens would serve on the city council. Indeed, the first mayor of the next century would be Potter Palmer's wife, Bertha Honoré Potter. Thus Stead evinced the prejudices of his class. City government by the well-born was not just Stead's personal daydream. Leading intellectuals and reformers of the time seriously urged denying the vote to the working and immigrant classes.[4]

Stead's baby, the Civic Federation, was incorporated on 31 January 1894 and had spectacular early successes. It first set up a Central Relief Association, which spent $135,000 to shelter the homeless and employ the jobless at public works tasks at ten cents an hour. Members of the federation even swept the city streets for six months to prove it could be done for ten dollars a mile, not the $18.50 the city was paying. Soon the city contracted for $10.50 a mile.

Reformers hoped they had a friend in the mayor's office. John Patrick Hopkins, the first Irish Catholic mayor, was elected to fill the remainder of the assassinated Harrison's term. Hopkins had risen to paymaster under the exacting George Pullman, who fired him, rehired him, and fired him again over religious and political differences.

Prudently, Hopkins had developed a sideline merchant business, his base to run for mayor. Newly inaugurated in 1893, he hornswoggled Stead, who found him "a presentable looking young man, whose countenance is good to look upon." Hopkins vetoed a transit ordinance for which Yerkes had bribed aldermen. Hopkins demanded that railroads build elevated viaducts to reduce the horrifying number of pedestrian accidents. He also called off regular raids on brothels as mere scams for bail bondsmen and justices of the peace. Stead rhapsodized that Hopkins "will not stop far short of the presidential chair."[5]

A clergyman from the Civic Federation called on the new mayor to demand the closing of "gambling hells," reprising a similar entreaty to the late Harrison. Hopkins agreeably allowed that stricter regulation might be possible. The next day, police closed every place of gambling. Hopkins said he knew nothing about it and speculated that the gambling operators had shut down of their own free will. Stead took this to mean "that the Mayor in addition to his other gifts possesses a broad sense of humor."[6] Within weeks gamblers were back in business.

The Civic Federation decided on direct action. Allan Pinkerton's detective agency, based in Chicago, functioned as a quasi-official security force for many residents and businesses owing to the chronic inadequacy of the police. The Civic Federation paid forty Pinkerton men sworn as special constables. They raided gambling houses, axes and crowbars swinging as tradition prescribed. Though some court writs stymied them, eventually one parlor's wheels and tables were burned in the furnace of city hall. Hopkins's reaction, characteristic for a Chicago politician, was to worry about loss of business. He noted that wholesalers told him their out-of-town business visitors expected their hosts to provide a three-night tour of the city's attractions: first theater, then a brothel, then gambling.

The federation's first president was the banker Lyman J. Gage, who was aided by Field and other millionaires, leading clergy, businessmen evangelists, and the redoubtable Mrs. Palmer. But with an exception or two, labor was excluded from the coalition. Thus it did not resemble Tammany Hall. Nor was it prepared for the next major labor uprising, the Pullman strike of 1894. As for Stead, he escaped the reformers' usual unhappy fate of outliving their reforms. Vice in Chicago indeed was being suppressed anew when he went down with the *Titanic* in 1912 after helping women and children into lifeboats.

In April 1894, the Union League Club invited aldermen, including known crooks, to a banquet with the commercial elite to discuss how to cleanse the city of corruption. The businessmen's endeavor was rather touching in that they imagined the problem might be resolved by negotiations around a boardroom table or in leather chairs before a fireplace in a walnut-paneled clubhouse, as their customs ordered. Actually, business and politics occupied different realms. Business aimed for profits, while politics strived to accommodate competing equities, including the claims of working-class immigrants. Such a misunderstanding of democratic processes thwarted reformers for the next hundred years. Some Progressives, such as Jane Addams and Lincoln Steffens, were not naïve about the divide between commerce and politics and wrote about it pointedly. Other bourgeois reformers often did not catch on. Diners at the Union League banquet had scarcely taken carriages home before their authority was challenged by another violent labor uprising.

On 11 May 1894, Pullman's workers struck. The depression induced Pullman to reduce his workers' wages and hours by 25 percent—but their rents not at all. Three thousand men walked out. Pullman laid off many others. The Civic Federation, fifty-six mayors, members of Pullman's family, and Bertha Honoré Palmer, queen of Chicago society, urged that most obstinate of tycoons to negotiate. He refused. Workers across the country then boycotted Pullman sleeping cars. The railroad industry's General Managers Association, based in Chicago, hired "deputy marshals," thugs recruited from the Levee, to protect their scabs.

To obtain federal intervention, the railroads astutely attached empty Pullman sleepers to mail cars, thus potentially hindering the mails under the workers' boycott. Over Governor Altgeld's angry objections, Democratic President Grover Cleveland dispatched troops from Fort Highwood to restore order and protect the mails. Thus the foresight of Marshall Field—Pullman's largest shareholder—in establishing that fort after the 1877 labor uprising was confirmed.

Soldiers were camped on the lakefront when a mob assaulted the stockyards and railroad yards. Federal and local armed officers in Chicago during the eighty-three-day strike numbered 14,186. Violence surpassed even that of 1877. The death toll over June and July was at least thirty-four. On 8 July in Hammond, Indiana, a railroad junction for Chicago, armed troops perched on train cowcatchers shot at protesters (or decoy provocateurs?) burning railroad cars. That action broke the strike, although no deaths were attributed to federal soldiers. Pullman reopened his factory on 2 August, refusing to accept a message from Altgeld appealing for amnesty for his workers until a National Guard officer forced it on him. Maybe without federal meddling, including a court injunction, Pullman would have been forced to arbitrate and American labor history much different. In any case, the turmoil weakened his health; he died three years later.

High-minded, public-spirited members of the Citizens' Association, Civic Federation, and Union League Club had failed to prevent the disaster or resolve its crisis of authority. They found not only that municipal government but personal upper-society pressures could not overcome the power of an industrialist during the Gilded Age, even one, Pullman, regarded by many as an enlightened reformer. Still, the Progressive movement was birthing an insurgency against industrial trusts as personified by Pullman and Yerkes. Before Progressivism flowered, reformers witnessed yet another outburst of municipal corruption.

Following the example of Yerkes, Mayor Hopkins formed a dummy corporation for a municipal franchise. Businessmen who actually intended to use the franchise then had to buy out the dummy for a ridiculously high price. The city council chartered Hopkins's Ogden Gas shell corporation on 25 February 1895. Ogden Gas still is cited as an egregious swindle, but there were no fewer than eight other franchise giveaways for utilities and railways that year. Franchises for the private use of public rights of way dated to a Chicago railroad clouting in the legislature in 1854. Hopkins stepped down as mayor, and when Ogden Gas finally was sold in 1906, his 17 percent share had grown eightfold in value to $1.3 million.

By 1895 reformers were close to despair. They had tried moral exhortation, depression relief, extralegal investigative means, judicial trials, even the jailing of boodlers; and had taken pragmatic steps, such as a revised city charter, stricter election laws, and the 1895 state civil service act. They had not solved the interlaced struggles of capital and labor, corruption and reform, or nativists and immigrants. Local government remained corrupt.

A concatenation of reform and business groups called a mass meeting in March to protest Ogden Gas and other boodle. The two hundred clubmen and the clergy who joined them were frustrated, frazzled, and at a loss. Lyman Gage, who chaired the meeting, said outright that they had failed. Historian Sidney I. Roberts wrote, "The simple fact was that Chicago reformers were bewildered and helpless in the face of intolerable municipal affairs. They were disgusted with their own impotency and their feckless civic associations."[7]

Tritely they appointed a committee of fifteen. One of them wrote up a plan for a third political party, but this old idea was rejected. Nearly a year was needed, until February 1896, for a new group blandly called the Municipal Voters' League to open shop. The league was one of the triumphs of Progressivism. It shunned the Citizens' Association tradition of gathering evidence for the indictments of political crooks. The league's initial purpose was to beat dishonest aldermen at the polls, pure and simple.

At this point, Democratic First Ward aldermen "Bathhouse" John Coughlin and Michael "Hinky Dink" Kenna walk on stage. Crooked and powerful politicians, they were the most vivid paragons of the type that inflamed reformers. Today they are regarded as quaint and amusing figures of Chicago legend. A bar and restaurant along the pedestrian walkway under Marshall Field's department store is called Hinky Dink's, meant to draw from patrons a chuckle over Chicago's tradition of corruption while the store itself continues to be sold to different transnational corporations.

Coughlin and Kenna controlled vice, police, and zoning in the central city for decades. Their naked display of vice and violence, especially in their annual First Ward Balls that enchant modern chroniclers, was so outlandish that reformers ultimately succeeded in ending the balls, if not the vice.

A description of the two men might explain their enduring personae as colorful rogues. Coughlin (1869–1938) grew up in a rugged Irish neighborhood called Connelly's (or Conley's) Patch along Twelfth and Sixteenth

streets between Michigan Avenue and the lake. He would express grati-
tude that the Fire destroyed his father's grocery, thus sparing him the fate
of being a rich man's son and the unthinkable horror of attending Yale.
"Bathhouse" earned his nickname as a masseur in a bathhouse. Later he
operated his own elegant bathhouses and saloons. A sartorial wonder, he
favored swallowtail coats of billiard-cloth green, striped Prince Albert
waistcoats with a plaid vest and plaid pants, and dark green patent leather
shoes, among other gruesome combinations. Not restricting himself to
male fashions, he introduced ordinances in the city council to regulate
the length of women's skirts. Also in the council, he happily recited awful poetry, which he sometimes published in newspapers as his own, although a *Tribune* reporter composed the doggerel for him as a gag. Refusing a bribe of $150,000 from Yerkes, he explained, "I was talking a while
back with [U.S. Representative] Billy Mason. Here's what he told me:
'Keep clear of the big stuff, John, it's dangerous. You and Mike [Kenna]
stick to the small stuff; there's little risk and in the long run it pays a damn
sight more!'"[8] This philosophy of stealing in small increments has guided
many Chicago politicians. In time Coughlin's power was eclipsed by that
of Al Capone, who followed a different school of thought.

Kenna (1857–1946), another son of Connelly's Patch, kept to the background, seeing to political organization and police protection of vice. He
quit school at age ten to hawk newspapers during Chicago's press wars
and at twelve bought a newsstand. Like many young men of the time, he
went west for adventure and landed a newspaper job in Leadville, Colo-
rado, with a letter of recommendation from Joseph Medill, who had given
the diminutive newsboy his nickname. After two years, Kenna returned
to Chicago because Leadville was, to his fastidious taste, too violent.

Kenna perfected methods of vote fraud, such as rounding up vagrants
and shuttling them from precinct to precinct to cast multiple ballots at
fifty cents a vote. Beyond the half-dollar, tramps were given lodging, food,
and beer for days before an election. No wonder politicians, including
nominal reformers, found the vote of the First Ward, which then housed
the Levee, critical.

Kenna was small and slope-shouldered, glum and closemouthed, unlike his partner Coughlin, who was large and voluble; both men were perhaps equally vain. Kenna dressed entirely in black. In a rare newspaper interview after a tour of Europe, he philosophized, "Most everybody in Rome has been dead for two thousand years."[9] During the 1890s depression, he fed eight thousand jobless men in his Workingman's Exchange saloon in a week. "Once a vagrant helped himself to the food too freely, and a bartender demanded a nickel from him. 'Hinky Dink' fired the bartender. Nobody forgets that sort of friend when election day comes."[10] Kenna was the First Ward committeeman for forty-nine years and spent his last days guarded by police and the mob both, compulsively counting and hiding coins in his hotel room lest they be stolen.

Why did working-class voters keep reelecting Bathhouse and Hinky Dink? The reformer Charles E. Merriam observed, "To be recognized and represented by a crook is better than not to be recognized or represented at all, from one point of view. This is not in fact the only alternative, but if it seems to be, the result is the same."[11] Many members of the Civic Federation did not grasp this insight.

When the federation spun off the Municipal Voters' League (MVL), Coughlin invited reporters to his saloon and declared, "This new movement is the mist which rises skyward before one's eyes, and while it may become thick enough to make a cloud and look scarlet and silver and gilt edged in the sunlight, it will yet be the cloud that will blind good political vision."[12]

After much deliberation, the MVL decided its first efforts must be practical, limited, and feasible. The group would elect honest men to at least 34 percent of the city council seats, thus preventing overrides of any mayoral vetoes of boodle ordinances. This goal was prosaic in contrast to the general ascent into glory sought by the likes of Stead. Accordingly, league leaders installed a tough guy as its president—George E. "Buzz-Saw" (or "Old King") Cole, a short, barrel-chested, bandy-legged businessman. Quickly, Cole outraged Coughlin and Kenna. When he reported that Coughlin was a tool of gamblers and thieves, they stormed into his stationery and printing office to demand a retraction: the MVL circular stated that Coughlin was born near Waukegan, Illinois, whereas in fact he was a native Chicagoan. Cole corrected this dreadful error. The two departed, satisfied.

In just two months before the 7 April 1896 elections, the MVL organized itself by ward and precinct. In this sense, it finally met Stead's mandate of mimicking Tammany Hall. It adopted machine tactics such as torchlight parades and door-to-door canvassing. The essential technique was to publicize each alderman's voting record on boodle ordinances. These were printed on placards waved through wards, emblazoned at the top with Coles's legend, A HUNDRED YEARS AGO IF PEOPLE WERE KNAVES, PEOPLE CALLED THEM SO.[13] Victor Lawson sent his *Daily News* reporters to assist the league's investigations. Reform alderman and league member William Kent fed the league inside information about council doings. The league also, following the precedent of the Citizens' Association honored still, hired private detectives to scour up dirt on politicians. Cole, unusual for a reformer, did not flinch at raw politics. His group denounced one candidate merely as an Italian who spoke poor English and ran a saloon. Reform leader Walter L. Fisher said, "Our methods were those of practical politics. We didn't call ourselves reformers. People don't like that word. It suggests long-haired dreamers and theorists—rainbow chasers."[14] The revelation that machine tactics need not always be used for corrupt ends lit the path of generations of reformers in train.

Hoyt King, secretary of the league, calculated that fifty-seven of the sixty-eight aldermen were crooked. The league targeted twenty-six of thirty-four incumbent candidates for defeat. Astonishingly, twenty of them lost. "In what was a peaceful election for Chicago—only two politicians were shot and only one serious gang fight occurred—reform candidates were swept into office."[15] After further MVL successes annually through 1900, only Kenna, Coughlin, Johnny Powers, and a few others known as "gray wolves" remained. Charles Merriam said, "As a result of the League's Herculean labors, Chicago for a twenty-year period had the best legislative body of any American city."[16] Perhaps this was damning with faint praise.

Whatever, reformers destroyed a "robber baron" of the era, Charles Tyson Yerkes, in 1898. Yerkes personified corruption for reformers in the way that

William Thompson, Al Capone, and Richard J. Daley served later, indicating how reformers tend to slight institutions in favor of personalities.

Having grown rich first in Philadelphia—a fact Chicago's upper class could never forgive—Yerkes (1837–1905) came to town in 1881. He had been imprisoned for seven months for mishandling Philadelphia city bonds. By 1886 he had bought control of the North Chicago City Railway. The next twelve years were spent hustling a monopoly over public transit. It was called "traction," after streetcar locomotion, which had switched from horses to below-grade cables in 1882. The term persisted even after overhead electric lines displaced cables twenty years later.

Yerkes openly extolled poor service and crowded, decrepit cars in the interests of profits. Perhaps his biggest mistake was in disdaining the pieties of his class. He did not seem bashful about his bribes, contract kickbacks, and womanizing, however much Medill and other editors vilified him as the "Goliath of Graft." Only once did he threaten a reprisal—actually, a death threat—when an editor wanted to print details of the private life of his wife. In time Yerkes capitalized his transit lines at $120 million with such a maze of overlapping corporations, inflated bonds, and watered stock that businessmen who joined his empire could scarcely sort it out. They were mainly eastern financiers, another fact Chicago could not pardon.

The commercial elite thought it could ruin Yerkes by calling in local loans for which his holdings were collateral. The showdown took place one night in 1896 at the home of meatpacker Philip D. Armour, then the city's richest man. Unknown to the group, Yerkes had placed enough of his wealth in government securities to guard against just such an exigency.

"My loans will be called?" Yerkes asked evenly. "My stock sold tomorrow?"

"That is right."

"All right, go ahead." Yerkes then threatened to dump all his stock on LaSalle Street at once. "If the stock exchange doesn't close tomorrow, your banks all will."

After he jauntily exited, the always pragmatic Marshall Field persuaded the conspirators, "Let Mr. Yerkes alone and he will come to his own end."[17]

In 1895 the legislature had enacted "eternal monopoly" bills granting Yerkes free, ninety-nine-year franchises to use Chicago streets for his transit lines. Yerkes not only bribed the lawmakers but bought the *Inter Ocean* to counter his opponents in the press. Then he approached Governor Altgeld with a proffered bribe of five hundred thousand dollars to sign the bills. Altgeld refused it and vetoed them. Yerkes in turnabout aided the effort to dump Altgeld for having pardoned the Haymarket defendants. The next governor, John R. Tanner, signed lesser legislation to allow the city council to give Yerkes fifty-year franchises.

Yerkes soon started spilling bribery money off city hall tables. The new mayor was Carter Harrison II, who ran in 1897 on a promise of public ownership of traction. The fifty-year ordinance was scheduled for a council vote on 19 December 1898. A mob filled city hall that day. Mistaking a photographer's flash powder for gunfire, aldermen dived for cover under their desks. Under threats shouted against them from the gallery, with hangman's nooses prominently waved, they defeated the franchise giveaway, 40-23. Yerkes shook the dust of Chicago off his feet and went to London, where he headed the syndicate that dug the Underground. He died in 1905 with his fortune down to $2 million while contemplating a divorce from his second wife to marry the daughter of one of his mistresses. History has not honored him for pioneering the mass transit that fathered suburbia and revolutionized land values.

What a strange compound of mob action, political self-interest, and rational good-government reform conspired to beat Yerkes down. One explanation might be that tyrannical pirates such as Yerkes were becoming anachronistic under the tide of Progressivism. Chicago's action, touted as the first municipal victory over monopoly capitalism, thrilled Progressives across the country.

What was Progressivism? Even now, the question has no straight answer. Historians have not agreed on the makings or a definition of the movement. Some say that Progressive reform was driven by a middle-class defense of its status against encroachments by the working class from below and barons of the trusts from above. Others assert that the real impulse for urban reform was the high value that wealthy capitalists attached to efficiency in all phases of life, including government. Further, a school of thought holds, the wealthy eventually killed muckraking because it hurt business. A more recent revisionism argues that municipal governments of the time were not really all that bad.[18] Progressivism is considered here as a political power struggle between *reformers* (fighters of corruption) and *regulars* (those who always supported their party).

The specific remedies sought initially by Progressives are easy enough to list. These reformers aimed to elect honest and competent officials, assure the integrity of the ballot, protect public employees under civil service rules, eliminate waste in government, and enact corrupt-practices laws. Some wanted to disenfranchise the lower class, and many joined crusades against vice. In Chicago, the men who led these efforts tended to share similar life stories.

William Stead, Walter L. Fisher, Henry Demarest Lloyd, and *Daily News* editor Melville Stone were sons of Protestant ministers. William Kent, son of a wealthy meatpacker, was influenced by his friendship with the Reverend Jenkin Lloyd Jones. Kent told a Municipal Voters' League banquet, "Fellow reformers: Our problem is how we can make the other fellow better, without being too damned good ourselves."[19] These men believed in the social gospel.

The social gospel preached that individuals should dedicate themselves to the redemption of others from societal as well as supernatural sins. The war against slavery had led many to clothe government with religious significance, to see the state as an agent of a New Jerusalem. Another tributary flowed from Marxian intellectual currents for the uplift of the working class. Also at the end of the century, the University of Chicago was refining the new disciplines of sociology and political science. The stream of empirical social science inspired Graham Taylor, of the university's theological seminary, to call the social gospel "sociology with God in it."[20] By 1908 the social gospel was formally codified as a creed by the American Methodist Episcopal Church. Still another inflow to Progressivism came from the rural Populist revolt, which climaxed in Chicago in 1896 with the Democratic presidential nomination of William Jennings Bryan after his "Cross of Gold" speech.

Evangelists and secular reformers found common ground in Progressive projects. In 1895 Governor Altgeld signed an enabling act for municipal civil service. To adopt it, cities had to hold a referendum. "The Civic Federation sent out a plea to every clergyman in the city to make civil service a topic for sermons, and almost every pulpit responded. . . . Mass meetings were held in every available hall and armory."[21] Chicago approved civil service by nearly a two-to-one margin, indicating that not only reformers but the electorate were tiring of boss rule. Of course, bosses managed to evade civil service regulations for many decades.

Social-gospel reformers did not operate in an atmosphere of religious comity. Protestants and Catholics still distrusted each other. During the mayoral campaign of 1895, the Loyal American Legion, a creature of the Masonic Temple, sent "personal and confidential" letters (emphases in original):

> Dear Sir: . . .
> For the past eighteen months this city has had an Irish Mayor [Hopkins], and now they want to give us a German Mayor in the person of Frank Wenter; the Democratic candidate for that office.
> For a great many years this city has been governed by foreigners, and *IT IS NOW TIME TO CALL A HALT.* The Irish are good enough in their place, and so are the Germans, but neither of these nationalities ought to be allowed to name a Mayor for a great city like Chicago. *Please keep this matter to yourself and uphold our American Institutions,* and let the foreigners take care of their own business, and allow the government of this city to be run by people who were born here. In other words, vote for
> GEORGE B. SWIFT,
> The candidate of all *TRUE AMERICANS* for Mayor.[22]

Swift was elected, enforced the midnight closing ordinance for saloons, closed gambling halls, and drove brothels disguised as massage parlors out of business. These endeavors were traditional and ineffective. Carter

Harrison's son, whose outlook on vice was not so harsh, replaced Swift. Reformers keep winning battles but losing wars.

Leaders of businessmen's civic groups eschewed the Loyal American Legion style of anti-Catholic bombast. These groups were, nominally and often in fact, secular and nonpartisan. Their leaders also were remarkably bound by class and politics. A study of a twenty-year sample of the membership of the Municipal Voters' League found forty-four Protestants, five Jews, and no Catholics. Forty-two had been born in the United States—although, tellingly, only twelve had been born in Chicago—and just seven were foreign born.[23]

Many reformers were younger holders of second-generation wealth, apostles of the social gospel, and relative newcomers to Chicago. They were less tolerant of municipal corruption than were the city's pioneer capitalists, Ogden and McCormick and the rest. For example, Walter Fisher was born in Wheeling, West Virginia, and went to Chicago to practice law in 1884 at twenty-two; Frank H. Scott, in 1903 the first president of the City Club, was then a forty-seven-year-old lawyer who had arrived from Tipton, Iowa.

Still one more factor behind the Progressive movement was the middle-class leisure afforded by industrialism. Such leisure produced the crazes for bicycles, baseball, and motion pictures—enthusiasms that incidentally undercut the popularity of parlor gambling so that it sought new forms. Leisure allowed businessmen their extracurricular activity of seeking good government. In 1904 the City Club encouraged its members that "the Saturday half-holiday, which is happily becoming so general the year round, should, during the cooler portion of the year, be devoted by City Club members to the consideration of public interests."[24]

Amid these phenomena—Progressivism, Populism, social gospel, social science, leisure, warfare between labor and capital and Protestants and Catholics—politics became respectable. Stead had said it was "bad form" to run for alderman and "a disgrace" to get elected.[25] But for the sons and daughters of the newly rich, politics was fashionable. Even aldermanic seats, ever the preserve of saloonkeepers and other lowlifes, attracted earnest young, wealthy candidates. Mayor Harrison II, for one, was shrewd enough to recognize this trend at the time and made the accommodations needed to win five terms.[26] William Kent, John Maynard Harlan (son of a U.S. Supreme Court justice), and Charles Merriam ran for and won city council seats. Harlan, in fact, was the Republican nominee for mayor in 1905, but the GOP leadership secretly backed the Democrat, Harrison II, in a crossover of partisan bosses that is still operative.

In reaction to business reformers, regular Democrats were consolidating. The Chicago Democratic party was not yet a true machine but was strong enough that Tammany Hall called on it for help. New York reformers were cracking down on Tammany Hall. With brotherly affection, the Cook County Democratic Central Committee chartered a train to New York to join Tammany in an election campaign march down Broadway in 1897. The Chicago party numbered 480, not counting servants, bartenders, and a band and bugle corps. In New York the press made sport of Bathhouse and Hinky Dink, who lived up to their reputations by marching in frock coats, silk hats, and white gloves. The spectacle inspired the writer Franklin Matthews to go to Chicago and pen an early muckrake, "'Wide-open' Chicago," for the 22 January 1898 *Harper's Weekly.* Soon Lincoln Steffens came to town.

Steffens's editor at *McClure's* magazine in New York was Bert Boyden. Boyden sent Steffens on a tour of cities to solicit reformist writers. In Chicago in 1902, Steffens dutifully called on Boyden's brother, attorney William C. Boyden. He suggested that Steffens interview his law partner, Walter Fisher, who was reforming Chicago. Steffens rejected the idea as preposterous: "'Reform, Chicago?' I laughed, and I must have expressed the idea that that might be news, if true, but—impossible."[27] Boyden shrugged and directed Steffens first to St. Paul, Minnesota, then to St. Louis, Missouri. There Steffens wrote "Tweed Days in St. Louis" for the October 1902 *McClure's,* which he claimed (inaccurately) to be the first muckraking article. His reviews of corrupt urban governments were collected in the epochal *Shame of the Cities* in 1904.

Steffens's publisher, Samuel S. McClure, explicitly told him to write that popular government had failed and that cities should be ruled by wise and wealthy men—for example, Samuel S. McClure. Steffens later wrote that he had fought a tough but losing battle against this editorial directive. But perhaps the directive was in his mind when he revisited Chicago in 1903 and ungallantly described it as "[f]irst in violence, deepest in dirt; loud, lawless, unlovely, ill-smelling, irreverent, new; an overgrown gawk of a village," and so on.[28]

Alienation from democracy united such odd reformist bedfellows as Stead, McClure, Pullman, and Field. Unlike Stead, Steffens sought a rational and scientific, not religious, plinth of ethics. He was enthralled by Buzz-saw Cole, Fisher, and the Municipal Voters' League, giving Fisher the benediction of a "reform boss." His October 1903 *McClure's* article was entitled "Chicago: Half Free and Fighting On." Even after a century, it reads as a bold document.

> [F]inancial leaders of Chicago were "mad." All but one of them became so enraged as they talked that they could not behave decently. They rose up, purple in the face, and cursed reform. They said it had hurt business; it had hurt the town. "Anarchy," they called it; "socialism." They named corporations that had left the city; they named others that had planned to come there and had gone elsewhere. They offered me facts and figures to prove that the city was damaged.
>
> "But isn't the reform Council honest?" I asked.
>
> "Honest! Yes, but—oh, h—l!"
>
> "And do you realize that all you say means that you regret the passing of boodle and would prefer to have back the old corrupt Council?"
>
> That brought a curse or a shrewd smile or a cynical laugh, but that they regretted the passing of the boodle regime is the fact, bitter, astonishing—but natural enough.[29]

Aside from another validation of the law of unintended consequences, this passage suggests the way the history of corruption and reform refuses to divide into neat ledgers of good guys and bad guys. Again, both bosses and businesses were invested in the status quo of corruption. Business members of reform groups were only a minority of their class. Early in the Municipal Voters' League campaign, George Cole noticed that prominent businessmen were boycotting his printing business. He said he coveted the approval of his wife and son and the rest could go to hell.

The political boss drew his votes from immigrant workers, his cash from vice lords and respectable businessmen alike—both seeking governmental boons. Often lost sight of are the intelligence, alertness, and astuteness of the boss playing these groups off one another. One can only imagine his puzzlement upon encountering the new breed of reformers, exponents of independent and ideological politics, while the boss understood politics as ethnocultural, partisan, entrepreneurial, and pragmatic.

Steffens's article also opened a literature of condemnation of reformers not just by bosses and grafters but by businessmen and reformers themselves. Mayor Harrison II struck an I've-seen-it-all, imagine-what-I-put-up-with pose late in life. He wrote,

> The reformer sat down daily to three square meals; he lived in a comfortable home, most often luxury surrounded him. What did he care for the necessities of hungry thousands, what did their needs amount to compared with the sacred cause to whose advancement he had committed his everlasting fortunes? . . .
>
> I had learned that many a professed reformer was not averse to accepting graft when it could be done with a modicum of safety.[30]

It was Jane Addams who whetted perhaps the keenest insight into the bosses, businessmen, and reformers of the era. Founder of Hull House in 1889, Addams (1860–1935) was also a women's suffragist, pacifist, and Nobel peace prize laureate. Born in Cedarville, Illinois, and reared in an affluent, pious Protestant home, Addams belonged to the first generation of American women to graduate from college. Hull House advocated the Progressive causes of child-labor and minimum-wage laws, the eight-hour day, and general social and intellectual uplift. By 1911 there were thirty-two settlement houses in Chicago built on the Hull House model of offering social and recreational services to the poor.

Italians, Greeks, and Polish and Russian Jews steadily displaced Irish in Addams's Nineteenth Ward neighborhood. She was confounded that they kept reelecting an Irishman, Johnny Powers. She came to understand why after twice failing to unseat him. On Christmas Eve, 1896, Powers gave away twenty-five thousand pounds of turkey, chickens, geese, and ducks to families in the ward. In an 1898 magazine article, "Why the Ward Boss Rules," Addams allowed that Powers took care of his people, albeit in a grubby, vulgar, political way, just as Hull House did on a higher plane. She estimated that one in five voters in the ward held a job arranged by the alderman. Years later, she wrote,

> [The boss] distributes each Christmas many tons of turkeys not only to voters, but to families who are represented by no vote. By a judicious management some families get three or four turkeys apiece; but, what of that, the alderman has none of the nagging rules of the charitable societies, nor does he declare that because a man wants two turkeys for Christmas, he is a scoundrel who should never be allowed to eat turkey again.[31]

With additional perception, Addams recognized the antidemocratic strain of Progressivism.

> The well-to-do men of the community think of politics as something off by itself. . . . [A]s a result of this detachment, "reform movements" started by businessmen and the better element are almost wholly occupied in the correction of political machinery and with a concern for the better method of administration, rather than with the ultimate purpose of securing the welfare of the people. They fix their attention so exclusively that they fail to consider the aims of city government. . . . [Bosses] are corrupt and often do their work badly; but at least they avoid the mistake of a certain type of businessmen who are frightened by democracy and have lost faith in the people.[32]

Even today, many reformers are fixated on "the correction of political machinery." Nonetheless, it should be noted that some business reformers were leaders of Hull House—George E. Hooker, a *Tribune* editorial writer, preacher, and attorney, actually lived there for forty years. The strands of political, social, and moral reform never divorced, although they did cohabit uneasily.

As for Alderman Johnny Powers, he took Addams's opposition with equanimity. He had prospered with a gambling den over his grocery during the world's fair, even as Mike McDonald took two-thirds of the profits. Powers was Yerkes's man in the city council, thus meriting the epithet "Prince of the Boodlers" under Yerkes, the "Goliath of Graft." Even so, Powers had a sense of propriety. Although like some of his fellow aldermen he owned saloons, dressed ostentatiously, and lived in a mansion despite official pay of three dollars per council session, he required that his confederates not sell out to more than one bidder. In Chicago, this rule amounted to political ethics.

The papers also called Powers the "Great Mourner" because he avidly attended constituents' wakes and sometimes paid for their funerals to spare families the disgrace of burial by the county. This activity was common of bosses in both history and fiction. Short, broad-chested, and soft-spoken on the council floor, Powers, when his Irish started fleeing the ward, insisted that Italians call him Johnny de Pow or even Gianni Pauli, an honorary son of Italy. (Despite this fraternal gesture, during the Capone regency of the 1920s, two of his precinct captains were murdered.) Addams grew grudgingly almost to like the man, who looked with favor on her uplift efforts. When his bandwagon passed Hull House at Halsted and Polk streets, Johnny threw nickels to children and cigars to men while the band played "Nearer My God to Thee."

Addams opposed him not with Italian candidates but with other Irishmen. She may have thereby demonstrated an ethnic preference of her class: the Irish at least spoke English. Even so, she largely ignored the Irish parishioners of the magnificent new Holy Family Church in her ward, preferring Italians "who reminded her of the picturesque quarters she had visited in Naples and Rome."[33] Addams in her writings expressed some anti-Jesuit sentiments. Class and religious biases apparently can encrust even someone as enlightened as Addams.

Her original beef against Powers was that he opposed a new public school in the ward. Hull House found that pupils there outnumbered seats in the local school by three thousand. Addams petitioned the board of education for a new school and won. Then Powers blocked it because he wanted a new parochial school in the ward and feared that another public school would prevent it. So in 1895, the Hull House Men's Club ran an independent candidate against Powers's allied Nineteenth Ward alderman, under the two-aldermen-per-ward system then, but lost.

The next year, Hull House unsuccessfully ran a man against Powers himself with the aid of George Cole and his Municipal Voters' League. During the next two years, the reelected Powers bought off nearly all of his opposition by giving them public jobs—even his election opponent, William Gleeson.

In 1898 Addams opened another campaign against Powers with a speech to the Chicago Ethical Culture Society. Powers proceeded to beat his Irish opponent by a larger margin even than against Gleeson. Addams then withdrew from electoral politics until Theodore Roosevelt's third-party Progressive campaign of 1912.

The heyday of muckraking lasted only several years; by 1906 it was moribund. President Roosevelt coined the term that year from a character, the Man with the Muckrake, in John Bunyan's seventeenth-century classic *Pilgrim's Progress.* Roosevelt said the muckrakers were going too far. As a good politician, he first praised honest reformers fulsomely. Then: "But, in addition to honesty, we need sanity." He knocked down "the wild preachers of unrest and discontent, the wild agitators against the entire existing order . . . the men who preach destruction without any substitute for what they intend to destroy," and so forth.[34]

Overall, though, Progressives accomplished tremendous things in the first decade of the twentieth century. Many features of public life taken for granted today, such as civil service, city planning and zoning, primary elections, and secret ballots are their handiwork. In Chicago they particularly improved the police, city budgeting, planning, and the courts. So-called justice shops run by justices of the peace, bail bondsmen, and police were legislated out of existence by the creation of the municipal court in 1907. The Citizens' Association waged a war against a lottery racket called "policy" from 1903 to 1907; as a result, 126 policy agents and nine bosses were indicted and twelve hundred policy wheels shut down (but policy remained a largely African American enterprise into the 1950s). The association stated that "its chosen plan of work is to remedy official abuses and non-enforcement of law by *publicity* and through the *grand jury*" (emphases in original).[35] This approach led to the epidemic of mass-mediated scandals, with reform reduced to public relations and law enforcement, that burgeoned in the 1970s.

Progressive failures included campaigns to win public ownership of mass transit and the enactment of a new city charter with home-rule powers. The charter effort traced, back through the nineteenth century, the everlasting struggle of Chicago to win independence from Springfield. Urban charters appear as dry, technical matters of government but actually are a stout plank of corruption and reform. The Chicago charters of 1837 and 1863 were frail patchworks. An 1875 referendum narrowly adopted a new charter that managed to favor both city aldermen and rural, railroad-controlled state legislators. Progressives were sure they could do better.

The staircase of events was familiar. In 1902 delegates from twenty-three civic groups met to frame a charter amendment, even though the language of the 1870 Illinois constitution seemed to preclude it. As the reformer Charles Merriam once complained, "With two million population, the City was still unable to grant a concession for checking hats or selling popcorn on the new municipal pier without a special act of the Legislature."[36] The Municipal Voters' League, having fought so hard and gained so much, was tired. George Cole, who had stepped down as MVL president in 1898, was enticed reluctantly to take over the Citizens' Association to win a new charter in conjunction with the Civic Federation. The groups' charter commission wrote a document, submitted it to the legislature, and the legislature monkeyed with it. Not until 1907 was the charter presented for a referendum.

There are two contrary explanations for the charter's defeat by a two-to-one margin. One is that politician Anton J. Cermak of the United Societies for Local Self-Government, in effect the saloon lobby, frightened the working class into believing the new charter would enable do-gooders to outlaw Sunday sales of alcohol. Another is that reformers disdained the proposal as defective after the legislature mucked up the charter commission's original work. Business reformers typically took the outcome as a victory of bad guys over good guys. The charter was beaten by a "combination of selfishness and stupidity with which every constructive movement has to contend," lamented Walter Fisher.[37] Either way, Chicago did not obtain substantive home-rule powers until 1971.

The transit issue was likewise disappointing. Mayoral candidates won and lost elections according to their stand on municipal ownership. The legislature in 1903 authorized cities to own, operate, or lease street railways. Legislative debate was so ferocious that the Speaker of the House fled his chair to take refuge in an anteroom. Mayor Harrison II and others said municipal ownership was a fine idea in the long run but, in the short run, financial and technical obstacles were insuperable. The short run always seemed to evolve into the long run. Harrison stepped down in 1905, citing family health reasons, and was replaced by former judge Edward F. Dunne, who campaigned for immediate municipal ownership to stop the depredations of such as streetcar king Yerkes.

Dunne was an Irish Democrat who espoused "Catholic social liberalism," a corollary of the Protestant social gospel. To administrative posts he named such worthies as Jane Addams and Clarence Darrow. This chronicle would not be a Chicago story without also noting that to get elected, Dunne joined hands with Hinky Dink Kenna and Bathhouse John Coughlin. Dunne took a committee of fifty to Springfield to lobby for local control of transit. The best he could do was to secure a pact with streetcar companies to upgrade their cars and grant the city an option to buy. Many reformers scorned this compromise as unsatisfactory. "Municipal ownership locally was killed in the house of its friends," Harrison II smugly recalled.[38] Not until 1947 was the public Chicago Transit Authority created.

To turn Progressive losses into wins, Walter Fisher, muckraker Lincoln Steffens's "reform boss," founded another civic group, the City Club, in 1903. At once the Club hired a former New York deputy police commissioner, Alexander R. Piper, to investigate Chicago's police force. His March 1904 report showed, for instance, the following:

Nineteenth Precinct, 6:30 P.M.

Civilians behind the desk smoking. Sergeant in shirt sleeves. At roll-call men stood in slouchy positions and talked to each other while orders were being read. . . . Not sufficient number of men to properly care for the precinct. Cellar in disgraceful condition, partly due to the taking care of tramps who used old paper for bedding which is a menace to the safety of the house on account of fire, and to the health of the men in the station.[39]

Piper uncovered worse offenses than poor posture and fire hazards. Twelve commanding officers were cited for dereliction of duty. Although Piper's job was to study administration and morale, not corruption, some patrolmen were indicted for taking kickbacks and bribes from slot machine owners, prostitutes, and taverns. The police chief was personally honest but had won his position because a woman friend had worked as Mayor Harrison's governess. Piper computed that the chief's manpower was short by at least two thousand men. "It is not necessary," he said, "for me to tell you that you have practically no protection on your streets."[40] The report created such a scandal that "Piperizing" the police became a vogue term for reformers in other cities.

The background was that police were controlled by gambling bosses Mont Tennes (McDonald's successor), "Hot Stove" Jimmy Quinn, and Jim O'Leary, son of the woman whose cow allegedly kicked over the lantern that ignited the Chicago Fire. Tennes's "gambling war" of 1907–8 fizzled out after twenty-three bombings but no fatalities or indictments. In 1904 a special grand jury indicted sixty-four gamblers, including Tennes and his brother Peter. Mont pleaded guilty and paid a fine of two hundred dollars. That same year, a five-year bookmaking war moved Harrison to close the Washington Park, Hawthorne, and Harlem racetracks, effectively ending thoroughbred racing for eighteen years, until it was revived with the ardent cooperation of Al Capone. Also in 1904, as the Citizens'

Association stamped out policy lotteries, the gambling ship *City of Traverse* embarked from Chicago for white people's betting excursions on Lake Michigan. In 1906 a grand jury exonerated police chief John M. Collins and his high-ranking officers on gambling protection charges. In 1908 Collins and his secretary were acquitted of further charges of conspiracy. And so it went.

The reform Mayor Dunne ran for reelection in 1907. A Democratic boss paid a call.

> He said to me, "Mr. Mayor, you are going to be beaten next Tuesday unless you make certain promises to some of the leaders in the party in the three river wards [notorious for vote fraud] about police inspections in those wards. Why don't you promise them what they want, then you will be elected for four years and after election you can tell them to go to hell." But I told him that while I appreciated his courtesy in calling on me, I could not comply with his suggestion or make any promises to the bosses about police inspectors who would have charge where gambling or prostitution might be carried on and that I would make no promises that I did not intend to keep. "All right, then," he said, "your goose is cooked next Tuesday."[41]

Despite this loftiness of purpose, Dunne's police were instructed to distribute his campaign literature and remove disorderly, meaning Republican, voters from the polls. Under attack by the newspapers, Dunne lost anyway to Republican Fred A. Busse (the first mayor to serve a four-year term).

Early Chicago Progressives were energized by the presidency of their hero Theodore Roosevelt. As a former president in 1909, he championed an unlikely cause, the rescue of Chicago police commissioner Edward McCann. West Side vice lords rebelled when McCann raised his monthly police protection fees. The vice lords testified against him; he was convicted and imprisoned. Once more, McCann's would not be a Chicago story without recording that he eliminated many brothels and returned "soiled doves" (prostitutes, also called "withered rose leaves") to their parents. He further forced bars to close at 1 A.M. and curbed the cocaine traffic.

Awaiting trial, sounding like a modern sensitive male, McCann said he "was glad to be suspended and have a chance to stay home and play with the kids."[42]

Many reformers refused to believe that McCann was not one of them. The state's attorney was suspected of bringing the case from mere political ambition. Thousands of reformers including Roosevelt petitioned for a pardon for McCann. The former president also wrote Governor Ed Dunne (the former mayor), imploring a pardon. And so it came to pass.

"Businessman Busse," like so many Chicago mayors, was a blend of a machine politician and a reformer. He owned stock in the company that sold the city manhole covers. His personal bodyguard was a pal of a leading gangster. But once, at a time when the seesaw of corruption and reform tilted toward reform, Charles Merriam persuaded Busse to appoint a commission on city spending. Busse probably came to regret the act. The panel included Merriam and Walter Fisher and exposed a network of graft and political favoritism. For instance, a contractor charged the city forty-five thousand dollars to remove a layer of shale at a new sewer site. Commission members visited the site and found only fine clay. The contractor was planning to use the clay to kiln bricks to sell the city. The panel's findings resulted in sixteen indictments—but no convictions.

Merriam's *Report on Municipal Revenues,* published by the City Club in January 1906, was funded by another Progressive type, Helen Culver. She came to Chicago from upstate New York to teach school and was asked by Mrs. Charles J. Hull, who was near death, to care for her two children. Charles Hull was a wealthy real estate broker and, after his wife's death, made his niece Culver his business partner. He died in 1889 and bequeathed his entire estate to her. Thus the Hull home became Jane Addams's Hull House.

Merriam found that Chicago's budget was just impossible: "Of the American cities, Chicago has the lowest tax-rate, the lowest revenue per capita, the lowest total revenues per capita. . . . The local revenue system is decentralized, unsystematic, necessarily expensive, and irresponsible."[43]

Consolidate, rationalize, professionalize government: these were Progressive watchwords. Merriam was elected alderman from Hyde Park in

1909, thrilling the entire reform movement. In hindsight it is equally significant that reformer George C. Sikes lost his aldermanic race in Austin, a West Side ward controlled by Democratic boss Roger C. Sullivan.
Sikes was the prime mover behind primary elections, held for the first time
in 1909 so that voters, not party bosses, would select aldermanic candidates. Sullivan, for his part, controlled a newspaper called *The Eagle,* which
reported that his

> dignified and manly appeal to the voters of the Thirty-fifth Ward
> resulted in the soaking of Sikes and the Municipal Voters' League
> in a way that was thorough and satisfactory. . . . The voters of Chi-
> cago have studied the career of the Municipal Voters' League with
> some interest. They have noticed how some of the men who coined
> the term "grey wolf," as applied to aldermen they could not con-
> trol, became hyenas and then tigers when the settlement of the trac-
> tion [transit] question came around.[44]

The regular politician's scorn for the MVL was not entirely without
cause. After its initial success, the group broadened its goal to seek not
just the right kind of aldermen but the right council committee chairs.
For its endorsement, the league extracted from candidates a signed pledge
to select the chairs on a nonpartisan basis. Then, after Republicans won
a council majority in 1900, the MVL concluded that nonpartisanship was
not a holy grail after all. With meal in its mouth, the group declared "that
most, even of the more prominent reform members, do not regard the
[nonpartisan] pledge as binding in the event it can be shown that better
results can be accomplished" otherwise.[45] Democratic bosses might have
laughed bitterly.

Since boodlers seldom get their say in chronicles of reform, the remarks
of Alderman Mike McInerny after Merriam joined the city council deserve to be recorded. McInerny's effort to overturn the MVL's selection
of a steering committee for the next council was beaten 40–19 in 1909.

> Here we find Ald. Walter Fourflusher Fisher, [McInerny said]. Af-
> ter Mr. Fisher got through with the vilification of the city council

members, what do the council do with him? They appoint him to a job which paid $10,000 a year as city traction attorney. There is not a jot or tittle of legal wisdom emanating from Mr. Fisher on traction litigation that could not as well be handled by the corporation counsel's office. His time is his own; his duties are few and far between. He got a job paying $10,000 a year of the people's money, and we are still in the control of that scorpion-like body, the Municipal Voters' League.

The *Tribune,* quoting McInerny's remarks, prefaced them by exulting,

Grey wolf fangs snapped impotently last night. Blood that was touted to be shed was unlapped as the pack went yelping and howling, galloping down the political alley, their hides stinging and smarting. . . .

Many a time during the McInerny deliverance, which he read in great part, the blush of shame was forced to the cheek of many a woman who was present in the crowded galleries. The big fellow from the stockyards, as he prides himself as being known, broke all possible restraining leashes and, to the silent applause of many a grin and leer on the faces of the fellows in the pack, dared the M.V.L. to do its worst.[46]

For the next ninety years, Chicago suffered public employees whose duties were "few and far between." In 1911 reformers believed that Chicago was ready to elect Merriam as mayor. He ran and lost to Harrison, in part because a playboy named William Hale Thompson and the corruption he represented were ascending as Progressivism receded.

4

Progressive to Prohibitionist

1910–20

There is something of [William H.] Thompson in Chicago, love of a show, distrust of the responsible powers that be, appetite for spoils and graft, drifting irresponsibility susceptible to demagogic appeals, a dangerous mood in every man and in every group.
—Charles E. Merriam, *Chicago: A More Intimate View of Urban Politics*

Charles E. Merriam expressed the fundamental creed of Progressivism when running for mayor in 1911. "You must decide," he told voters, "whether the next four years in Chicago are to be years of graft, crime, lawlessness, waste, extravagance, and defiance of our desires, or whether they will be years of honest, efficient administration."[1] *Honest, efficient:* holy writ for reformers to this day. Harold L. Ickes, Progressive Republican leader, had persuaded Merriam to run for mayor. Financial backers included Julius Rosenwald, chief of Sears, Roebuck and a major civic philanthropist. Victor F. Lawson contributed ten thousand dollars and favored Merriam in his *Daily News*. Even the Irish president of the Chicago Federation of Labor endorsed Merriam for the general election (the labor vote split).

"I like the fellow," Mayor Busse said of Merriam, "but I can't be too familiar with him, otherwise they'd think I was a reformer."[2] Avoiding that horrific label and yet dogged by reformers, Busse withdrew from the Republican primary. Aldermen had first been nominated by means of primary elections in 1909; mayoral candidates got their turn to bypass nominating conclaves of bosses in 1911. Rosenwald was in Europe on a business trip when he learned that Merriam had won the GOP primary. Rosenwald cabled Ickes: "My hat is off to you. I am returning by the first steamer."[3]

The Democratic nominee was Carter Harrison II, previously mayor from 1897 to 1905. It was a classic, brass-knuckled Chicago campaign. On 4 April 1911, ward bosses who controlled vice and patronage elected Harrison over Merriam by four percentage points. Much of the Republican organization under boss William Lorimer secretly backed the Democrat, Harrison, over Merriam in a typical party-leader crossover. Merriam wrote,

> The truth was that the opposition succeeded in convincing many that I was a "reformer," and I was unable to escape from the implications of that pregnant term. . . . [W]as I not from a silk-stocking district? Was I not in the University [of Chicago]? Had I not pursued the grafters, and beaten the machine? . . . If in reality I had been rich and in reality a puritanical reformer of the type described, perhaps I might have enjoyed the situation. . . . If my managers had been thoughtful enough to produce some woman at the psychological moment, demanding that I take care of some bastard son, I should probably have been elected.[4]

Although Merriam returned to the city council in 1913, his mayoral defeat took the steam out of the Progressive movement in Chicago. Its denouement came in 1912 with former President Theodore Roosevelt's "Bull Moose" third-party campaign against his chosen successor, President William Howard Taft. In 1911 Taft had fired Roosevelt's holdover secretary of the interior for plotting against his administration, naming Walter Fisher to replace him. This action enraged Roosevelt, spurring his launch of an independent candidacy. Merriam, Ickes, Addams, and other Progressives led their followers through the Bull Moose door. Fisher and others thought the movement was madness. The GOP schism assured the election of Democratic President Woodrow Wilson. More than ninety years later, the Chicago Republican party still has not regained its footing.

Was Mayor Harrison II a reformer? The question has no clear answer. For one thing, there was no consensus definition of *reform*, represented

as it was by liberal businessmen, the settlement-house social gospel, prohibitionists, evangelical clergy, labor leaders, wealthy uplifters, populists,
and socialists. In turn, Harrison and his ilk disagreed with reformers over
the components of *corruption.*

The Harrisons, father and son, were wealthy, European-educated, and
distantly related to presidents William and Benjamin Harrison. Harrison
II was a Protestant who studied both at Yale and at the Irish-Catholic St.
Ignatius College in Chicago (now Loyola University). He was married to
a Catholic who served as a courtier to Bertha Palmer, queen of Chicago
society, and who reared their children in the Catholic faith. In his own
person, Harrison was an ethnically balanced ticket.

Harrison supported the magnificent Chicago Plan of 1909, pressed by
businessmen's clubs, with its classic mandate for an open and free lakefront. Harrison finally shut down the Levee, although he once ducked out
of city hall to avoid a confrontation with the saloon buster Carry A. Nation. He also was the only mayor to face potential criminal charges while
in office. During his fourth (two-year) term back in 1903, a fire at the
Iroquois Theater killed 602 people, double the toll of the Chicago Fire. Free
tickets had helped city inspectors overlook violations of the fire code, written so assiduously by the Citizens' Association in 1874. The theater manager, Harrison, and other officials were cited by a grand jury, but charges
were not prosecuted. The disaster provoked stricter fire regulations, cop-
ied by other cities in the way that reformers make incremental gains.

William Stead had catalogued forty-six saloons and thirty-seven brothels in the Levee. The numbers did not unduly trouble Harrison, who favored open but geographically confined vice. Like Mayor Wentworth in
the 1850s, he faced pressures when downtown business interests started
to lap against the vice district. Accordingly, Harrison cut a deal with
Kenna and Coughlin to shift the Levee two blocks south but keep it officially unmolested.

Harrison's first term saw the start of the annual First Ward Balls in 1898,
political shindigs with mock-stately sarabands, led by Coughlin and Kenna
at the stroke of a December midnight, followed by mayhem and fornica-
tion. The last alcohol-fueled ball was held in 1908. The businessman evan-

gelist Arthur Burrage Farwell, horrified when he attended one of the fetes, deployed his Law and Order League to city hall, the courts, and newspapers to revoke the balls' liquor license. When these efforts naturally failed, Farwell said, "There is no legal means of stopping the ball. However, there are other strings to our bow."[5] Clergymen took to their pulpits to shame businessmen into boycotting the ball. Kenna tolerantly opined, "I ain't got any grouch against preachers. They're all right in their place. I know some preachers who are mighty decent men. But whenever you hear one of them fellows shout that Hinky Dink is a menace to society, keep your hand on your watch."[6] Whether or not congregations gripped their watches, enough businessmen stayed away from the 1908 ball to undercut its revenues for First Ward coffers. That is the real reason Kenna and Coughlin stopped the balls.

Reformers soldiered on. English evangelist Rodney "Gipsy" Smith led a march on the Levee in October 1909. In January 1910, the Women's Christian Temperance Union marched on city hall. Later that month, the Church Federation, an umbrella group of Protestant denominations founded in 1907, called on Mayor Busse to name a vice commission. Busse complied, but it fell to Harrison to receive the commission's study in 1911. The Reverend Graham Taylor trumpeted that it "proved that the 'regulation' of vicious resorts did not regulate them, and that 'segregation' did not segregate them, and that 'sanitation' did not and could not protect their inmates and patrons from the most infectious diseases. . . . For two years, the report of the Vice Commission to the City Council was pigeonholed by the mayor's office. But its facts had gone abroad. The papers had spread the knowledge of them more widely than the printed report."[7]

Thus reformers had learned the value of newspaper publicity. The 311-page report was banned from the mails as obscene for counting more than one thousand brothels, eighteen hundred madams and pimps, and four thousand prostitutes. Annual revenues were estimated at $15 million, of which one-fourth was profit. Commission members put the matter in terms the business class could understand: the capitalized value of a whore was computed at twenty-six thousand dollars versus that of a "girl" store clerk at six thousand dollars.

Pigeonholing the explosive document or no, Harrison professed shock upon seeing, while attending a convention in St. Louis, an illustrated brochure promoting Chicago's Everleigh Club. Everybody knew about the genteel brothel at 2131–33 South Dearborn Street, opened in 1900 by two sisters from Harrison's ancestral Kentucky bluegrass. On 24 October 1911, Harrison ordered the place padlocked, assuring Kenna that he was not kidding. Police held off until obtaining consent from Kenna and Coughlin, then informing the proprietors and their patrons of the impending raid. Harrison claimed to be angered by the resulting delay until 1 A.M. on 25 October. A Chicago slogan of the time was *Be a Booster Not a Knocker* and the sisters accepted the end with fatalistic good cheer. After all, Minna Everleigh said, she was not a knocker. Harrison, who had presidential ambitions, is remembered largely just for putting the Everleigh Club out of business. In 1912 there was another Levee march led by evangelists, formation of a new committee of fifteen, and indictments of five gambling resort owners.

Graham Taylor, founder of the Chicago Commons settlement, bragged, "[W]e have put the owners of segregated vice 'on the run.' . . . We must put up the strongest kind of fight against restoring the red light district and inviting its inmates to return to the shambles. It is really coming. [State's Attorney John E. W.] Wayman assures me personally that he will not only keep it closed, but will suppress any house or district of which I or others will inform him."[8] The next year, 1913, saw the issuance of 135 vice warrants. Police served only twenty of them. Wayman resigned his office and soon committed suicide. On 16 July 1914 came the raids that finally doomed the Levee and the official policy of geographically enclosed vice (although it enjoyed unofficial revivals). Harrison said in 1915, "There has been no official corruption in these twelve years, nor have friends grown rich at the expense of the public."[9]

Despite this heartening pronouncement, Harrison was defeated in that year's Democratic primary. Later he wrote what could serve as a career summary for all twentieth-century reform mayors: "I have always been a little in advance of public opinion in Chicago. It is true I have not been so far ahead the people could not see me."[10] Harrison's departure cleared the way for a radically antireform mayor, William Hale "Big Bill" Thompson.

"Civic Chicago," the collection of urban uplift groups, tried to keep its chin up as the drive to suppress vice and drink overtook structural reforms of government. Reformers found that extinguishing vice was not universally approved, nor were their own good intentions always assumed. In December 1913, State's Attorney Maclay Hoyne indicted the semisainted Julius Rosenwald, philanthropist and chief of Sears, Roebuck, for property tax evasion. The case was nakedly political and went nowhere, but reformers must have wondered where so many of their friends had gone.

In the first decade of the century, feverish civic improvement efforts were so numerous that reformers could hardly keep them straight. Directors of the City Club grudgingly decided in 1905 to allow women "at committee rooms and occasionally in the general [clubhouse] rooms"—if properly escorted.[11] Jane Addams took advantage of this liberality, venturing into the clubhouse for committee luncheons. The elevator boy "who knew me well said casually: 'What are you eating with today—with garbage or with the social evil?' I replied: 'Garbage,' with as much dignity as I could command under the circumstances, and he deposited me on the fourth floor where I found Mary McDowell, head of the University of Chicago Settlement [House], pinning on the wall blueprints of a certain garbage reduction plant."[12]

Such had been the energy that was ebbing. After Merriam's mayoral defeat, the abashed City Club resolved to thwart the middle-class flight to the suburbs—far from a post–World War II development. Vacant land was still available in the north and southwest sections of the city, so in December 1912, the club invited architects to submit plans to lay out a residential district in an imaginary quarter section, a square 2,640 feet on a side.

The club awarded prizes, but Mayor Harrison and the commercial elite took little notice. In June 1914, the club sponsored a new awards competition to design a community center incorporating schools, libraries, churches, offices, shops, and theaters "in an actual or assumed neighborhood." Hull House reformer George Hooker said it would "reduce the social isolation of the family [and] restore in part the neighborhood life which has so largely vanished from our big cities."[13] Both projects fell flat. Other city leaders shrugged them off, saying the designated areas were too far from the lake and public transportation. Problems of land acquisition and financing, they said, were insuperable. City Club documents do not indicate that members foresaw mass transit or automobiles as instruments of what they lamented as the decline of a sense of local community. By 1916, registered automobiles outnumbered horse-drawn vehicles in the city.

The Progressive concern with planning and zoning was caused in part by steady forays of industry, immigrants, and vice into residential areas. Prairie Avenue near the lake on the South Side was the first locus of Chicago millionaires' mansions, housing such people as Marshall Field, at one time the largest individual taxpayer in the United States. In 1885 Bertha Potter had stunned the beau monde by moving into an awesome mansion on North Michigan Avenue. Instantly it became the new epicenter of the wealthy. Just as creeping industrialism had encroached on vice in the Levee, vice had seeped against the estates on Prairie Avenue. The avenue became a sad remnant of a few wealthy widowers. And so it came to pass that in 1922, one of George M. Pullman's daughters razed her father's vacated old mansion lest it become a whorehouse.

The nineteenth-century Prairie Avenue puritans—Armour, Field, Potter, Pullman, and their descendants—had lost not only their patented street of residence but their moral authority. Businessmen intended to prevent such misfortunes by planning and zoning. A civic drive to zone the city was launched in 1913 and won its enabling legislation from Springfield in 1919. Reformers suspected that Mayor Thompson would regard zoning as another goo-goo love affair that needed to be humored, like planning. Thompson was "for" the Chicago Plan of 1909 in the sense that it required two hundred miles of street extensions, widenings, and improvements, along with the shuffling of railroad passenger and freight terminals: opportunities to mete out boodle in contracts and patronage. Under "Big Bill the Builder," nominal bridge tenders actually were paid to run Thompson's political office. Each generation of reformers seems to have to learn the essence of public works anew. A visiting journalist understood it at the time:

> [C]ivic pride was high in Chicago. It stung, in particular, a few rich men, and these decided that they must have the finest city on the globe. They formed a Plan Commission and gave it money to employ engineers. And although this Commission has never had any authority except that of general public enthusiasm, its edicts have been obeyed as explicitly as Napoleon's were when he commanded Baron Haussmann to rebuild Paris. Through shifting administrations and the worst city government on earth, their work has progressed. "How?" I asked. The answer was a wink. "Remember—there is always big graft in letting such huge contracts for improvements."[14]

To their surprise, reformers found that Thompson favored zoning. Reformers saw zoning as a means to preserve their residential neighborhoods. Thompson perceived conversely that factory and retail districts, once designated, were protected. Businessmen might pay him for such protection. The enactment of the city's first zoning ordinance in 1923 was not the first or last time that reformers and politicians found common ground. In this case, zoning was an endeavor by the middle class to preserve its assets, a practicality distinct from the ardor of early Progressives to build a New Jerusalem on tides of idealism. As tides of reformist idealism ebb and flow, the defense of class interests is the oceanic constant.

"Big Bill" Thompson's type, the idle rich sportsman, is now extinct. Thompson (1867–1944, mayor 1915–23, 1927–31), the son of a Chicago developer, ventured west to find adventure, like Kenna and other young men of the time. Again like Kenna, Thompson now is a source of nostalgic civic merriment. He worked as a railroad brakeman and a ranch cook. Returning to head the family business after his father's death in 1891, Thompson spent his days with the Chicago Athletic Association. He led its water polo and football teams and played cowboy on horseback on city streets. Tall and imposing, if round-shouldered and chubby, he signed up with the William Lorimer Republican organization.

Senator Lorimer was, in the view of some historians, the first Chicago politician truly to merit the title *boss*. A GOP leader introduced Thompson to Lorimer with the comment, "Locally us Republicans always pay too much court to the church element and to reformers. The people want liberality. Let's find a young chap like this one, Billie, an American of good connections and a believer in personal liberty."[15] ("Personal liberty" was code for "wet" support for legal alcohol; "social legislation" its "dry" opposite.) Lorimer, a native of England, a Catholic convert, and a former streetcar driver, prospered on the West Side through an alliance with Irish and Jews. Lorimer had been Yerkes's champion in the state legislature, which in 1909 elevated Lorimer from the U.S. House to the Senate after a four-month deadlock. Declining to rely only on its own reporters, the *Tribune* hired private detectives to investigate allegations that Lorimer bought the office by bribing legislators who happened to be—not a small matter to the *Tribune*—Democrats. Progressives were outraged in particular because the direct popular election of senators, replacing election by legislatures, was one of their causes. Lorimer fought hard to keep his seat, but on 13 July 1912, the Senate voted 55-28 to expel the "Blond Boss" for bribery. Lorimer's biographer concluded that there was a bribery "jackpot" in the legislature, but whether Lorimer personally was guilty is unproven.[16]

The Lorimer affair had many political twists and turns over three years, but its real importance lay in expressing the abiding antagonism between Protestants and Catholics. At the bar of the Union League Club shortly after Lorimer was elected, wealthy lumber merchant Edward Hines, a Catholic, encountered another businessman, Protestant Clarence Funk of International Harvester. Hines said he had spent one hundred thousand dollars to "put Lorimer over in Springfield." International Harvester's share of replenishing the standing "jackpot," Hines casually informed Funk, would be about ten thousand dollars. Funk said, gentleman to gentleman, that he did not do business that way and dropped the matter.

Inevitably, word of this conversation leaked. The Union League Club fell into an uproar, finally taking the excruciating step of dumping Hines from membership. The *Western Catholic* newspaper then devoted its front page and a sixteen-page special section to a defense of Hines, inviting its readers to ask the archbishop of Chicago "what kind of man is this Edward Hines. The answer will convince you that he is a model Christian, an honest businessman—a friend to be loved and admired."

Lorimer, ousted by the Senate, returned home to a hero's welcome organized by Mayor Thompson. Seeing an opportunity to attract Catholic votes, Thompson called Lorimer "a living example that a press trust [meaning the reformist Protestant *Tribune, Daily News,* and others] controls this city and nation, and that a man who will not bend his knees to its dictates can be driven from political or public life."[17]

The Protestant Thompson also reached out to African Americans. Early in his term, he hired blacks for city sanitation crews, spurring Italians, who regarded sanitation as their bailiwick, to fierce protests. Fifteen thousand people heard Thompson defend his employment practices at an unprecedented rally of white and black supporters in 1915.

However disturbed respectable Protestants might be by black city workers, some took comfort in Thompson's vigilance against Catholic hires. "Do you know why my people don't mind this spoils talk in the newspapers?" a member of a women's church group asked a reporter. "Well, I'll tell you. They tell us that the city hall has filled up with Catholics, that the Pope is the real power in Chicago. . . . [I]t may be necessary to crack the civil service law a little to get the Catholics out. My people are willing to see the law broken for that reason."[18]

"Big Bill" had learned from Lorimer the value of cynically assembling ethnic coalitions. One of the Municipal Voters' League's embarrassments was that it had backed Thompson for an aldermanic seat in 1902 on the ground that "the worst you can say of him is that he's stupid."[19] In hindsight the best that can be said about him is that he favored the enfranchisement of blacks—because he needed their votes—and championed public playgrounds, parks, bridges, and paved streets.

Within his first five months as mayor, Thompson settled a transit strike, helped to break a teacher's union, and supposedly enforced the Sunday closing law. In short, he was more or less an ordinary Republican. Then Thompson's career sank steadily from mediocrity to squalor to pathos. The rest of his first two terms traced a familiar pattern: rallies and raids, investigations and indictments, acquittals and survival of the system. In 1916, Thompson and Democratic state's attorney Maclay Hoyne promised a bipartisan campaign to clean up the city together—without notable success. Thompson would say anything. When the city council passed a Merriam resolution asking Thompson to dismiss his two cronies from the three-member civil service commission, he said, "Those fellows in the council who are against me are all a bunch of crooks, and that Merriam from the University of Chicago is the biggest crook of all."[20]

Reformers now had an outright ogre to fight, in contrast to the quasi reformer Harrison. But the fight seemed to have gone out of them. At least it flagged soon after the death of Theodore B. Sachs. Born in Russia in 1868, Sachs fled pogroms there to arrive in the United States at age twenty-one, penniless and ignorant of English. He became a physician and in March 1915 opened a public tuberculosis hospital in Chicago. The White Death then was as terrifying as the epidemics of polio in the 1950s and AIDS in the 1980s.

Thompson was distressed that the sanitarium was not a patronage playground and moved to oust Sachs. A political naïf who took no public salary, Sachs did not grasp Thompson's purpose until the mayor ordered a "civil service reform" investigation of the facility. Sachs caught on at last and resigned in protest on 20 March 1916. Before killing himself on 2 April with an overdose of morphine, he wrote a note "to the people of Chicago":

> The Chicago Municipal Tuberculosis Sanitarium was built to the glory of Chicago. It was conceived in a boundless love of humanity and made possible by years of toil. . . . Every penny of the people's money is in the buildings, equipment and organization.
>
> The city council of Chicago should make a most thorough inquiry into the entire history of the institution, and the community should resist any attempt of unscrupulous contractors to appropriate money which belongs to the sick and the poor. . . . The institution should remain as it was built: unsoiled by graft and politics— the heritage of the people.
>
> In the course of this every man and woman in Chicago will know that Dr. Sachs loved Chicago and that he has given his life to it. My

death has little to do with the present controversy. I would not dig-
nify it.

I am simply weary.[21]

Thompson had called Sachs the worst appointment he ever made. After
the suicide, he protested that the doctor had resisted his efforts to upset
Sachs's own patronage at the sanitarium. The eternally exasperating nature of Chicago corruption and reform was expressed by a physician friend
of Sachs who said that Thompson's city hall was to blame for Sachs's
death—"But it won't touch them in the least. Politicians are not senti-
mentalists. There will be no good result come out of his death. It is just
one good man less."[22]

The City Club on 30 March had called on the city council to appoint
an impartial commission to investigate Sachs's resignation. Nothing happened, so after his death, the Union League Club and the Woman's City
Club took the lead in forming a committee of one hundred to produce a
"good result" from the death by driving the spoils system out of the sanitarium. The committee was perforce a Republican group, and Thompson eventually took over a remnant of it for the 1920 elections.

Not that the threat of popery alone could unite Protestant sectarians.
Open warfare between the social gospel and fundamentalism broke out
in 1917. The liberal divinity school at the University of Chicago on the
South Side turned its cannons against the North Side's Moody Bible Institute, founded by Dwight L. Moody. Both the theological and geo-
graphical divisions are important, signifying class conflicts. Partisan divisions were in play as well. During the presidential campaign of 1916,
prominent national Republicans privately assured leading German American clergy that a GOP administration would not fight Germany in the
world war. German Americans feared that President Wilson, despite the
Democratic campaign slogan that "he kept us out of war," would join
England in the strife.

Anglophile and Democratic-leaning University of Chicago theologians
accused Moody preachers of national treachery for taking money from
Germans and later by favoring Russian Bolsheviks after America joined

the war. Moody-type conservatives countered that liberal intellectuals such as those at the university had befriended Germany more so by their pre-war pacifism, further by their adoption of the Higher Criticism's scientific analyses of Scripture, birthed in Germany.[23] Protestantism, America's majority religion, was rancorously sectarian during World War I and Prohibition, and could not settle on the proper role of the state. Reform movements thereby were constrained.

The social and cultural conflicts that both reformers and Thompson faced would daunt anyone. Wartime industry invited new waves of immigration—especially African Americans from the South—at seemingly supersonic speed. A half-million blacks arrived in just three years. Rapid industrialization and immigration undercut the sense of class-bound, coherent community that businessmen reformers had labored so earnestly to uphold. Thompson sought political shelter and called it "America First."

When the war came, Irish and other Catholics, German Protestants, and Jews all had their own reasons to despise America's main ally, the British. Thompson calculated to unite these groups by demagogically assailing, of all possible villains, British royalty. His most celebrated asininity came in 1927 when he threatened to punch out the king of England should that monarch dare to set foot in Chicago from a state visit to Canada.[24] Thompson also made a big deal out of purging from the public schools allegedly pro-British textbooks that slighted the heroism of George Washington.

There was a price to pay for such trifling with ethnic emotions, and after the war, the bill was presented during the race riots of July 1919. Forgotten is that a riot nearly had broken out in the previous month between Poles and Jews over Jewish pogroms in Poland. Eight thousand Jews gathered in a then-Jewish section of the Lawndale neighborhood on the South Side to resist an expected invasion by five thousand Poles. Police got advance word and were able to prevent violence. Then on 27 July, a black teenager on a homemade raft floated south from the Twenty-fifth Street beach to the Twenty-ninth Street beach. He had crossed an invisible line between the African American and white beaches, a fatal error. Five days of race riots killed thirty-eight people, injured five hundred, and burned a thousand homes. An official investigation blamed much of the violence on Irish social and athletic clubs such as Ragen's Colts and the Hamburg Club. These clubs formed auto caravans that raced up and down the Black Belt along State Street from Twenty-fifth to Fifty-seventh streets, firing gunshots from both sides of their cars in premonitory gangland style.

Thompson was paralyzed by the anarchy and could not bring himself to ask Governor Len Small to call up the militia, forcing Small to do so on his own. (Small was acquitted of unrelated corruption charges in 1922 by a bribed jury.) Pointedly, Small did not mobilize among his four militia regiments one that was billeted in the riot area but was black. Thompson had his faults, but his job of mediating among ethnic and religious enmities was impossible. He suffered nervous breakdowns in 1915 and 1928.

Civil liberties were thrashed during the war and its aftermath. U.S. attorney general A. Mitchell Palmer, in effect the acting president under the stroke-disabled Wilson, in January 1920 ordered the arrests of more than six thousand suspected Communists and radicals. Many were held without bail, many extradited without due process. At least Palmer had an explanation for his xenophobia, because in 1919 he had escaped death in an anarchist bombing near his home. There was little excuse for other leaders of the "Red Scare" who threw one socialist out of Congress and five from the New York legislature.

Chicago joined in the enthusiasm. In September 1917, federal agents raided Socialist party headquarters in the city. William D. Haywood, president of the International Workers of the World, founded in Chicago in 1905 and called "Wobblies," was arrested. Federal judge Kenesaw Mountain Landis in 1918 sentenced fifteen IWW leaders each to twenty years in prison for opposing U.S. involvement in the Great War. Landis's reputation for rectitude won him the post of commissioner of major league baseball after the Chicago "Black Sox" threw the World Series in 1919.

Democratic Cook County state's attorney Maclay Hoyne would not be left behind. He raided three hundred suspected radical hangouts in Chicago, arresting 150 people. Hoyne was a reformer in the sense that reform reduces to the prosecution of public officials when the mayor and state's attorney belong to different political parties.

The new technology of telephone wiretaps was abused by government officials and private reformers both. In this aspect of corruption, Thompson was more sinned against than sinner. Hoyne tapped 1,740 telephone conversations to prosecute Thompson's police chief and a pro-Thompson, African American alderman. The two were wise enough to retain Clarence Darrow as defense attorney. In 1917 they were acquitted, an event that moved Charles Merriam to call Chicago the only completely corrupt city in America.

The next police chief set up a police espionage unit to spy on antiwar dissidents (a strategy revived by Mayor Daley in the 1960s). Thompson was distressed by all this gumshoeing. He saw a "conspiracy against me [in which] my enemies have recently bored holes in the walls of my apartment, installed dictagraphs [an early stenographic device], tapped telephone wires, stationed operators in adjoining rooms and employed spies to hound me." Thompson's most studious biographer adds, "According to Justice Department files, it was true."[25] But at the time, Thompson was disbelieved.

Civic Chicago did not rise up against the repression of civil rights. The City Club board in 1920 "discussed plans for having a public statement issued by a group of prominent citizens in regard to the governmental activities against Radicals." Soon the board rejected a call by activists to stage "a mass meeting [at the Club] to protest the campaign against, and the deportation of, Radicals" because the directors "could exercise no control" over such a rally.[26] That was the end of that.

Instead, Progressives had one last gasp at electoral politics, Merriam's 1919 campaign against Thompson for the GOP mayoral nomination, and two more struggles to rearrange the formal structures of government. Having learned a sorrowful lesson after being branded as a reformer in 1911, Merriam campaigned in 1919 as a war veteran armed for a home-front fight. He and other reformers tried to make an issue of the Sachs suicide. Thompson was a better politician than Merriam, the political scientist, and won renomination and reelection.

Still, reformers managed in 1921 to replace the system of thirty-five wards, each with two aldermen elected in alternate years, with fifty wards of one alderman each—and they were elected on nonpartisan ballots! Bosses did not cry tears on their pillows at this recasting of governmental process because they still effectively controlled it. Reformers also called a state convention to write a new Illinois constitution allowing home-rule powers for Chicago at last. The old warhorse George Cole of the Municipal Voters' League was summoned from civic retirement once again to head the Constitutional Convention League. Illinois voters approved the convention in 1918 and elected delegates in 1919. The new document was placed before voters in 1922 and soundly beaten. As its price for home rule, the legislature had demanded severe limits on Cook County representation in Springfield. Reformers such as Harold Ickes, Edward Dunne, Clarence Darrow, and the publishers of Chicago newspapers could not swallow this and formed the Peoples' Protective League to defeat the proposal. In Cook County, the vote was twenty-to-one against.

Prohibitionists, with their radical idea of social and moral reform, had gotten ahead of the tinkers of political, structural reform. The Eighteenth Amendment was ratified on 16 January 1919. The view that Prohibition was a punishment visited on urban Catholics by rural Protestants has become commonplace. The Volstead Act enforcing Prohibition took effect on 17 January 1920, the twenty-first birthday of Al Capone.

QUIT CLAIM.

"You've got the possession, you shall have the title."

"Quit Claim," an 1859 cartoon from *The Tricks & Traps of Chicago* that mocks the city's 1830s origins in a land boom on a lakefront swamp. *Chicago Historical Society, ICHi-32380.*

The Reverend Jeremiah L. Porter, Chicago's first reformer. *Photo by Max Plain, Chicago Historical Society, Cabinet Card Photographs Collection.*

William Butler Ogden, Chicago's first mayor, booster-politician, and railroad builder. *Chicago Historical Society, ICHi-32561.*

THE ALDERMAN'S DECLARATION
OF INDEPENDENCE

"The Alderman's Declaration of Independence," a view of aldermen, with portraits of streetcar pirate "Charley" Yerkes and alderman Johnny Powers on the walls, by Progressive-Era *Chicago Tribune* cartoonist John McCutcheon. *Chicago Historical Society, ICHi-14902.*

HE WON'T BE REFORMED.

The Bad Little Boy of the Nineteenth Ward Still Persists
in Throwing Stones at Hull House.

"He Won't Be Reformed," an 1898 *Chicago Times-Herald* cartoon that shows Powers, one of the "gray wolves" of the city council, stoning Hull House after its founder, Jane Addams, tried to unseat him. *Chicago Historical Society, ICHi-30814.*

"Buzz-Saw Reformer" businessman George E. Cole, whose Municipal Voters' League threw many crooked aldermen out of office. *Chicago Historical Society, Cabinet Card Photographs Collection.*

"Carter H. Harrison Against the Boodlers!," an 1898 poster with which Carter H. Harrison II, a blend of reformer and machine politician like many other Chicago mayors, condemned "Boodlers," especially Yerkes. *Chicago Historical Society, Broadsides Collection.*

"Harrison and Chicago," a campaign poster for Mayor Harrison, who defeated reform challenger Charles E. Merriam in 1911, taking the heart out of the local Progressive movement. *Chicago Historical Society, Broadsides Collection.*

First Ward aldermen Michael "Hinky Dink" Kenna and "Bathhouse John" Coughlin, whose nakedly flamboyant corruption inflamed reformers for decades. *Chicago Historical Society, ICHi-10972.*

Mayors William Hale "Big Bill the Builder" Thompson and William "The Mayor Who Cleaned Up Chicago" Dever with their wives in 1927. *Chicago Historical Society, ICHi-10024.*

Cook County Democratic chairman Patrick A. Nash and Mayor Edward J. Kelly, whose "Nelly-Cash" machine led the city through the Depression and World War II. *Chicago Historical Society, ICHi-25538.*

"The Warning," a *Chicago Tribune* cartoon by Carey Orr that expressed the fear that Richard J. Daley, when first elected mayor in 1955, would be controlled by "the Bosses." *Chicago Historical Society, ICHi-09943.*

Women marchers from Daley's ancestral Eleventh Ward, which indicated how Daley's genius for organization made him the undisputed boss. *Chicago Historical Society, ICHi-34722.*

The archetypal cigar-chomping, fedora-adorned Chicago ward boss (unidentified) from the Daley era. *Photo by Stephen Deutch, Chicago Historical Society, ICHi-35542.*

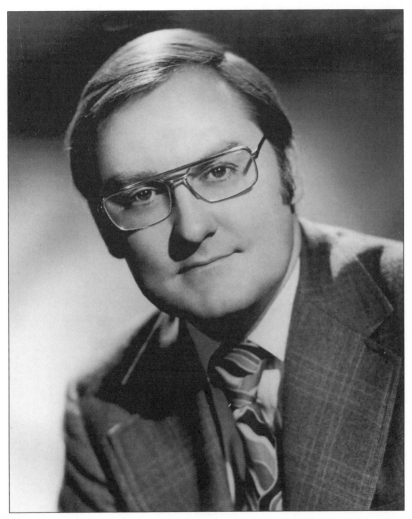

James R. Thompson, the U.S. attorney for the Northern District of Illinois, who put many Daley associates in prison in the 1970s and served as governor from 1977 to 1991. *Author's collection.*

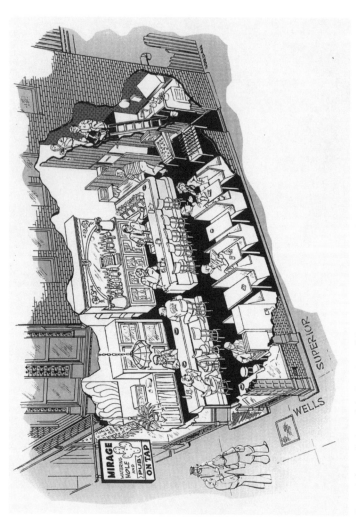

An artist's rendering of the interior of the Mirage tavern, secretly owned by the *Chicago Sun-Times* and used in a sting operation against crooked inspectors in 1978. *Photo by Jack Jordan; reprinted with special permission from the Chicago Sun-Times, Inc. © 2003.*

A 1986 shot of Mayor Harold L. Washington (with sledgehammer), the city's most successful reformer, though attacked for ethical missteps himself. *Chicago Historical Society, ICHi-22781.*

Alderman Lawrence S. Bloom, Chicago's "last" reformer and a convicted felon, savoring his reelection in 1995. *Photo by Bob Ringham; reprinted with special permission from the Chicago Sun-Times, Inc.* © *2003.*

5

"Big Bill" and Bootleggers

1921–33

[T]he story of Al Capone and the Prohibition Era is not only one of crime, it is also the story of a valiant struggle, led by the people of Chicago, against a powerful criminal underworld . . . that was not the result of an alien conspiracy in the form of a transplanted Sicilian Mafia as is popularly believed, but . . . was the result of the history of Chicago itself.
—sociology professor and former
Chicago policeman Robert M. Lombardo

Al Capone was not an organizational genius, and Eliot Ness did not single-handedly take him down. Those are two major myths. Lesser ones are that Capone poured as much as $260,000 into Thompson's 1927 reelection campaign and that the gangster then hung a portrait of the mayor on his office wall in homage. Supposedly flanking it were images of his other heroes, Washington and Lincoln, in a gangster's triptych of honor. Only recently have those latter two tales been debunked.[1] Meanwhile, what traditional reformers were doing during Prohibition gangsterism is a mostly untold story.

The rat-a-tat-tat rubouts of competing bootleggers in Chicago have won such a hold on the national mythology that only the essential facts need be listed here. Mob boss "Big Jim" Colosimo imported Johnny Torrio from New York as a bodyguard in 1910. In 1919 Torrio likewise imported Capone as *his* bodyguard. Colosimo was murdered in 1920. Torrio took over his operations. In 1923 Torrio and Capone were forced out of Chicago to Cicero, a Bohemian suburb nine miles west of the Loop. Serious gang warfare broke out in November 1924 among Italian, Irish, and Jewish crime bosses.

Decades before, Chicago established the customs of street violence. Even before Capone and Torrio decamped for Cicero, the city was having one of its periodic labor wars. In 1921, during the transition to a peacetime economy, the construction industry ordered wage cuts of 20 percent for skilled workers and 30 percent for unskilled. A lockout followed inevitable resistance by the Irish-dominated trade unions. Eventually the unions accepted federal judge Kenesaw Mountain Landis, who had cracked down on the Standard Oil monopoly with a $29-million fine, as arbitrator. Landis found the local construction industry "rotten with manipulative combinations, uneconomic rules and graft, which caused the stagnation of building" even during a chronic housing shortage.[2] Despite his bashing of industry, Landis's settlement was so antilabor that capitalists quickly formed a Citizens' Committee to Enforce the Landis Award. Members included Julius Rosenwald of Sears, Roebuck, benefactor of reform groups.

Ensuing bombings became known as the building-trades war. In 1922 alone, fourteen buildings were bombed, two policemen were shot and killed, and State's Attorney Robert E. Crowe played to the galleries by ordering wholesale arrests. The head of the Building Trades Council was a Torrio gangster. Only one small-time figure was convicted. Bombings occurred on 10 and 12 April 1922, but bombers took a day off for election day, 11 April, lest voters be frightened from the polls and fail to reelect the bosses. A judge sentenced some election officials to jail for vote fraud, but another court released them. By 1929 the Employers' Association published *It's a Racket!*, a catalogue of allegedly horrific things done by organized labor. For instance, during a single month, fifty thousand tires were slashed on cars parked in the garages of businessmen who declined to pay protection money to the Midwest Garage Owners Association. That same year, the Citizens' Committee to Enforce the Landis Award considered its work done and disbanded.

In the previous decade, the newspaper circulation war differed in purpose but not in kind from the city's gambling and labor wars. William

Randolph Hearst, the model for Charles Foster Kane of the cinema classic *Citizen Kane,* had launched the *Chicago American* in 1900. Hearst's desire to overtake the *Tribune* and other Chicago papers found expression in the armed seizure of *Tribune* delivery trucks and the disposal of their contents in the Chicago River in 1907. Carriers and newsstand dealers who resisted dropping the *Tribune* were beaten, but a *Tribune* lawsuit quelled the violence for a while. Then, after Hearst's penny press caused a newspaper price war in 1910, the *Tribune* found it expedient to hire away Hearst's top thug, Max Annenberg, enraging Hearst. Next came competing acts of truck hijackings, driver kidnappings, newsstand bombings, and gunfire. Those times are a platform of the fond mythology of the Chicago press. Over two years, twenty-seven people were killed. Only a small socialist daily reported the mayhem, as the major papers honored a news blackout. Eventually the *Tribune* won the conflict by means of capitalistic enterprise—it secured cheaper newsprint by buying timber rights and building paper mills in Canada, moves accomplished by Robert R. McCormick.

Max Annenberg once approached Al Capone at the behest of *Tribune* boss McCormick to prevent a *Tribune* drivers' strike. After Capone did as asked, he remarked, "Them circulation fights was murder. They knifed each other like hell. . . . And who do you think settled all them strikes and fights? Me, I'm the guy."[3]

Violence intended to serve the ends of labor, capital, or ethnicity was not invented in Chicago by Prohibition mobsters. As for old-fashioned political violence, the city obliged as Prohibition dawned. In the primary of February 1921, bombs were exploded successively at a meeting of people supporting Anthony D'Andrea, a nonpartisan opponent of Alderman Johnny Powers; at the home of a man whose son-in-law worked for D'Andrea, and finally at the headquarters of the candidate himself. These detonations might have been recriminatory. Powers's home had been bombed months earlier, after which he posted a constant armed guard. In March, two supporters of Powers were killed. In May, D'Andrea was ambushed and killed with a shotgun.

Where was Mayor Thompson during this carnage? He ordered his police chief to conduct gambling raids, with the usual outcome and with the added twist of a feud with the Republican state's attorney, Robert Crowe. When it came to vice crusades, Crowe claimed the franchise.

Another demand on Thompson's time was lawsuits and countersuits involving the newspapers. Libel suits became something of a mayoral avocation. Thompson did not conform to the *Tribune*'s idea of a proper Republican, so the paper printed the news that he had allowed private lawyers to batten on transit contracts. Further, he exhausted the city's borrowing authority by shoveling transit funds into municipal operating costs. In 1920 Thompson, on behalf of the city, sued the *Tribune* and *Daily News* in separate $10-million libel cases. The *Tribune* reactively sued Thompson for $2.9 million in 1921, seeking to recover excessive fees boodled to consultants who appraised private land needed for public works. In response, Thompson appealed to President Warren G. Harding's White House for help. Harding sided with the big-city Republican mayor by instructing his administration not to aid the *Tribune*'s case. Thus, officials up to the secretary of commerce, who then was Herbert Hoover, and even the attorney general thwarted the paper's fact-finding efforts.[4]

Meanwhile, Crowe was hard at work prosecuting Thompson's cronies. He indicted the mayor's political strategist Fred "The Big Swede" Lundin and fifteen others for conspiring to defraud the public schools of a million dollars. Testimony in the four-week trial described offenses such as the purchase of $133 potato peelers. In 1923 all defendants were acquitted. Lundin's defense attorney was Clarence Darrow.

Labor wars, circulation wars, political bombings, meretricious gambling raids, finagled lawsuits, criminal acquittals—that Prohibition criminals might find a welcome in such a city was no anomaly. Moreover, Chicago simply detested Prohibition. Irish, Jews, African Americans, and other immigrants to the city had long national histories of reasons to distrust official authority and its laws. Even the *Tribune,* mouthpiece of the Protestant bourgeoisie, opposed Prohibition. In 1922 the city council voted to spend no city funds to help enforce the Volstead Act. In four advisory referenda, voters expressed their own disapproval.

The spectacle of Prohibition gangsterism eclipses Chicago's business-as-usual activity during the 1920s. The South Park Board built Soldier Field on the lakefront, never mind the 1909 Chicago Plan's mandate for an open lakefront, for $8.5 million. At the same time, Los Angeles built a bigger and better Civic Stadium for $1.7 million. The 1926 Army-Navy football game at the new Soldier Field gathered $625,000 in receipts. Each service academy got $150,000, leaving $325,000 for so-called expenses, craftily allocated by South Park Board president (later mayor) Edward J. Kelly. Total construction costs for Soldier Field in three stages from 1922 to 1939 amounted to $13 million.

Traditional reformers in the 1920s hardly knew what to do. Businessmen reformers founded the Chicago Crime Commission, the first of its kind in the country, in 1919. At first its basic task, before wandering into outright vigilantism, was gathering data. The Civic Federation concerned itself with public budgets, bond issues, and taxes. The Citizens' Association fought the age-old battle against vote fraud. E. J. Davis, superintendent of the Anti-Saloon League, founded the Better Government Association in 1923 to fight bootlegging; it soon found itself engaged mostly against vote fraud.

George C. Sikes, father of the fifty-ward law and former investigator for the Bureau of Public Efficiency, scolded the Municipal Voters' League in particular and the reform movement in general in 1922.

> The league in its later days has become stale and conventional. It has gained standing in highly respectable quarters and lost the favor with the common people which it once had. Its refusal to publish the names of its executive committee was so stupidly inexcusable that even its friends could not defend it from attacks on this ground by Mayor Thompson. Unless the league can thoroughly rejuvenate itself soon by fresh popular contacts and reorganize on democratic lines the community would be better off if it should cease to exist. . . .
>
> The trouble with Chicago is that its newspapers, civic agencies and capable citizens do not develop and support leaders of the [Detroit reform mayor James] Couzens type.[5]

With Thompson's city hall representing crime, vice, and spoils run amok, reformers sought a Couzens type. Late in 1922, the City Club held a forum with the primly nonpartisan title "What Are the Issues and What Kind of Man Do We Need for Mayor?" It was organized by Graham Taylor and Mrs. Kellogg Fairbank, a novelist, socialite, and Democratic national committeewoman. The day after Christmas, businessmen and clergy from numerous civic groups convened at a Loop hotel to form a committee of one hundred. At first its job was to find a goo-goo Republican to run against Big Bill. On 3 January 1923, the City Club held a public luncheon at which the committee evolved into the Nonpartisan Citizens' Mayoralty Committee, headed by Mrs. Fairbank.

On 11 January, that group listed two Democrats and five Republicans as acceptable reform candidates. Soon the school graft scandal broke. After Crowe got word to Thompson that another round of city hall indictments might come soon, Thompson, always full of surprises, declined to run for reelection. The reform movement ended up backing Democratic nominee William Dever. Though an Irish Catholic, Dever was a respectable judge and former alderman—an honorary WASP, as it were, to reformers.

The Republican nominee was the obscure postmaster Arthur Lueder, himself a reformer. That both major candidates were true reformers was a first. So was Dever's bipartisan showing. He won a landslide, running well even in the outlying Republican wards ringing the Democratic inner city.

Not a naïve goo goo as sometimes portrayed, Dever had agreed to hand over city hall patronage to Cook County Democratic chairman George E. Brennan. This deal, presumably necessary to gain party backing, sustained the power of the ward bosses—as with Mayor Dunne's alliance with Kenna and Coughlin in 1905. Previous and successive examples of such collusion could be cited.

An archetypal boss, chairman Brennan was a former coal miner who grew rich via a bonding company whose services were retained by city employees. Brennan once related to reformer Charles Merriam a conversation he had with a crook:

George, what about the liquor privileges for the Loop district?"

"Why, I don't know."

"I'll give you $100,000 a year for those privileges, George."

"No, no, I don't think so."

"Well, I'll come back again."

Well, when he came back the second time he pulled out the biggest roll of bills and slammed it down and said, "George, here is $100,000."[6]

Brennan said he spurned the cash because Dever would not tolerate what then was called *collection*. In Merriam's view, Prohibition gangsterism was an iatrogenic disease caused by such reform. Because Dever shut bootleggers out of their normal transactions with politicians, they had to organize separately. Gangsters thus became city hall's parent company, so to speak, not its joint venture. The upshot was modern organized crime. This theory was not just Merriam's own. As late as 2001, an anticrime authority wrote that the Capone gang became "the official mediator between the underworld and Chicago's established political structure. Independent gamblers could no longer seek out their own deals with local politicians."[7]

Dever's first action in office, like that of the original reform mayor Medill, was to raid gambling dens and brothels. For good measure, Dever added "black and tan" saloons that fostered racial mixing in the South Side's Black Belt. Closing the black and tans gratified many white voters—racial mingling had been officially cited as one of the causes of the 1919 race riots.

Then, backed by the Chicago Law Enforcement Committee and prudently having secured promises of support from law enforcement at all levels of government, Dever waged the "Beer War" of 1923. Although it failed in the end, Dever's courage cannot be denied. Four thousand saloons were padlocked and sixteen hundred business licenses revoked from drugstores and the like that sold liquor on the side. Within a hundred days, the city effectively was dry and Dever a national celebrity—"the mayor who cleaned up Chicago."[8]

Dever's blunder was in thinking that the crackdown settled the Prohibition issue for his administration. Personally "wet," be believed Prohibition was a bad idea but that rigid enforcement would lead to its repeal. (In the long run, he was right.) In the meantime, he might win the reformers' hoary goal of municipal transit ownership. Cutting deals, Dever passed a limited form of public ownership through the city council. Duly was formed the Nonpartisan Citizens' Committee of One Thousand to support Dever's plan. Reformers scorned its imperfections, and it was beaten in a 1926 referendum.

That same spring, a U.S. Senate subcommittee convened hearings on Prohibition. Members of Chicago's Better Government Association testified that mobsters and politicians were in cahoots to subvert Prohibition. Miffed, the city council sent its own delegation to Washington to protest that Prohibition was failing only because the public would not tolerate it. Next, Chicago's U.S. attorney said state courts and local police tied his hands on enforcement. That provoked an indignant Dever to take the next train to Washington to defend his own and Chicago's honor. His two days of testimony can be read as the lament of a good man blocked from attaining real reform because of the national obsession with the ultimate reform, Prohibition. Dever's earnestness was so compelling that he was mentioned as a potential presidential candidate, and when he stepped off the train back in Chicago, thousands cheered.

Two lesser episodes of the Capone saga might illustrate why Dever failed. The first is now forgotten, maybe because it was not murderous. It features another reform type, the fearless, crusading, and independent journalist. Robert St. John was not a capitalist autocrat like Medill or McCormick of the *Tribune* or Lawson of the *Daily News*. Nor was he a Graham Taylor or Mrs. Fairbank. St. John was a kid, really, just twenty-two when he became editor of the *Cicero Tribune* after Dever had driven Capone and Torrio to Cicero.

The two gangsters controlled the suburb's government. On 24 January 1925, Torrio was shot while carrying groceries into his home but survived. Discouraged by this event, he moved back to New York and then Italy, yielding the Chicago mob to Capone. Capone cut a deal with local officials that the mob could run gambling in Cicero but not prostitution. St. John started reporting Capone's double-cross openings of brothels there and elsewhere. Capone, modestly by his lights, assigned the rival *Cicero Life* all of the town's public-notice ads. Then he pressured merchants not to advertise in the *Cicero Tribune* on pain of having their property tax assessments increased or of facing a forest of "No Parking" signs in front of their shops.

St. John, undaunted, interviewed prostitutes in a local Capone brothel, scrupulously paying ten dollars for each fifteen minutes. "I had been to France and had had 'experiences,' " St. John confessed, but he was "nauseated" by the place. Al's brother Frank supposedly arrived at 4 A.M., perceived what the editor was doing, and fled down a fire escape. The whores "insisted I [St. John] depart by the window of a second-floor toilet from which I could jump to the roof of a lean-to and then to the ground. I was grateful for their concern, but as I jumped I wondered what my chances were of staying alive."[9]

His resulting article filled an entire edition. "The next issue of the *Cicero Tribune* carried very little social news," he wrote. "The story was continued from page to page . . . For years after that I used to say that I had one distinction which I thought unique: I had written the lengthiest and most thorough exposé of a house of prostitution that had ever appeared in a newspaper."[10] Among the "repercussions" he noted was the formation of a Ministers' and Citizens' Association. This group appealed to the state's attorney and sheriff for law enforcement, of course without satisfaction. The Cook County sheriff was Peter B. Hoffman, so inept and corrupt that he was lampooned in the play *The Front Page* and its movie versions as Sheriff Peter B. Hartman.

The Ministers' and Citizens' Association raided a Cicero gambling resort. Alerted, Al Capone sped to the place and complained to the leading raider, a Congregationalist minister, that reformers were picking on him. "Reverend, can't you and I get together—come to some understanding? . . . If you will let up on me in Cicero, I'll withdraw from [southwest suburban] Stickney."[11] The clergyman refused this peace entreaty, but the gambling shop was back in business that afternoon.

Prostitution, gambling, and bootlegging thrived even when goo goos resorted to extralegal methods. The Ministers' and Citizens' Association named an action committee and gave it one thousand dollars to spend as it saw fit, no questions asked. The money allegedly was given to Hymie Weiss, a Polish Jewish gangster and enemy of Capone. Soon the new brothel was destroyed by fire.[12] The Capone gang did not see the newspaper exposé and the fire as just coincidental. Three days later, three thugs superintended by Frank Capone beat St. John in broad daylight. On two corners of the intersection stood Cicero policemen to interdict any interference.

Upon leaving the hospital, St. John found that Al Capone had paid his bill. The editor went straight to town hall and demanded arrest warrants against Frank Capone, one other thug, and two John Does. The desk sergeant refused but at length asked St. John to return the next morning for the warrants. Then, St. John found himself alone in a room with Al Capone.

> He was impeccably dressed in a blue shirt, white stiff collar, blue tie pierced by a sizable diamond, black well-polished shoes, blue pocket handkerchief, and black hat at a jaunty angle. . . .
>
> "I'm an all-right guy, St. John, whatever they say. Sure I got a racket. So's everybody. Name me a guy that ain't got a racket. Name me one!" . . .
>
> "I'm taking a lot of my valuable time telling you about me so you'll get me straight, see? I don't hurt nobody, especially you newspaper boys. I like all of you. You don't do me no harm. You advertise me. What more could I ask for?
>
> "Take the Ship. That's a big operation. Lots of overhead. But how can I advertise? I'd like to buy a page in the Chicago *Tribune* every day. Come to the Ship. Best gambling joint in the country. But I can't advertise. So you guys write stories, exposures or whatever you want to call them, and they get right on the front page and I get my advertising for free. Why should I get sore? I ain't no heel."[13]

Soon the nonheel started peeling off bills from a wad of hundreds—first three, then two more, then another before St. John lost count. "I was juvenile enough to like dramatic gestures, so without saying a word I turned abruptly, opened the door, went out, and slammed the door shut as hard as I could. My only regret years later was that I had been unable to see the facial reaction of Mr. A. Capone, antique dealer, after I left."[14]

Capone probably did not worry too much about it because he bought out the *Cicero Tribune*'s partners, who fired St. John. He left Chicago for a distinguished career as a national and foreign correspondent.

The second damaging episode for Dever, an outright assassination, came just three days after he returned from his Washington triumph. William H. McSwiggin was the twenty-six-year-old star prosecutor under State's Attorney Crowe, having sent seven minor criminals to death row in eight months. On 27 April 1926, McSwiggin and five pals walked out of an illegal saloon in Cicero. Twenty bullets hit McSwiggin; two other men were killed and two were shot but lived. The evidence indicates that the leading triggerman was Capone, mistaking McSwiggin for Weiss—although, as always, Capone had arranged a reliable alibi. Six grand juries were impaneled. The number of indictments was none.

Chicago was inured to gangsters killing gangsters, perhaps even satisfied by the idea. The British philosopher Gilbert K. Chesterton visited the city and wrote, "I do not mean to be at all Pharasaic about Chicago. It has many beauties, including the fine fastidiousness and good taste to assassinate nobody except assassins. . . . In the advanced, inventive, scientifically equipped and eminently post-Victorian city of Chicago the criminal class is quite as advanced, inventive and scientifically equipped as the government, if not more so."[15] As Chesterton suggested, the average Chicagoan did not live in fear of wanton gunfire (although, businessmen noted, such fear engendered by the media inhibited the city's convention and tourist trade). Still, the murder of an assistant state's attorney in the illegal drinking company of hoodlums shocked even Chicago. This crime, as much as the defeat of the transit plan, took the remaining heart out of Dever's administration.

State's Attorney Crowe vowed yet another ultimate crackdown and asserted that his young deputy merely had been gathering evidence at that Cicero saloon. The claim was disbelieved. On 11 October the Capone mob, having improved in identifying targets, managed to kill Weiss. That murder prompted a peace conference among mobsters, whose ensuing territory-sharing treaty characteristically was announced to the press by Capone. He abrogated it with the St. Valentine's Day massacre of 1929.

The Bureau of Internal Revenue estimated the 1927 income of Capone's gang at $100 million, of which $10 million was Capone's profit. Thirty million dollars was budgeted for graft to buy politicians and police. Once more, such data are imprecise. The *Chicago Daily News* estimated the combined revenue from bootlegging and gambling for all gangs at $6.26 million a week, or $326 million a year.

Julius Rosenwald and others implored Dever to seek another term in 1927 to drive a stake through "Big Bill." Thompson ran for mayor and beat Dever by nine percentage points. Often recorded is that Capone gave Thompson's campaign $260,000; a more reliable source put the figure at $150,000; the true amount cannot be known. Not disputed is that the election followed violence and vote fraud in the mid-1920s or that the civic carpet of burning coals of racism seared the 1927 election.

Presiding circuit court judge Edmund K. Jarecki, a Polish goo-goo hero, had sentenced eleven election judges and clerks to jail after the 1925 elections. A legal technicality invalidated the proceedings, and Crowe declined to sign a writ of mandamus to correct it. An officer of the Citizens' Association finally signed the petition for the writ. A study by the association in 1926 took special notice of the sixteenth precinct of the Forty-second Ward.

> When there were not voters in the polling place, [ward heeler John] Sherry would walk to the back door and holler "all right." Then men would come in from the rear room and from the second floor with bunches of ballots that they had marked, and Sherry would open the ballot box and the men would drop the ballots in the box. At intervals during the day Sherry and O'Malley (an official who has never been apprehended) would take about ten ballots at a time and go into a polling booth and mark them and put them in the ballot box.[16]

And so on. Jarecki canceled his summer vacation to continue prosecuting vote-fraud cases without pause. By September 1927, 169 defendants had been named, of whom twenty-three were found guilty and fifteen sentenced to jail. This success rate in punishing polling dishonesty was unprecedented.

The taste of victory was temporary once again, for Capone repatriated to Chicago after Thompson's reelection. Dever's partisans had tried exploiting working-class white racism just as Republicans exploited the threat of popery. Democratic boss Brennan had warned that Thompson's election would turn the city over to the Black Belt and gangsters. Democrats slyly dispatched blacks into white neighborhoods to canvass for Thompson and staged a fake rally of blacks for Thompson in the Loop, where black faces were seldom seen. On Loop streets, a calliope played *Bye Bye Blackbird.* Voters apparently were so disgusted with Prohibition, or at least so enamored of Thompson's demagogy, that these tactics were unavailing. Thompson's reelection provoked the historian Will Durant to ponder whether the Western experiment of democracy was finished.

The character of Thompson's third term might be conveyed by another obscure incident. Fred Mann arrived from Germany as a boy and became a waiter at the Green Mill, a famed nightclub. Later he ran the Million Dollar Rainbo Gardens, a popular nightclub on North Clark Street. Wishing to celebrate the reelection of his pal Thompson, Mann staged a victory party at Rainbo Gardens with three thousand guests and two orchestras. Supporters gave the mayor a Lincoln sports coupe. He traded it for a touring car with a spotlight installed to illuminate his face as he drove city streets. After a discreet delay, Mann sent Thompson a ten-thousand-dollar bill for the cost of the party.

Imagine Mann's surprise when federal Prohibition agents suddenly threatened prosecution for his having served alcohol at the Thompson fete. Mann's next step was to call on the mayor for help. Mere clerks rebuffed him. The feds padlocked Rainbo Gardens. Soon who called on the nightclub owner but a mobster who suggested he might reopen under a partnership giving a cut of the profits to the mob. Mann again entreated city hall without result. Scorning the mob, he tried importing jai alai games to his now-dry club but lost money. On 8 October 1930, Mann took a walk in Lincoln Park, sat on a bench, and shot himself in the head. A bloodstained envelope in a coat pocket contained four notes to family members. He told his widow, "I am going insane seeing you suffer from my misfortunes. Had I only listened to you all would have been different. Have mercy on me."[17] He was fifty-seven years old.

The *New York Times* reported on its front page the day after the 10 April 1928 primary, "Chicago went to the polls with sluggings, kidnappings and other forms of violence accompanied by the rat-tat-tat of machine guns." So many bombs were thrown that it became known as the "pineapple primary." Election violence had begun in January when bombs exploded at the homes of the city comptroller and of an adviser to Thompson. On 21 March "Diamond Joe" Esposito, a gangster and GOP ward leader, was shot to death on a sidewalk as he walked between two bodyguards. The homes of a U.S. senator and of a candidate for state's attorney were bombed on 26 March. Octavius Granady, who challenged a mobster for a Republican committeeman post, was slain on election day. Within six months, sixty-two bombings occurred in Chicago. Thompson was defeated for reelection to his GOP ward committeeman slot and State's Attorney Crowe was beaten. So, despite the "pineapple primary," jubilant was the mood of reformers.

Inspired reformers won for the venerable Frank J. Loesch, head of the Chicago Crime Commission, an appointment as a special assistant Illinois attorney general. Twenty persons were indicted for assault, kidnapping, and conspiracy to murder, along with routine charges of vote fraud. A women's reform group recorded that of seventeen defendants actually tried, sixteen were convicted. "Among them was a state senator. Nine were office holders, and the others were saloon keepers; gamblers and hotel [brothel] keepers. This was the only conviction ever obtained in this city which showed the plain alliance of crime and politics."[18] Reformers sometimes seemed ignorant of their city's history. For demonstrating the entente of crime and politics, surely the Great Boodle Trial of 1887 sufficed. Anyway, reformers took some additional solace because former judge John Swanson, after beating Crowe in the Republican primary, was elected state's attorney in November.

A more significant date for Thompson personally might have been 20 June 1928. That was when he and others were found liable in the $2,245,604 real estate appraisal boodle suit brought by the *Tribune*. The mayor had his second nervous breakdown.

After the St. Valentine's Day Massacre of 1929, State's Attorney Swanson ordered all Cook County speakeasies and brothels closed. The outcome was predictable. Anyway, the massacre had so horrified business reformers that they paid a visit to the new president, Herbert Hoover, in Washington. His predecessor, Calvin Coolidge, already had launched an investigation of Capone for tax evasion at the request of his vice president, Charles G. Dawes, a banker from the Chicago suburb of Evanston. Hoover recalled in his memoirs,

> In March, 1929, a committee of prominent Chicago citizens, under the leadership of Walter Strong, the publisher of the *Daily News,* and Judge Frank Loesch, president of the Chicago Crime Commission, called upon me to reveal the situation in that city. They gave chapter and verse for their statement that Chicago was in the hands of the gangsters, that the police and magistrates were completely under their control, that the governor of the state [Republican Louis Emmerson] was futile, that the Federal government was the only force by which the city's ability to govern itself could be restored. At once I directed that all the Federal agencies concentrate upon Mr. Capone and his allies. . . . It required two years to assemble the evidence and conduct the trials, but in the end we restored the freedom of Chicago.
>
> In the subsequent [1932] Presidential campaign Vice President [Charles] Curtis informed me he had been approached by an important lawyer who said he was in a position to deliver the bootleg vote in the large cities if I would agree to pardon Capone. I asked the Vice President what answer he made. He said: "I told him he really could think up a better joke than that."[19]

At the time, Hoover assured the Chicago envoys that he soon would redeem a campaign promise by naming an impartial commission to study

Prohibition. The eventual report of the Wickersham Commission in 1931 was dismaying. Federal agents had killed about two hundred bootleggers and 269,584 people were jailed for a total of 26,613 years, all at a cost of $300 million, while anyone who wanted a drink could get one without much strain.[20] In his conference with the Chicagoans, Hoover did not disclose some of his other maneuvers on the Capone front.

Also in March 1929, the president met with Republican publisher Robert R. McCormick in the White House. The St. Valentine's Day Massacre had moved McCormick's *Tribune* to editorial despair: "The butchering of seven men by open daylight raises this question for Chicago: Is it helpless?"[21] McCormick, like the goo goos, implored Hoover to sic the Treasury Department on Capone. The president carefully wrote out Capone's name on a memo pad, as though it might slip his mind.

During one of his daily postbreakfast exercises, Hoover tossed an eight-pound medicine ball over a net on the White House South Lawn to treasury secretary Andrew Mellon while demanding, "Have you got that fellow Capone yet? Remember, I want that man Capone in jail!"[22] Supposedly, Capone offered the government $4 million to settle his tax problems but was spurned. Capone incidentally never met Eliot Ness and, at his trial, asked his attorney to point him out. Prosecutors doubtless felt pressured to ship Capone off to prison before Hoover's reelection campaign. Methods used to nail Capone by federal agents and private citizens alike were impure. Capone was indicted on 5 January 1931, convicted on 24 October, and sent to prison on 4 May 1932 with a ten-year sentence. But only the most obdurate optimist could agree with Hoover that he had restored the freedom of Chicago. Cynics wondered why the Republican White House never prosecuted Mayor Thompson despite his obvious partnership with Capone.

Somewhere there is a line between eccentricity and madness, and a common debate in Chicago concerned on which side of that demarcation Colonel Robert R. "Bertie" McCormick stood. The state of his mental health would be of no particular interest to anyone except his family and biographers but for the fact that psychic distress often was evinced by figures of Chicago corruption and reform. To say that the conflicts were so intense and soul-consuming as to generate emotional disorder would be facile. Perhaps nothing more than the ordinary incidence of mental illness is reflected. All the same, the roster is intriguing. Pioneer settler, businessman, publisher, and educational reformer John S. Wright ended his life in insane asylums. Mayor Medill fled Chicago for Europe during a nervous breakdown. Muckraker Henry Demarest Lloyd broke down. State's Attorney John E. W. Wayman, sanitarium chief Theodore B. Sachs, Republican leader Edward J. Brundage, and U.S. senator J. Medill McCormick, the *Tribune* publisher's brother, committed suicide. Reformist *Chicago Daily News* publisher Victor F. Lawson had an episode in which he could not sleep or bear to be left alone. White Sox owner Charles A. Comiskey died as a recluse after the "Black Sox" scandal of 1919. Depression-era mayor Ed Kelly, fearing conviction in an earlier sanitary district scandal, "took to a hospital bed where a friend saw him writhing in terror while a nurse on either side of the bed held his hand."[23] Michael Kenna ended his life as a reclusive crank. Mayor Richard J. Daley showed traits that his critics called paranoid. Due for surgery after a stroke in 1974, Daley underwent the operation a day before it was officially scheduled and posted police around the hospital, lest assassins try to cut the power supply. Donald A. Neltnor, former executive director of the City Club, committed suicide in 1999.[24]

When *Tribune* reporter Alfred "Jake" (or "Lucky") Lingle was gunned down on 9 June 1930, the reactions of neither publisher McCormick nor Mayor Thompson made up their finest hour. McCormick had served as a colonel in World War I and later wrote a letter claiming credit for inventing nearly all modern military tactics, which even his supporters conceded was ludicrous. McCormick's mother once said, "Bertie's not quite right in the head."[25]

Lingle had started as a *Tribune* copyboy in 1918 via the favored route to employment in Chicago—he was recommended by a ward boss. Lingle had known police chief William F. Russell as a boyhood chum on the West Side. Lingle had met Capone in 1920 when Capone was a lowly assistant to Torrio. Such contacts made Lingle a valuable police reporter, although he never wrote a line of copy. In those days, many "legmen" reporters phoned in their tips to "rewrite men" in the newsroom, who cranked out the copy. Lingle was one of those freewheeling reporters.

Earning sixty-five dollars a week, he lived like a millionaire. No fool, Lingle commented to a policeman that he was being tailed as he entered stairs down to a pedestrian tunnel under Michigan Avenue to catch an afternoon train to a suburban racetrack. Soon a man shot him in the head, tossed aside the handgun, and disappeared in the crowd. Lingle fell face-down, stubbing the cigar between his teeth into the floor.

Just the day before, McCormick had met in his *Tribune* office with a federal official in hot pursuit of Capone. The agent mentioned that Lingle was familiar with Capone, even accompanied him sometimes to his Miami resort. McCormick pledged cooperation and arranged an appointment with Lingle two days hence. Reasonably, McCormick concluded that his thirty-eight-year-old reporter—whom he did not know—was killed to prevent his becoming a government informant.

The *Tribune* at once offered a reward of twenty-five thousand dollars for information leading to the conviction of the killer or killers. Even McCormick's enemy William Randolph Hearst posted rewards. The murder of a reporter was as shocking as that of assistant state's attorney McSwiggin in 1926. The mob was a fixture in Chicago but sometimes went too far. A *Tribune* editorial of 11 June 1930 was a chest-beating call to arms: "It is war. There will be casualties, but that is to be expected. . . . The challenge of crime to the community . . . . has been given with bravado. It is accepted."

The publisher did not take well the evolving news that Lingle had been a crook. Lingle's diamond-studded belt buckle was identified as a gift from Capone. Supposedly he had boasted to another reporter of fixing the price of beer in Chicago. Lingle helped businessmen get political favors, policemen obtain promotions and transfers, and criminals ward off police. He also borrowed heavily from businessmen, aldermen, and the city's corporation counsel—who in effect was the acting mayor under the ailing Thompson. On 30 June the *Tribune* admitted that Lingle was no martyred hero: "That he is not a soldier dead in the discharge of duty is unfortunate considering that he is dead." While the editorial was unsigned, that sentence carried the unmistakable stamp of McCormickesque prose.

Thompson had installed William F. Russell as police chief under a reputed deal to stay the $2.2 million judgment of 1928 in the case brought by the *Tribune* against improper city real estate assessments. The *Tribune* favored Russell, a crony of crime reporter Lingle, for the chief's job. It happened that the Illinois Supreme Court in 1930 ruled in Thompson's favor in the assessment case.

After it was disclosed that Lingle and Russell had shared a brokerage account, Russell was forced to resign. Thompson, still recuperating from a breakdown, did not grasp the severity of the crisis and ignored calls for him to step down as well. He merely jeered at "the Lingle-Tribune Evangelistic Institute."[26]

Rival newspaper executives also took some glee at the puncturing of McCormick's sanctimony. Hearst's *Chicago American* demanded that *Tribune* executives explain to a grand jury how their editors could have been ignorant of Lingle's criminal activities. WHO KILLED JAKE LINGLE AND WHY? the *American* twice headlined in shouting, 120-point type. The first part of the question beckoned fingers to point at Capone, but Capone passed word to the state's attorney that he was innocent and indeed had assigned his men to find the killer. Meanwhile, the *St. Louis Star* sent a reporter to Chicago to investigate the case. This diligent journalist revealed that the city editor of the *Chicago Evening American* was a frequent guest at Capone's Miami resort, that a police reporter for the *Herald* and *Examiner* enjoyed a sideline income as press agent for a mob-controlled dog track, that another reporter got a kickback of a nickel on every sack of cement sold to local builders, and that still another participated in Cook County graft.

Ten months after Lingle's death, a St. Louis hoodlum named Leo Vincent Brothers was convicted and sentenced to fourteen years in prison for the killing. The minimum sentence reflected the judge's belief that Brothers had not acted alone. The identity of his employer and accomplices, if any, or whether Brothers was paid to "take the fall" for a Chicago mobster remains a mystery. When Thompson visited him in his cell in 1936, Brothers still would not talk, although he did tell the former mayor that police had hung him over a door and burned him with lit cigars in trying to force a confession.

A North Side casino called the Sheridan Wave Tournament Club was closed by police after the St. Valentine's Day Massacre. Mobsters planned to reopen it in June 1930, but Lingle allegedly had raised his protection fee from 10 percent to 50 percent of the net revenues (the ordinary rake-off was 40 percent). Therefore, North Side racketeer Jack Zuta or Capone himself ordered Lingle killed. This theory is as plausible as any.

Zuta, the reputed boss of "white slavery," was murdered on 1 August 1930. With foresight he had arranged for prosecutors to find incriminating evidence in the event of his death. The files included canceled checks to judges, senators, a newspaper city editor, and Thompson's Republican club. Lingle's murder had tugged a thread to unravel a cover over corruption of a depth and breadth that appalled even jaded Chicagoans. Previously, crime had been easily personified: It was the fault of Capone, who ran the rackets, and Thompson, who permitted him to do it. Now it was undeniable that corruption was not the monopoly of a few evildoers but, instead, was pervasive and endemic. Not since Prohibition began had this periodic lesson for reformers slammed with such force.

In any case, "Lingle's betrayal left McCormick feeling more suspicious than ever about human nature. . . . Learning exactly the wrong lesson from the debacle, the Colonel became more, not less, reclusive."[27] His isolation and rancor reached outposts of extremity. Thompson's reelection defeat in 1931 twitched the *Tribune* to splatter its most toxic venom:

> For Chicago Thompson has meant filth, corruption, idiocy and bankruptcy. He has given our city an international reputation for moronic buffoonery, barbaric crime, triumphant hoodlumism, unchecked graft and a dejected citizenship. He has ruined the property and completely destroyed the pride of the city. He made Chicago a byword for the collapse of American civilization.[28]

Actually, Thompson's successor, Anton Cermak, might have been even more corrupt. Thompson, unable to bear the loss of public office, tried to found a third party, dabbled in anti-Semitism and Nazism, forlornly sought the GOP mayoral nomination in 1939, and died as a recluse, attended only by his mistress, in a Chicago hotel in 1944. Unhappy deaths seem to visit Chicago wrongdoers and reformers both.

A new coterie of wealthy Protestants resolved that only upright citizens such as they could rid the city of its Italian American crime syndicate and the malfeasance of Thompson's multiethnic, working-class political machine. While the Municipal Voters' League had adopted machine tactics and the Ministers' and Citizens' Association tried a fraternity with the underworld against Capone in Cicero, this group journeyed into utter vigilantism. Its leader, Robert Isham Randolph, said, "No honest man needs to defend his liberties nowadays; constitutional rights are invoked only as evasions and loopholes to escape the law."[29] In due course, Randolph himself was moved to invoke the Fifth Amendment against self-incrimination.

First calling itself the Committee of Courage, later the Citizens' Committee for the Prevention and Punishment of Crime, the group came to be known as the Secret Six. Members took the modifier seriously. Its membership and finances have never been fully disclosed. FBI files on the matter gained by writers under the Freedom of Information Act are still censored. For sure, it is known that the panel was organized in February 1930 by the Chicago Association of Commerce, linking with the Chicago Crime Commission. Two of the six members belonged to the Sons of the American Revolution. Where local and federal law enforcement had failed, they believed they would succeed by virtue of their rectitude and money.

The group hired undercover agents, tapped telephones, and passed out cash. Seventy-five thousand dollars was dropped on the Treasury Department's enforcement branch to help investigate Capone.[30] The Citizens' Association had made sure to escort its two major witnesses out of state before the Great Boodle Trial. The Secret Six sent its star witness off the continent, to South America, until he was needed to testify at Capone's trial.

Chief financier of the six was Samuel L. Insull Jr. (1859–1938), like George Pullman, a dubious reformer-as-tycoon. The son of an English dairyman, Insull went to America to become the top assistant to inventor Thomas Edison. In Chicago, like many other capitalists, he borrowed a stake from the Marshall Field family. During the 1920s, he controlled the electric and gas utilities, elevated railways, and commuter rails between the city and suburbs. In 1926 Insull in effect bought a U.S. Senate seat for Frank Smith, provoking the Senate to refuse to swear Smith into office. After William Lorimer's ejection in 1912, Chicago surely won a national record by seeing two of its elected U.S. senators ushered out of the chamber's doors within fourteen years.

As an employer, Insull was enlightened for the times, unlike his predecessors Pullman and Yerkes. When the Depression hit, Insull extended $50 million in credit to Chicago so that it might pay its schoolteachers and police, reprising the actions of Mayor Ogden in the panic of 1837 and the Citizens' Association in 1876. Later the Depression broke Insull. He ruined many smaller investors in what was then the largest corporate collapse in history. He departed to Europe to evade prosecution for breaking mail-fraud and bankruptcy laws. In 1934 he returned to Chicago, was tried three times, and thrice acquitted. Insull died in a Paris subway with eighty-five cents in his pocket and $14 million in debts. This was the man who believed his money, probity, and influence might stamp out corruption.

At first the Secret Six was allied with State's Attorney Swanson, an enemy of Thompson. But Swanson broke with the group in 1932 amid accusations that the state's attorney and the six were wiretapping each other's offices. The Secret Six went so far as to open its own illegal speakeasy, the Garage Cafe at 60 East Thirtieth Street, as a convenient place to buy information from low-level criminals and police.

The chief investigator for the six eventually claimed the group had spent a million dollars, handled 595 cases, and aided in winning fifty-five convictions. One member of the Chicago Crime Commission scoffed, "The Secret Six never fought crime, never brought about any real information that led to prosecutions, but did gather a lot of information which could be used for blackmail. . . . The Secret Six accomplished nothing in the purification of Chicago."[31]

A grand jury called the leader of the six, Robert Isham Randolph, to testify about the group's wiretaps and other activities in 1932; Randolph pleaded the Fifth Amendment. He was accused of conflict of interest for taking a salary of twelve thousand dollars from businessmen to run the six while drawing another twelve thousand as an engineer for the corrupt sanitary district. Meanwhile, Insull had fled to Europe and another of the six, Julius Rosenwald, died in 1932. With the Depression drying up the group's funds, in December of that year, a jury awarded damages of thirty thousand dollars to a man falsely arrested by Secret Six agents. In April 1933, the Association of Commerce, ending the posing of businessmen as a posse saddled up to ride horseback down dusty western streets, disbanded the six.

The story of the six is a modern one: they inspired a Hollywood movie. As a businessmen's interest group, they employed private funding of prosecutions after the pattern of the Citizens' Association in the Great Boodle Trial of 1887 and exploited mass-media publicity, including some in the *Saturday Evening Post*. A 1931 gangster movie, *The Secret Six* starred Wallace Beery, Jean Harlow, and Clark Gable in a story obviously based on Chicago and Capone. The film featured a chase scene and much gunfire, scenarios now all too familiar. The hero was Gable as a reporter who aided the private six. The public notion of reform was moving from a good-government enterprise of moral entrepreneurs into dimensions of scandal, mass media, cops-and-robbers thrillers, public entertainment, and the cult of celebrity. These trends would reach dismaying extremes by the end of the century. In Chicago, at least, their genesis might have dated to 1868 when Alderman "Honest John" Comisky summoned to testify before his investigative committee the infamous madam Carrie Watson. Upscale reformers gradually shifted their targets from specific governmental bodies to a mass-mediated audience for scandal.

With the debacle of the Secret Six that accompanied the Depression, the Republican party as a factor for reform in Chicago left the field of play for good to become mostly a heckler on the sidelines. The new Democratic mayor, Anton J. Cermak, was, with Fiorello La Guardia of New York, the best urban ethnic politician ever.[32]

On 19 December 1932, Cermak did something predictable, almost banal— he ordered a raid on the headquarters of the old Capone mob. During the fracas, Frank "The Enforcer" Nitti was bodily held by policemen and then shot and wounded by another policeman who thereupon shot himself in the hand, or arranged to be so shot, to stake a claim that Nitti had shot first. The raid reflected Cermak's attempts to shift control of North Side gambling to persons friendlier to his administration. In his inaugural address, Cermak had promised to solve "the so-called crime situation" by naming a police commissioner who "will not be interfered with in the slightest degree by me."[33] Then he appointed a man who would safeguard gambling for ward committeemen.

His corruption aside, and despite an utter lack of what now is loosely called charisma, Cermak was an uneducated political genius. He expanded the ethnic makeup of the machine while professionalizing its operations. "A house for all peoples" was his slogan. A sign of Cermak's farsightedness is that he publicly met at city hall with African American leaders protesting police brutality in 1931. Not that Cermak should be credited with enlightenment on the matter of race. Even so, Cermak's outreach and then the New Deal sparked the migration of black voters, Republican since Lincoln, to the Democratic party.

Cermak's original power base was the hatred by all saloonkeepers and most voters for Prohibition—not repealed until 5 December 1933 after nearly fourteen years. Cermak, born in 1875 in Bohemia, assembled Bohemians (Czechs), Poles, Scandinavians, Germans, Italians, African Americans, and others to outnumber the Irish and sunder, temporarily, their hegemony.

Partly as an olive branch to the angry Irish, Cermak supported the presidential renomination of the Irish Catholic candidate of 1928, Al Smith, over Roosevelt at the Democratic National Convention in Chicago in 1932. FDR bested his fellow New Yorker Smith on the third ballot. To punish Cermak, Roosevelt as president-elect did not favor him with federal patronage. Cermak traveled to Miami to meet with Roosevelt and eat some crow.

The mayor was fatally shot there on 15 February 1933 by a gunman who supposedly aimed for Roosevelt instead. That the dying Cermak told FDR, "I'm glad it was me instead of you," is probably mythical. Also unverified, but a newspaper staple repeated here for the sake of legend, is the story that when a Cermak aide telephoned a ward boss back in Chicago to report that Cermak had been shot, he was asked, "Is he dead yet?"

"I don't know."

"Well, put a hunnert under his nose, and if he doesn't twitch, then you know he's gone."[34]

After his death on 6 March 1933, $1,466,250 was found in one of Cermak's safe-deposit boxes, the sources of the cash never identified, as with the opening of former mayor Thompson's lockboxes upon his death in 1944. Meanwhile, the rumor that the Miami killer's real target was Cermak and not Roosevelt, on orders from the mob, has never died. Cermak took two slugs to the chest while Roosevelt was unharmed, indicating that the assassin's marksmanship was either good or poor.[35]

Irish politicians swiftly arranged a counterputsch. Edward J. Kelly (1876–1950, mayor 1933–47) was installed by the city council after the usual frantic and devious maneuvers. Kelly and his successors kept together for fifty years the ethnic jumble that Cermak had built, while in other cities such machines fell to pieces.

Kelly's father was a saloonkeeper and firefighter. The junior Kelly, although he dropped out of school in the fifth grade, clouted his way to the post of chief engineer of the Metropolitan Sanitary District (MSD).

The Citizens' Association and other reformers had created that district in 1889 as a separate taxing authority because the state refused the city adequate taxing powers. The MSD achieved the miracle of finally making the Chicago River flow backward to cleanse the city's drinking water. The MSD was yet another public body with overlapping jurisdictions that offered opportunities for corruption. Quickly the MSD became an epicenter of patronage and graft with scandals erupting into the 1990s. In the 1890s, there was no true citywide machine but the embryonic machines of Republican William Lorimer and Democrat Thomas Sullivan split the spoils. The district's twenty-eight-mile Sanitary and Ship Canal opened on 2 January 1900 without the usual ceremony but with the usual institutional finagling. St. Louis stood ready to file a request for a court injunction because downriver Chicago sewage might pollute St. Louis, Chicago's historical rival for Midwestern dominance. To evade a possible injunction, the canal was opened secretly. But the *New York Times* noticed and sarcastically headlined, WATER IN THE CHICAGO RIVER NOW RESEMBLES LIQUID.[36] Incredibly, the project had removed more earth than did the Panama Canal.

MSD employee Kelly in 1908 resolved a dispute with his boss, the son-in-law of a Republican leader, by decking him with a single punch. Kelly walked out, resigned to seeking new employment. But he was rehired by "Bertie" McCormick, then president of the sanitary district. McCormick reasoned that "any man who punched another who had greater political power, and punched him justly was a good man."[37] McCormick became a national leader of reaction against the New Deal and American involvement in World War II, yet his *Tribune* stayed strangely friendly toward Democratic Mayor Kelly.

In 1930 Kelly had been one of twelve sanitary district officials indicted in the Whoopee Scandal, another newspaper and businessmen-reformist enthusiasm. One of the district's bid-rigging techniques was to require businesses to submit bids in identical envelopes provided by the district. In this way, they could be secretly opened before the public opening, then resealed in fresh envelopes with no evidence of tampering in the event that an outsider had underbid the ring. The Association of Commerce, father of the Secret Six, assigned private auditors to the district. An independent muckraker named Elmer Lynn Williams published a newsletter about corruption, *Lightnin'*, without excessive worry about libel laws. Among Williams's lesser findings:

> The central Auto Service received for various "rides," $72,000 in 1928. In these cars rode [sanitary] district officials, accompanied by young women procured for these tired business men by an older woman who was on the pay roll. The taxpayers were charged for vanity cases, whiskey and the time of the "entertainers." A committee from the legislature examined the records of this auto livery and were so shocked at the revelations that they suppressed the evidence as too indecent to disclose.[38]

A grand jury pegged the total thievery at $5 million. Seven hundred witnesses built a case that district officials had gained wealth on payoffs, bribes, and kickbacks. Kelly's indictment was dropped for reasons never satisfactorily explained.[39] Some defendants went to prison, and only Kelly was unpunished. Later charged with income tax evasion, Kelly settled with the government in 1933, paying $105,000 in penalties and interest on unreported income from 1926–28.

Kelly was corrupt, but he ably led the city through the Depression and a second world war. Reform groups, bereft and broke, kept plodding along the road to a New Jerusalem faintly visible in the haze on the horizon.

6

Depression and War

1934–45

[I]n a decentralized and fragmented system such as the United States, corruption is indispensable for government and for the application of the decisions of public policy; if Chicago functions, if the programs of the New Deal have been applied locally, it is partly thanks to the corruption of politicians and local bureaucrats.

—Jeanne Becquart-Leclercq, "Paradoxes of
Political Corruption: A French View"

The Depression had nearly everyone—reformers, regulars, and ordinary people—discouraged and bitter, if not despairing. Al Capone, with his shrewd if singular sense of public relations, set up a soup kitchen before he went to prison. No number of soup kitchens, however, could answer the pervasive misery. Chicago author Studs Terkel recalled growing up in his parents' residential hotel in the 1930s: "[A]fter the Depression, you saw a change. There were men in the hotel lobby during the day. They were idle, frustrated. They drank. Tempers grew short, and the men fought over nothing. The card decks wore out faster, and then there were fewer and fewer men."[1]

By 1933, fourteen thousand public schoolteachers, denied paychecks for several months, picketed the Loop financial district. Tear gas tossed by police broke up the crowd, but teachers and city workers both continued to demand their pay. Besides the schools, city hall was $280 million in debt, with unpaid employees numbering 40,123. Unlike Mayor Ogden in 1837, Mayor Kelly could not personally bail out the city. Unlike Mayor

Heath in 1876, he could not call on the Citizens' Association to tide things over with a mere million-dollar loan. Not only were the city's debts too huge but civic groups themselves were going broke.

Each summer, the Urban League and the City Club gathered old clothes for the needy. When the league asked for help with another such "Bundle Day" in 1932, the club replied that its *Bulletin* had suspended publication. There was thus no way to reach its members except by a special mailing—which would cost more than the value of the clothing collected. The clothing drive was postponed indefinitely. The next year, the City Club declared bankruptcy, put its assets into receivership, and then reincorporated in 1934. Even the Union League Club, redoubt of rich businessmen, filed for bankruptcy.

Facing such an unprecedented crisis of bare cupboards everywhere, Kelly reacted professionally and nimbly. He assuaged teachers and city workers for the moment by signing tax anticipation warrants. In the longer run, he kept the city solvent with two revenue streams. One was federal aid from Franklin D. Roosevelt's New Deal. The other was organized crime. The *Daily News* reported in a series of articles in October 1934 that a million dollars a month fell on Kelly's machine from vice. This estimate perhaps was modest; another pegs the sum at $20 million a year.[2] If the machine was healthy, it could keep city government operating—provided that the city made severe cutbacks, especially in schools, and manipulated accounts to ensure that paychecks for patronage workers were honored.

Running for election to keep his seat in 1935, Kelly calculated that a large victory would persuade Roosevelt that he would need the Chicago machine for his 1936 reelection campaign. Cermak had beaten Thompson in 1931 by 194,000 votes, an impressive margin. Kelly defeated a Republican nobody by 632,000 votes, an astounding margin. FDR got the point and bypassed his White House political apparatus to put Kelly directly in charge of federal patronage in Chicago. (This situation was reprised by President Lyndon B. Johnson and Mayor Richard J. Daley in the 1960s.) New Deal money built roads, subways, sewerage, and the city's first ten public housing projects. Moreover, it put the jobless to work.

The Chicago Republican Progressive turned New Dealer Harold Ickes wrote that Roosevelt stayed his Justice Department from moving against Chicago's city hall. Attorney General Frank Murphy, according to Interior Secretary Ickes, "said he wanted very much to clean up Chicago because he thought it was the worst mess in the country and that he hoped 'they' would let him go ahead. I found out that it was surmised that the President would not permit Murphy to go ahead with this investigation on account of Ed Kelly." The frustrated attorney general held that his office had "all the goods that it needed on the Chicago crooks."[3]

FDR also did a big favor for Cook County state's attorney Thomas J. Courtney, elected in 1932 as yet another putatively reformist lawman. The case that drew Roosevelt's attention was that of Roger Touhy. A successful but second-rank mobster, he was called "Terrible Touhy" by newspapers. Touhy was a labor organizer and bootlegger who sold high-quality beer during Prohibition. With cunning and artifice, Touhy fended off the Capone mob's efforts to annex his northwest suburban Cook County turf as well as his labor unions. Thereby he survived as the last Irish-American bootlegger. Touhy was one of those intelligent, discreet criminals who live quietly in the suburbs, doting on their families while ruthlessly, violently managing their enterprises.

Another Chicago gangster was John "Jake the Barber" Factor, the half-brother of cosmetics tycoon Max Factor. England sought the extradition of Factor, an English native, for trial on a $7-million stock swindle there. In June 1933, Factor arranged to be kidnapped in a ploy to evade extradition. Courtney prosecuted Touhy for the fake kidnapping. In December, Courtney went to Washington to implore Roosevelt to delay Factor's extradition pending Touhy's trial. FDR agreed, risking a quarrel with America's closest ally for the sake of alleged law enforcement in Chicago. Touhy was railroaded to prison for a bogus kidnapping he had nothing to do with, as federal court proceedings in the 1950s proved.

In August 1938, Courtney dispatched his cops into offtrack betting parlors, axes and crowbars swinging once more. However, the prosecutor did not bother with the technicality of obtaining judicial warrants. More than six hundred raids produced zero convictions. Courtney was grabbing headlines to challenge Kelly in the 1939 mayoral primary. He lost but continued as state's attorney until 1944.

John Gunther, later the author of *Inside USA* and other acclaimed *Inside* books, was home on leave as Vienna correspondent of the *Daily News* in 1934. He wrote two articles lionizing Courtney, "a brash young giant with the hardest job in the world, cleaning up crime in Cook county. He is 6 feet 4; he is just 40; he is hard-boiled as a professional riveter; he has a handsome voice and much magnetism; and he knows his stuff." Courtney told the writer, "When I took office, Chicago was virtually controlled by hoodlums. Invisible government by thugs and gangsters and racketeers dominated the life of the city. That is all ended now. There are no organized gangs left. There is no racketeering on the old basis." Gunther cited statistics offered by Courtney's office as evidence for these spectacular claims.[4]

Gunther's credulity, like William Stead's admiration of Mayor John P. Hopkins, seems astonishing now in a cynical age. Courtney, a former state senator and ghost payroller under Kelly in the sanitary district, once held four simultaneous public jobs. As sergeant at arms for the city council, he was hauled before a grand jury (but not indicted) because city contractors accused him of demanding a fifty-thousand-dollar kickback. Shots were fired at a car containing State's Attorney Courtney, an alderman, and two police detectives in 1935. This assault was more or less ordinary.

Gunfire was something of an occupational hazard for Chicago politicians in the 1930s, as well as the 1920s. Republican alderman and candidate for assessor James C. Moreland was eating dinner at home when shotgun fire blasted the chandelier off his dining room ceiling in 1934. GOP committeeman and state representative Albert J. Prignano was shot to death on his home doorstep in front of his wife, mother, and eight-year-old son that same year. Republican state representative John Bolton, a member of organized crime's delegation in Springfield known as the West Side Bloc, was lethally shotgunned while driving his car in 1936. Two ward heelers for Democratic alderman and committeeman Joseph P. Rostenkowski were shot to death outside Rostenkowski's home in 1938. Courtney's office solved none of these crimes.[5]

A destitute citizenry, a nearly broke city, a corrupt government—what were respectable reformers to do? By and large, they were grateful to Kelly for keeping Chicago stable at a time when the survival of capitalism itself seemed in jeopardy. The director of the Civic Federation said, "Mayor Kelly is giving Chicago better government than it has had in many years. He has made several strong appointments and is a man of good judgment and great strength."[6]

Some old Progressives, though, were displeased that so many of their brothers had joined hands with the likes of Cermak and Kelly. At a banquet in his honor, Graham Taylor said, "It is my unwavering faith in democracy, in the belief in the ultimate good judgment of the average man—that keeps me going. Those reformers who have recanted have my greatest contempt."[7]

The commercial elite undertook to revive Chicago with, of all things in the pits of Depression, another world's fair. The planners of the Century of Progress Exposition of 1933 spurned public subsidies for it. Such fastidiousness upheld their respectability by avoiding unsavory entanglement with the crooked municipality. They might be unhappy to learn that the fair, so surprisingly popular that it was extended into 1934, now is remembered mostly for the performances of nude fan-dancer Sally Rand. She thoughtfully considered, "I cannot sincerely say that I would have chosen this road to fortune. At any rate, I haven't been out of work since the day I took my pants off."[8]

Rand's date for the opening night of the ornate Empire Room in the Palmer House hotel in 1933 was Abraham Lincoln Marovitz. This trivial event is mentioned because the young lawyer Marovitz (1905–2001) already was getting his name in the newspapers. He came to represent another Chicago type—the quasi-official civic grand old man—and figured in the political history of the next sixty years. Marovitz delighted in joking that his Lithuanian immigrant mother believed she had named him for a Jewish martyr after reading that Abraham Lincoln was shot in the temple. Serving as a senior federal judge into his nineties, Marovitz consistently was honored by the news media. Talking with a reporter in his chambers, he might interrupt by saying, "Sorry, but I've got to take this call from Frank"—Frank Sinatra.

Once again, his would not be a true Chicago story without noting that his legal clients had included gangsters. "In my younger days I wanted to make a lot of money," Marovitz said, so he "defended people who were some of the dirtiest, the most disgusting people around." Among them was a Capone hit man. Marovitz would stroll the streets of Springfield with state senate colleagues Richard J. Daley and Benjamin Adamowski and remark, "Some day the three of us will run Chicago, a Pole, an Irishman, and a Jew."[9] Daley eventually elevated Marovitz to the federal bench. The point is not that Marovitz was venal. The point is that he was a Chicagoan.

Marovitz's 1930s looked much like the 1890s, only more so—world's fair, depression, labor turmoil, police attacks on strikers, endemic vice, ethnic enmities, ferocious fights over control of local government—even an assassinated mayor (Harrison I in 1893 and Cermak in 1933). As personalities, Kelly, Courtney, Marovitz, Daley, and others kept intact the machine cobbled by Cermak, while machines fell apart in other cities. Cermak in his turn had built on the protomachines of McDonald, Hopkins, Lorimer, Sullivan, Brendan, and the rest.

Confronting such personalities as well as the institutions of the machine, traditional reformers gamely kept working to fix the formal, mechanical arrangements of government. They did so as a national left wing grew ever more militant in asserting that the Depression proved the failure of the American experiment in democratic government and free markets. Reformers' faith in rational, incremental reform in an age of radical dissent was remarkably constant.

Its days of glory long past, the Municipal Voters' League was absorbed by the Citizens' Association. The Legislative Voters' League, an offshoot of the MVL to monitor General Assembly elections, suspended operations. The Better Government Association was discredited by its officers' secret funding of a candidate for state's attorney in the 1920s. The Bureau of Public Efficiency, the pet creation of Charles Merriam and Julius Rosenwald, withered until it merged with the Civic Federation. The fed-

eration and other groups sought lower taxes through efficiency while root-
ing out more public funds for relief (the Depression word for welfare).
Reformers spent other energies in defeating state legislation to legalize
offtrack betting, the "handbook bill," sought by Mayor Kelly in hopes that
wager tax revenues might rescue municipal finances.

Despite all Depression obstacles, these reform organizations, along with
freshly militant women's groups, soldiered on, seeking good government
in the sense understood by the middle class. In the mid-1930s, the Citizens'
Association took credit for beating the handbook bill, blocking commercial development on the downtown lakefront, and preventing a new airport on landfill in the lake. More than that, though, reformers wanted to
rebuild the structure of city government and assure the integrity of the ballot.

The City Club was in front of a struggle to scrap Chicago's mayor-
council form of government in favor of a city-manager system. The idea
was that professional managers, instead of wicked politicians, would provide cleaner and more efficient government. The scheme was another old
Progressive enthusiasm. The first council-manager plan had been installed
in Staunton, Virginia, in 1908.

Meanwhile, the City Club had another project going, the renaming
of streets and the systematizing of street numbers after decades of annex-
ations had endowed the city with duplicate street names and other con-
fusions. In the way that alley-cat politics so often astounds reformers, some
aldermen opposed the Club's street plan merely as a payback for the Club's
advocacy of a loathsome city-manager plan.

The brilliant Paul H. Douglas, who became one of the leading U.S.
senators of the century, served a Depression term in the city council and
came to understand aldermen better than did many other reformers. His
memoirs describe the rough democratic equilibrium of reform and corruption that could teeter-totter one way or the other but was never
knocked off its fulcrum.

"As alderman, I was introduced into a strange new world. Gambling
was prevalent all over the city, and it was commonly known that City Hall,
the ward organizations, and the police all shared in the payoffs." Douglas delineated similar graft in other city departments and public schools,

then considered his city council seatmates. "[F]ew of my new associates had ever gone to college. But in terms of innate intelligence most of them would have held their own with my colleagues on the Midway [the University of Chicago]. I liked them and believed them better persons than most of the well-educated and wealthy utility lawyers."[10]

This was not an idiosyncratic observation. Other reformers such as Harold Ickes also recorded that machine politicians were more likable than their reformist opponents: "The reformers were aloof and austere. They had a veneer that was like the polish on a slab of granite, and contrasted unfavorably with the warm joviality of the Irish political chieftains. I am grateful that I was never in a position where I felt that I had to go either to the politicians or the reformers for help. But had I needed help I am sure that I would have been more certain of getting it from the politicians."[11]

Douglas, for his part, swiftly learned that an honest man could not live on an alderman's pay. After office expenses, "there was only $200 left from my monthly salary of $417." Requests from "churches and charitable organizations to support their benefits" took the rest and more, and "the last straw came when a solicitor for a church benefit demanded $50. I explained my problem, which did not impress her in the least. She repeated that she wanted the money, and if I didn't give it, the members of her church would be told and would act accordingly at the next election."

Here was the fulcrum of the reform-corruption balance, the tacit complicity of reformers in corrupt power. Douglas made a public appeal for goo goos to "help me be an honest alderman," and

> [W]hat frustrated many was not just their failure to get the money, but that they, good, pious church people, were being given a lesson in ethics by a despised politician. My situation was not unique, for, talking to my [aldermanic] colleagues, I found that they gave many thousands of dollars a year to churches and charities. Evidently, the "good" people of the community contributed to the moral downfall of politicians as much as did the "bad." The "bad" gave money to the politician; the "good" took most of it away.[12]

During the Depression, the "good people" believed the council-manager system should be adopted just on its merits. Their proposal was this: Replace Chicago's mayor-council government—that is, a mayor elected citywide and aldermen elected from fifty wards—with nine councilmen elected at large. The council would elect one of its own as a figurehead mayor, then hire a city manager who was above politics (a fantasy). Aldermen would be paid twelve thousand dollars a year, up from five thousand, and the manager at least twenty-five thousand.

Professionalize, systematize, consolidate. Further, aldermen would be elected under a complex proportional representation plan with voters ranking candidates by their order of preference.

Whatever their failings, political bosses are shrewd in protecting their own interests. They saw the city-manager plan for what is was: a scheme to replace them with the upper middle class. Citywide aldermanic elections would undercut the clout of ethnicities allocated by wards. The City Club hired a consultant and lobbied in Springfield for enabling legislation. The club recorded in wonderment, "It is interesting to note that the merits of the bill or the fundamentals involved were never an issue or seriously questioned during the hearings before the legislature or on the floor of the House."[13] Rather, the bill failed by three votes after representatives objected in debate that the Chicago press had called some of them hoodlums. Politicians have their pride, after all.

The city-manager system never had a chance in Chicago, considering the city's stubborn history of ward politics, and decades of reformist efforts to install the system were wasted. The durability of the status quo, maintaining always a rough equilibrium between the forces of corruption and reform, is a stout fortress. Reformers kept pressing for a city-manager plan until the 1950s when Mayor Richard J. Daley finally put a stop to such nonsense. Nonetheless, the question of whether government should be run by experts or by common citizens is still unresolved, in theory at least.

Ballot integrity was another frustrated reformist drive, some concrete successes in the 1930s notwithstanding. For much of the nineteenth century, ballots were printed by political parties, not civic government. Not until 1891 did Illinois adopt the unified, secret ballot. Early in the twentieth century, the use of voting machines was allowed in Illinois; they were not adopted in Chicago until 1948 and then the purchase contracts were corrupt and the devices inadequate.

A related campaign was that for a short ballot. The American system of eager localism wrote such long ballots with so many offices and candidates that voters could hardly be blamed for obeying their precinct captains' instructions to mark a straight ticket. The short-ballot effort in Chicago dated at least to 1912. By 1927 reformers called the city's ballot "the largest, clumsiest, most confusing and absurd to be found anywhere in the world."[14] It measured thirty by thirty-six inches.

With reformers unable to restructure the electoral system, the Women's Civic Council of the Chicago Area revived the old Citizens' Association technique of finding and prosecuting individual wrongdoers. This straightway avenue of reform beckons U.S. attorneys for the northern district of Illinois even now, while Cook County state's attorneys remain largely indifferent. The Women's Civic Council got its hands dirty, tediously studying six years of public records and mining for other documents. In 1934 the group reported these findings:

> The lack of proper examination of [election] judges and clerks, before appointment by the County Judge, results in the appointment of large numbers of judges and clerks whom the police records show have been arrested many times and many times sentenced for crimes.
>
> On this docket, according to reports in our possession, are the names of persons sentenced for contributing to the delinquency of children, larceny, robbery with a gun, rape, assault with intent to kill, jewel thief, gangster and gunman, train robbery and kidnapping. . . .
>
> Only about 65 percent of the names of judges and clerks are published (as the statutes provide) before appointment by the County Judge. This leaves many vacancies to be filled with temporary appointments and records show that many persons of bad character are appointed to such vacancies. . . .
>
> In many precincts the voters were openly paid $.50 for their vote. [Apparently, inflation had not impacted the price paid by Hinky

Dink Kenna forty years earlier.] In one instance practically every voter was paid at the door of the polling place as he left, by the precinct captain.[15]

This study had a surprising outcome: In 1935 ninety-nine officials were convicted of vote fraud and thirty-seven received light jail sentences. Equally significant is that the machine run by Kelly and his confederate, Democratic chairman Patrick A. Nash, was hardly upset. No matter how many officials were prosecuted, clean elections awaited a statewide, uniform voter registration system (enacted in 1935), reliable voting machines, and periodic, serious purges of the registry, the latter project still a work in progress and still open to mischief.

What did upset Kelly and Nash ("Nelly-Cash," mirthful Chicagoans called the machine) was labor violence. On 26 May 1937, workers struck the Republic Steel Corporation in the southeast corner of the city. On Memorial Day, some two thousand workers marched on the plant to block scabs from crossing picket lines. About 150 police, tipped off to the action, confronted the marchers and ordered them to disperse. Some strikers' tossing of bricks and swinging of metal pipes and wooden boards provoked police to draw their pistols. Officers killed ten strikers, some shot from behind, and injured sixty others. Twenty-six policemen were hospitalized with injuries.

Like its predecessors, the Memorial Day Massacre scripted rosters of heroes and villains still in dispute. Also like previous incidents, it galvanized Congress to convene a special investigative committee. Still again: a local reformist committee of fifteen was chartered. As with Haymarket, the political fallout descended for decades. The machine dumped Kelly in 1947 for reasons including organized labor's anger over the Memorial Day Massacre.

After a decade of Depression with its tenaciously attendant corruption, gangsterism, and violence, traditional reformers were fed up. A 1939 City Club pamphlet, "Rebuilding Chicago," was outlandish in the baldness of its language.

Chicago today is a city which industrial enterprise generally avoids. In the measure of its economic recovery it lags behind the other great cities of the nation. Ten years of depression threaten to become permanent economic decline for Chicago. Potential expansion is checked by business and labor racketeering. Real estate and social development has been demoralized by an absence of effective city planning or zoning. Chicago lacks decent housing for a great proportion of its people. . . . Its tax rate, adjusted to a comparable basis, is the second highest in the country. Its local government is exorbitantly costly for the services rendered.

There are many assets, it is true—significant assets—to be set off against these and other liabilities which could be listed, but on any objective social and political balance sheet, Chicago today is bankrupt, and only a few aggressive, far-sighted citizens seem to understand or care about its plight. The whole future of the citizens of Chicago is jeopardized by their acquiescence. . . . Time after time the request for help goes out. Time after time the answer comes back: "I agree with what you want to do, but I can't afford to stick my neck out." Or: "Here's my check, but for heaven's sake don't let my name be connected with this project." Or: "I consider my own work vital to the community, and it takes all my time to do it well." Such answers kill no civic dragons. They symbolize the apathy and fear on which such dragons flourish.[16]

In case this screed did not drive the point home, another pamphlet tried to slay dragons by specifying "Your Job." It asked frankly, "Do You Believe in Democracy?" and recited the following:

Industries are leaving Chicago.
Families are moving to the suburbs.
Housing is becoming more inadequate.
Blighted areas are becoming more blighted.
Taxes are constantly increasing. . . .
Some agency must take a start toward the cleaning up of Chicago's many business, political and labor rackets. There have been many requests that the Club take such action but due to lack of adequate funds the Board has hesitated to authorize an extensive study of this

subject. As a beginning, however, the Board has decided to organize a committee to collect and organize the easily accessible information and rumors concerning harmfully unethical business, labor, and political practices.[17]

Few people noted whether such a committee was organized or what it did. Instead, the tail end of the Depression birthed a radical reformer of a new type, unworried about sticking his neck out or letting his name be connected with a project. Ralph Waldo Emerson once declared that an institution is but the lengthened shadow of an individual. This new institution's name was Saul Alinsky.

Alinsky might best be described by first stating what he was not. Clearly, he was not a middle-class reformer of the ilk of Citizens' Association members and the rest. Nor was he a Protestant revivalist heir of the Great Awakenings.

Saul Alinsky (1909–72), in contrast that could hardly be sharper, was profane, sharp-tongued, Jewish, allegedly atheist, even Communist. He was the polar opposite of William Stead, the genteel revivalist; muckraker Lincoln Steffens, the genteel Progressive; or Dwight Moody, the Christian evangelist, all exponents of bourgeois rectitude. Alinsky, on his face a bearded intellectual (rather like Steffens in that regard), studied criminology at the University of Chicago but always favored action over academics. Many of his quotations reside in anthologies. "The means-and-ends moralists, or non-doers, always wind up on their ends without any means." He despised goo goos as "the kind of guys who walk out of the room when the argument turns into a fight."[18] Alinsky's legacy is such a touchstone for liberals that Hillary Rodham Clinton wrote her Wellesley College senior thesis on his organizing tactics.

On any day during the Depression, a reformer could visit the Back of the Yards neighborhood southwest of ("back of") the stockyards and find living conditions scarcely improved since Upton Sinclair's scandalous 1905 muckraking novel *The Jungle*. That was the book that moved President Theodore Roosevelt to create the Food and Drug Administration. The original stockyards workers were Irishmen. In ticktock fashion, they were joined or shouldered out by Germans, Poles, Lithuanians, Slovaks, Russians, Ukrainians, and Jews. Meatpackers imported southern blacks to break strikes, starting in 1904, but they were excluded from Back of the Yards and forced to live in the Black Belt. The white ethnicities created their own churches, synagogues, and business, labor, and fraternal organizations. By 1939 these groups numbered no fewer than 185. Even in hindsight, it is amazing that Alinsky managed to combine most of them into united protests.

His Back of the Yards Neighborhood Council was not, as sometimes believed, the first neighborhood reform organization. But it was probably the most hell-raising. Alinsky's innovations included boycotts, sit-ins, and demonstrations. On 16 July 1939, a rally at the Chicago Coliseum drew thirteen thousand people to denounce management practices at the stockyards. Soon the meatpackers accepted a deal that opened up labor organizing and improved working conditions. The Coliseum's outpouring of front-stoop-level outrage was something different from the mass meetings of middle-class reformers, setting up their enumerated committees, or from William Thompson's original biracial political rally of 1915, or even from labor union demonstrations in support of strikes. Traditional reformers tried to centralize reform and government; Alinsky meant to decentralize it with sidewalk activism that the 1960s would call participatory democracy. The seesaw of centralization and decentralization is another dialectic behind corruption and reform. Chicago neighborhood clubs proliferated to an extent that by the 1960s they were eclipsing citywide reform organizations.

Among Alinsky's other qualities was his apparent ability to prophesy. Protestant gentility as an essential trait of reformers was steadily slipping away. Moral reform yielded much ground to social and political reform, including its ever more radical cells into the 1970s. Even now, establishment politicians confront social protest inspired by the example of Alinsky. When the University of Chicago moved to acquire property in the Woodlawn neighborhood in 1961, thereby uprooting poor black families, Alinsky launched the Temporary Woodlawn Organization (TWO). Eventually

President Nixon's administration had to appease TWO with a million-dollar grant, despite the fact that by then it was run by criminal gangs. Maybe not even Alinsky could have foretold this outcome of reform struggles. By that time, he was something of a national grand old man of leftist revolt, organizing in other cities under his Industrial Areas Foundation. In yet another example of the curiously entwined kinship of some radicals and some capitalists, the foundation was underwritten by the wealth of Marshall Field's family.

After many decades of alternating prosperity and depression, peace and war, religious revival and secularism, there still was no settled notion of reform and corruption. Reform had become such a slippery concept that there was no accepted reformist model: Stead, Steffens, Moody, Fisher, Ickes, the Secret Six, the Women's Civic Council, Alinsky? The imprisonment of Capone, who personified corruption, jailed by prosecutorial excesses? Abraham Lincoln Marovitz, Ed Kelly, Dick Daley, FDR, all striving earnestly to alleviate the Depression with their own connections to corruption?

The nation was about to join another world war. Like the first, the second war pushed governmental reform to the sidelines. With a war to be won amid oceanic societal changes, it is small wonder that Chicagoans paid little mind to continuing crime and corruption or, for that matter, ongoing political follies. Mayor Kelly cracked down, like previous mayors, on infractions of liquor laws without seriously threatening the liquor industry. He enlisted Mrs. Loyal Davis, a socialite and the mother of Nancy Reagan, to corral underage soldiers in uniform and send them into bars to test whether they would serve alcohol to teenagers (of course, most did).

Only the rapid rebuilding after the Chicago Fire of 1871 could compare with the breakneck frenzy of work. From 1939 to the peak of the war five years later, the area's factory production rose from $4.3 billion to $11.9 billion, an increase of 277 percent, besting even the expansion during the Civil War.

Kelly led the city through the war after meeting the usual quota of unsuccessful prosecutions of mayoral underlings. Daniel A. Serritella held the now-defunct post of city sealer, charged to assure that merchants gave their customers honest weights. The Republican boss of the First Ward, he was convicted of fraud but was elected to the state senate after the verdict was reversed on appeal. Also, an audit of the books of the city treasurer showed a shortage of four hundred thousand dollars, never accounted for and never repaid. Another Kelly functionary was his city clerk. He was acquitted of embezzling $733,817.

During the war, African Americans remained confined to a South Side Black Belt also called Bronzeville. It developed jazz, invented urban blues, and generally created a high, uniquely American culture. Reform groups convened a conference on "The Negro and the War," urging tolerance. As always, though, the subterranean Chicago history was written by vice. Cook County had impaneled a grand jury in 1941 to investigate gambling. What did it find? "Shocking conditions." Negroes gambled even if they were on relief, the panel was appalled to note. Blacks would place bets of a nickel, dime, or quarter on a "policy wheel," a canister from which lottery numbers were drawn. Policy had been the target of a Citizens' Association antivice campaign forty years earlier. Blacks did not totally control this racket, although that myth was propagated. Annual revenues were estimated at $7 million. Neither the mob nor the political machine disregarded the attraction of $7 million. A black policeman once tried to explain policy to a reformer: "We arrested one woman 16 times, and here's what she said to me: 'I'm not going to steal, but I'm going to write policy until I die.' Good people make policy bets every day. Many women going to work make bets on one or two sets of numbers. They're buoyed up all day by the thought that they may win."[19]

January 1942 saw the indictments of twenty-six policy defendants, of whom seven were black. Among the whites indicted, three had been implicated in a separate scandal involving $910,000 of Retail Clerks Union funds for which only sixty-two dollars could be accounted. A county prosecutor complained that Kelly's city hall was trying to derail the policy case. In the end, twelve defendants were found not guilty and the other cases were ruled nolle prosequi, that is, dismissed.

Forms of gambling favored by whites seemed to endure fewer official disturbances than did policy. In August 1941, State's Attorney Courtney's county police launched another raid against handbook betting. It fizzled. A grand jury urged the disbanding of the police "morals squad" and the punishment of four of its officers for protecting Loop gambling. In July 1942, the city's civil service commission cleared a police captain and three morals squad officers of these charges.

In 1943 bogus gambling raids were conducted in Chicago by state's attorney's police on 8 September and in Cicero by Cook County highway police on 7 October. In the former raid on a gambling resort run by Al Capone's brother Matt, cops seized roulette wheels, craps tables, and blackjack tables. A court fined thirteen of Capone's workers and ordered the gambling equipment destroyed. Court officers discovered that much of it already had been returned to the mob. At the latter event, Chicago Crime Commission investigators noted the collusion between police and gamblers at a Cicero club. The commission's evidence was presented to a grand jury. It "conducted the most sweeping probe of organized gambling and racketeering in the history of the city," according to the *Chicago Sun.*[20] The chiefs of the highway police and Cicero police, nine Chicago police captains, and various rank-and-file officers were indicted. Almost all were freed on legal technicalities.

In June 1944, the civil service commission found its backbone and fired the police chief and seven police captains for allowing gambling in their districts. A little more than a year later, the new police chief reinstated the seven. From March through December 1944, another gambling war killed six persons while three were shot but survived. When it was over, the American Publishing and News Service, which the Capone gang had launched, enjoyed a monopoly on disseminating racing information necessary for handbook betting. Soon the firm expanded nationwide.

In the thick of the war, December 1943, Charles E. Merriam reflected on forty years of Progressive struggles.

> Our tax system which was crumbling in 1906 is crumbling still more in 1943. Our difficulties with the general property tax, which were bad enough then, are far worse now. . . .
>
> Many efforts have been made to bring about [an urban revenue

amendment to the Illinois Constitution of 1870] and thus far have
failed. . . .

There were in 1933 some 1,642 governmental agencies in the region and there is still something like that. You must get the services
of an expert if you are going to count them all.

Then the old reformist lion expressed once more the abiding Progressive
credo:

It is my belief that the world is entering a great age—beyond the
dreams of men—when war and unemployment have been put out
of date by human intelligence and faith.[21]

World War II soldiers came home and created the biggest, most consistent and expansive prosperity the world has ever seen. At the time, though,
Americans feared that the end of wartime production would bring back
another depression. The ruling classes, returning soldiers, and their Rosie
the Riveter wives and girlfriends were afraid. Whatever President Harry
Truman's achievements in postwar geopolitics, his immediate domestic
problem was avoiding another peacetime depression amid bitter national
labor strikes. Housing and jobs were scarce. Veterans were abandoning
their native cities for hastily erected suburbs. Chicagoans faced a difficult
transition to a peacetime economy, just as after World War I. Traditional
reformers valiantly continued trying to improve education, secure clean
elections, and put men in jobs through public works.

The City Club, the Woman's City Club, the League of Women Voters, the Chicago Citizens Schools Committee, and others in 1944 asked
the National Education Association (NEA) to straighten out the mess in
city schools. The board of education refused to cooperate and questioned
the NEA's patriotism. The NEA's report of May 1945 was a typically damning goo-goo study. It noted that the state's attorney had begun a probe of
the school board back in 1939.

This investigation was never completed but it revealed, among other
things, evidence of payments of bribes to public-school officials, the

awarding of contracts to relatives of public-school officials, the contribution of money to political campaign funds by firms that received school-board contracts, the rejection of low bids in certain cases, the substitution of low-grade material for first-class material specified in contracts, and the awarding of contracts to firms owned by a well-known racketeer. This report, in many places other than Chicago, would have resulted in a grand jury investigation.[22]

Aside from the snide remark about "places other than Chicago," the NEA found that political interference extended even into academic matters. An alderman's daughter won a teaching certificate after she failed a teacher's college. Meanwhile, the superintendent of schools got the board of education to adopt textbooks he had, at least nominally, written or coauthored. (More than forty years later, during another wave of school reform, similar abuses were revealed.)

A parade of goo-goo groups demanded that the city council call hearings on the NEA findings. Duly was named a committee of five aldermen—each man a Kelly stooge. The committee listened to two days of testimony, considered the evidence, and concluded that the NEA charges were unfounded.

On another front, the drive for ballot integrity was revived after former reform alderman Paul H. Douglas lost a primary election for the U.S. Senate. Believing that vote fraud had sunk Douglas, reformers founded the Independent Voters of Illinois in 1944. The IVI affiliated itself with Americans for Democratic Action, a new organ of the anti-Communist left, in 1947. Both groups would find themselves under attack during the Red Scare of the 1950s, but the IVI lasted as a significant political force into the 1980s.

The field of public works was perhaps the most important postwar salient. If returning veterans could not find work, the City Club urged, the government should give them public works jobs. In light of past opposition by the business class to New Deal "boondoggles," this stance was an unexpected one that the club took some pains to explain. "During the depression years we spent a good deal of money wastefully, some for relief and some for 'boondoggling' projects which had little social value."[23] Public works had alternately thrilled and disappointed reformers since the days of the Illinois and Michigan Canal. However,

> [t]he end of the war will terminate the present employment of approximately 10,000,000 men and women who are serving in the armed forces and of approximately 30,000,000 who are now working in wartime industries. Many of the women who are now employed will return to their homes, many of the younger men and women will resume their interrupted education and many of the older men will retire, but the vast majority—probably between 20 and 30 million—will seek peacetime jobs in the production of goods and services.[24]

That statement from 1944 in "Public Works as an Element in Full Employment after the War" was followed by proposals for huge governmental projects "to prevent mass unemployment after the war is won." Suggested programs included "a super highway system," public buildings, parks and playgrounds, forestry and soil conservation, "slum clearance and housing," and so forth. The club continued,

> Practical businessmen through [various organizations] are carrying on what appears to be the first crusade for post-war planning in the history of democratic nations. . . . This does not mean that we ought to overemphasize public as against private enterprise. It simply implies that to the extent that private enterprise is unable to make use of employables who want to work, public enterprise must step in to fill the gap.[25]

In other words, we are middle-class business reformers, believers in free markets but not unsophisticated about the public sector either. Most of the public works advocated by the Club in 1944 actually happened in the years following. Once again: corrupt government, public works, an appeased populace. Even so, the expansion of the welfare state and the secularization of society had displaced old-style evangelistic reform.

In the postwar era, the city's traditions of crime and public and labor union corruption did not serve it well. Much of the groundwork for that baleful history was being laid in Washington. In 1947 four Chicago gangsters clouted early paroles from the Justice Department, which made not even a pretense of following standard parole procedures. Harry Truman, as a senator from Missouri, had led a wartime investigative committee that exposed much defense-plant fraud and contract rigging. The mortally ill Franklin Roosevelt made Truman his vice president at the Democratic National Convention in Chicago in 1944 by characteristically devious means never made fully clear. After Truman became president upon Roosevelt's death in April 1945, the key Senate investigative mantle fell to a man Truman detested, Estes Kefauver of Tennessee.

7

Big Nineteen, Big Nine

1946–59

There IS graft in the [police] department. It's no secret! But it is just a symptom of what is wrong with Chicago. I don't know when it started, but everybody in this crazy town, big people and little people, would rather pay somebody off than obey the law. Chicago people don't WANT strict law enforcement!

—anonymous Chicago police officer,
letter to a *Chicago Daily News* columnist, 1953

Senator Estes Kefauver's Committee to Investigate Organized Crime in Interstate Commerce held explosive hearings in Miami, Kansas City, and St. Louis in 1950. Kefauver planned to take his show to Chicago that fall. He went there in October to make preparations, staying at the famed Drake Hotel on the lakefront Gold Coast. Chicago labor attorney Sidney R. Korshak suggested that Kefauver might delay his hearings until after the November 1950 elections—it was shaping up as a bad year for Democrats—and Kefauver assented.

In 1976 the *New York Times,* in a four-part investigation of Korshak's mob-connected career, charged that he had blackmailed Kefauver with infrared photographs secretly taken by the mob that showed the senator and a call girl in his hotel room. During the height of the Watergate era's journalistic reliance on "blind" or unnamed sources to reveal wrongdoing, the newspaper identified its source only as a "highly respected business executive." Though the senator had a reputation as a womanizer, his

153

former associates denied the allegation and apparently it was not otherwise corroborated until 2002.[1]

Both the *Times* and Kefauver's defenders missed the point that if Korshak did blackmail Kefauver, it might have been unnecessary. Chastened by President Truman (who called him "Senator Cow Fever") and others, including Cook County Democrats, Kefauver already appreciated the need to minimize the political damage to his party in the upcoming elections.

The Kefauver hearings were the Alamogordo of televised national scandal. Like the first atomic-bomb explosion in that New Mexican desert, it rained fallout all over the political terrain. The rubrics of *corruption* and *reform* gradually faded into the concept of constant, mass-mediated *scandal* with its consequent public cynicism about government. Corruption and scandal might seem to walk hand in hand, but they are different things. Corruption can exist without scandal, but not vice versa. Corruption is the effort to transmute improper public influence into private gain. Reform is the effort to prevent that activity. Scandal is a publicized episode that brings disgrace to individuals and offends the moral norms of a community. The key word is publicized. Corruption often is not made public because its participants desire secrecy.

Kefauver's publicized hearings established, among other innovations, the practice of witnesses invoking the Fifth Amendment against self-incrimination, offending the public's sense of rectitude, without which there is no scandal. After a half-century of televised political scandals, a group of scholars considered "why people don't trust government" (also the title of their book).[2] The usual suspects were rounded up, including negative framing of the news by the media. Although none of the writers said so explicitly, they viewed public cynicism as a social pathology. Whether skepticism toward government is unhealthful or realistic was not debated.

Publicity from his crime hearings, as it happened, helped win Kefauver the Democratic nomination for vice president in Chicago in 1956. Kefauver's hearings anticipated McCarthyite Communist hunting in the 1950s, Vietnam War probes in the 1960s, Watergate in the 1970s, Iran-contra in the 1980s, and the Clinton impeachment in the 1990s. In the early 1970s in

Chicago, U.S. attorney James R. Thompson artfully used television news in his campaign to convict Mayor Daley's associates of corruption. Thompson was an author of the modern culture of scandal, of reform considered as a branch of law enforcement, as the following chapters will explore.

Kefauver, despite his priority in video images of investigative gavel banging, did not invent televised scandal any more than Richard Nixon fathered illegal bugging or Jim Thompson zealous prosecution. The political landscape is littered with such as Carey Estes Kefauver, able politicians who wanted to be president but never made it for reasons including bad luck as much as anything else. Dignified, slender, and soft-spoken, yet never living down an image as an Appalachian bumpkin with a jack-o-lantern grin, the Tennessee senator did not know he was foretelling televised scandal as a fixture of the national polity. He merely coveted headlines and movie newsreel footage. He understood the new medium of TV little more than did other politicians of the time. Adlai E. Stevenson, for one, was ignorant even of how to turn on the TV in his hotel room during the 1952 Democratic convention in Chicago that nominated him for president. He called in an aide for technical support.

Kefauver was appalled by the power of organized crime, as was Robert F. Kennedy, a former aide to Wisconsin senator Joseph R. McCarthy. Both Kefauver and Kennedy revived the muckraking tradition by writing books in the 1950s about crime in America. By that time, organized crime might have been more pervasive, if less bellicose, than during the Roaring Twenties. Since the 1920s, the mob steadily had expanded from illegal alcohol, gambling, and commercial sex into labor racketeering and infiltration of legitimate businesses.

Kefauver had violated protocol by staging hearings in Truman's native Kansas City in July 1950, even calling to testify a relative of the president's original political patron, city boss Thomas Pendergast. No political expertise was needed to discern that focus on urban crime would hurt the Democratic party and boost the more rural- and small-town-oriented Republicans.

Certainly, Kefauver had no shortage of matters to investigate in Chicago. A rash of murders stoked the energy not only of his committee but of local reformers. As usual, Chicago reformers met fierce and ingrained resistance.

The city's tradition of political violence had continued from the 1920s. John J. Hoellen, on the day in January 1947 that he filed the first of many Republican candidacies as a reform alderman, was called at home by a man who said he was a reporter. Hoellen opened his front door to meet him and faced a shotgun blast from ten feet away. The shell was a dud, and Hoellen suffered only some pellet holes in his overcoat. The gunman said Hoellen's death would enable him to take over gambling in the North Side's Forty-seventh Ward. A machine judge dismissed the charges against him.

In October 1948, William J. Granata, a Republican candidate for clerk of the circuit court, was hacked to death. In December 1949 in Cicero, township assessor and former assistant state's attorney Frank J. Christensen was shot to death outside his home. He was helping former village president John C. Stoffel try to eradicate Capone's old gambling racket there. Soon after, mobsters blocked Stoffel's car, but he managed to get away.

Despite the enticement of calling witnesses such as Hoellen and Stoffel, Kefauver, at mob lawyer Sidney Korshak's alleged behest, consented to lay off Chicago until 1951, safely past the election. Then two sensational new murders impelled him to schedule hearings there anyway on 5–7 and 17–19 October 1950. He took care to keep them behind closed doors.

On 25 September, former police captain and prospective chief Kefauver witness William Drury backed his Cadillac into his home garage on the North Side and was shot dead. As his widow gave her statement to police, attorney Marvin J. Bas, who had been working with Drury and other informants, was gunned down on a West Side street. Whether the two killings were coordinated or separate events, and who pulled the triggers, are unknown. At the time, an alderman conventionally complained, "The people resent the great publicity given these killings. Chicago is not the crime center of the nation."[3]

On 17 October, Kefauver's witness was the Democratic nominee for Cook County sheriff, Daniel A. "Tubbo" Gilbert, who, although not subpoenaed, agreed to tell the committee how he had earned a newspaper sobriquet as the world's richest cop. He innocently thought he could allay negative publicity by taking this voluntary step (even now, some indicted politicians are unschooled in media rituals.) Gilbert had been the state's attorney's chief investigator for eighteen years, during which time not one mobster was convicted of murder. Asked to account for this, he explained to the committee, "They don't leave no evidence."

Gilbert showed six years of his tax returns and estimated his net worth at $360,000, allegedly gained from investment tips from friends and gambling on football games, prize fights, and elections. "I have been a gambler at heart," he said cheerfully.

Perplexed by Gilbert's savoir-faire, Kefauver asked, "Is that legal?"

"Well, I don't know whether it is legal. I would say it was legal if a fellow wants to make a bet on an election, there is nothing illegal about it. No violation of the law."

Not willing to accept this, the committee counsel repeated the query, to which Gilbert replied, sounding surprised as though the question had never occurred to him, "Well, no, it is not legal, no." In fact, it was a misdemeanor.[4]

Chicago Sun-Times reporter Ray Brennan posed as an employee of a stenographic service hired by the committee and obtained a transcript of Gilbert's testimony. (This impersonation now would be regarded as a transgression of journalistic ethics.) The *Sun-Times* headline of 2 November 1950 screamed, EXCLUSIVE! WHAT GILBERT TOLD KEFAUVER. The story helped defeat Truman's Senate Democratic majority leader, Scott Lucas of Illinois. Lucas was beaten that month by Everett Dirksen, who became the Senate Republican leader under President Johnson, helping to pass his Great Society bills and wage the Vietnam War.

Beyond making news splashes, the Kefauver committee did not seriously investigate political corruption in Chicago or effect its cleanup. Still, it embarrassed politicians, including Mayor Martin H. Kennelly, yet another unhappy reformer. His predecessor, Kelly, saw his clout decline after the 1943 death of his partner in running the machine, Cook County Democratic chairman Patrick A. Nash. As sanitary district chief and mayor, Kelly had cemented Nash's friendship by giving millions of dollars in public works to Nash's sewerage contracting companies. By 1947, organized labor disfavored a mayor whose police caused the Republic Steel Massacre and who, moreover, promoted racially integrated public housing. As the legend goes, when party bosses visited Kelly in 1947 to tell him he was out, he brightened after a minute of glumness and suggested his fellow son of Bridgeport, Kennelly, as his replacement.

Kennelly's failing, like that of mayors Medill and Dever, was not that he scorned the game of politics so much as that he played it only haphazardly and badly. In Kennelly's case, his status as a bachelor who lived with his widowed sister did not enhance the machine's estimation of his manhood.

Once again the legacy of retailer Marshall Field writes some of the city's political history. Kennelly's father died when he was two years old. Kennelly worked in Field's packing and shipping warehouse, earning a warm letter of recommendation when he left. Later he launched his own moving company, submitting a bid to ship the Field Museum of Natural History from its crumbling building dating from the 1893 world's fair in Jackson Park to its present temple in Grant Park on the downtown lakefront. Kennelly's fledgling firm was given little chance until he showed a Field family member the old warehouse letter of recommendation: "He did his work very well and we found him honest. He left of his own accord."[5] Kennelly got the job and sent an invoice for forty thousand dollars—half the amount the Fields had budgeted. Thereafter the Fields backed him as a good-government figurehead and patron of public works. As with Dever in the 1920s, respectable business believed it had a friend as mayor and need not worry too much about systemic corruption.

Meanwhile, Nash's successor as Democratic chairman was Jacob M. Arvey, son of Eastern European Jewish immigrants, who held the unorthodox view that it was better to win with a reformer than to lose with a regular. World War II veterans were moving to the suburbs in a renunciation of the crowded, corrupt city. Ahead of his time, Arvey perceived that the machine needed to appeal to them somehow. After slating Kennelly for mayor in 1947, Arvey sought the liberal intellectuals Adlai Stevenson and Paul Douglas for high office in 1948. The machine said, fine, we'll have two clean faces atop the ticket, but we won't take that University of Chicago economics professor and one-time reform alderman Douglas as governor. Arvey cut a deal. If Stevenson would run for governor and Douglas for the U.S. Senate—who in the machine cared about the distant Senate?—both would have the party's support. After a characteristic period of solitary agonizing, Stevenson took the deal. His gubernatorial victory margin of more than a half-million votes helped carry Truman to his presidential election, an amazing upset.

Stevenson campaigned against corruption in Springfield, accusing Republican Governor Dwight H. Green, who as a federal prosecutor had helped put Capone in jail, of tolerating illegal slot machines in Illinois. The allegation was true, even though Green had run a reform campaign for mayor against Kelly in 1939. During Green's governorship, a reporter for the *St. Louis Post-Dispatch* exposed gambling graft in Peoria, Illinois, prompting the convening of a grand jury. When that jury indicted only the *reporter,* Stevenson's win was assured. As governor, Stevenson raided illegal gambling shops in downstate St. Clair County but not in Cook County.

Mayor Kennelly reacted to the Kefauver episode by ardently stepping up raids against the policy wheel racket in black wards. In four years starting in January 1951, he conducted 11,562 police raids that produced 24,476 arrests.[6] For good measure, he rounded up unlicensed black "jitney cabs" in Bronzeville, where white taxi drivers refused to go. That will show them that Chicago is serious about cracking down on crime, Kennelly thought. Let Kefauver make his headlines! I am cleaning up the city! In March 1951, Kennelly's police commissioner, Timothy J. O'Connor, told the Kefauver committee that there was no syndicated, organized crime in Chicago.

Kennelly's Bronzeville raids enraged U.S. Representative William L. Dawson (1886–1970), a one-legged, profane, and secretive lawyer and boss, one of the multitudes of southern blacks who moved north during the Great Migration. He had taken control of six wards in the days when a black man was fortunate enough to run a single precinct. His organization reaped ten thousand dollars a month from policy, some of which was returned to the community by way of the informal welfare system that characterized political machines. Dawson appealed to Kennelly to call off his policy raiders but was haughtily refused. This obscure incident had far-reaching outcomes. The Italian American mob was moving in on the black gambling racket, and perhaps Kennelly did not even know his raids were abetting that hostile takeover. Theodore Roe, the last black holdout, was wounded in a gun battle in 1951 and finally killed in 1952. Kennelly and police chief O'Connor said they had been unaware that Roe was a policy boss.

During that time, a nonviolent scandal disgusted the citizenry. In 1952 federal agents revealed that Chicagoans had eaten 4.5 million pounds of horse meat in the preceding two years. Ground beef adulterated with 40 percent horse meat, as arranged by organized crime, was sold. The state superintendent of food and dairies and state meat inspectors had been bribed to look the other way. The Chicago health commissioner was forced to resign and then was indicted, but a machine judge dismissed the charges.

Horse meat aside, it was still another murder in 1952, so soon after the Kefauver hearings, that shocked the city into we're-mad-as-hell-and-not-going-to-take-it-anymore citizen outrage redolent of the Progressive and Prohibition eras. Depression and world war had blunted reform endeavors, but they were resurrected in the early 1950s as a secular reprise of revivalist campaigns to shut down the Levee. On 6 February 1952, Charles Gross, acting Republican committeeman of the Thirty-first Ward and avowed enemy of the West Side Bloc, was felled on a sidewalk by shotgun blasts from a passing car. The murder puzzled police because Gross did not seem important enough for the mob to kill. The press said he was a retired soft-drink businessman, also a bookie, who had taken to carrying a handgun for protection at the behest of family and friends. They had futilely advised him to keep out of politics.

As rumors roiled, goo-goo groups called an anticrime rally on 11 February, drawing more than three hundred people into the LaSalle Hotel ballroom as scores of others milled outside the doors. It was the city's last mass citizen rally convened to combat organized crime. A sponsor of the event called it "the greatest outpouring of Chicago emotion in history." That was hyperbole, but the crowd was inflamed like Stead's of 1894.

Chicago Crime Commission chairman Austin L. Wyman told the Cook County GOP chairman, "You know there are hoodlums in your party," then turned to county clerk Daley to add, "Dick, you know you have them in the Democratic Party." For extra measure, he demanded of U.S. attorney Otto Kerner, "Why have there been so few prosecutions of big-time hoodlums?"[7] (Kerner had said, "There is no such thing as organized crime or syndicated crime or gambling. It is only newspaper talk."[8] Later he became governor, the head of a federal commission to analyze 1960s race riots, a federal appellate judge, and a convicted felon.) The officials sat stone-faced under chairman Wyman's assault. Next, reformers bravely but tritely created a committee of nineteen. They came to be called the Big Nineteen.

Four days later, Kennelly named nine aldermen to investigate crime, fending off reformist demands for an independent civilian commissar. Members of the Emergency Committee on Crime, who became known as the Big Nine, comprised five machine aldermen and four independent aldermen. Their votes routinely split 5-4 as expected. The politics of corruption and reform in Chicago once again was seen as a polar opposition, the nineteen versus the nine, good guys and bad guys.

The Big Nineteen opened offices in the Loop. "The reason the Crime Commission has failed," a speaker told the City Club, "is that it has fought a little private duel with the underworld instead of carrying on a campaign. The job of the Committee of 19 is to take advantage of the tremendous strength that is latent in the desire of hundreds and thousands of Chicagoans to do something if you will just tell them what to do and how to do it."[9] Reformers, who had been trying to articulate just such directives for more than a century, fell again upon the weapons of money, electoral activism, and sermonizing. The nineteen solicited "Dollars for Decency." On 27 March, a dinner meeting of one thousand representatives of 225 churches called for citizen activism in the 8 April primary.

Meanwhile, the Big Nine's chief investigator, Charles A. Bane, questioned police officers about their personal finances. At once he was stymied by legal challenges. Police chief O'Connor said he doubted he could compel his officers to answer the questionnaire. The nine called public hearings on the matter. Corporation counsel John Mortimer, who had machine connections, ruled the inquiry unlawful. As for the state's attorney, John S. Boyle, he had been the lawyer for the mob-controlled Trans-America News Service, a racing wire. He told the Kefauver committee he had not known it was a criminal outfit at the time. This was like not knowing that the Chicago Cubs were a baseball team. Boyle's record as Cook County prosecutor upheld the traditions of the office. In 1951 he secreted away in posh hotels a prominent madam as a grand-jury witness and indicted a prostitution ring including a doctor, a nurse, an orchestra leader, and eleven madams. All were acquitted except for five madams who were placed on probation.

On 16 July 1952, the city council voted 40-7 against ordering police to disclose their finances. The next day, Bane resigned in disgust. Later he observed that aldermen cast their votes from fear that after the police, they next would be forced to explain their finances—as indeed was secretly his plan.

The nineteen responded with a rally called by the Church Federation on 27 July 1952, a gathering of eleven thousand Protestant clergy and parishioners at the International Amphitheater. By a standing vote, they implored the council to set aside the 40-7 vote. The federation also issued an eight-point citizens' code with the initial proviso: "1. I commit myself to the idea that the intelligent and honest exercise of my citizenship is a religious obligation."[10] Jeremiah Porter, abolitionists, William Stead, prohibitionists, and many others would have understood and endorsed this declaration.

The remaining history of the nine and nineteen is complex as *scandal* steadily overran the substance and process of *reform*. Italian Americans were especially perturbed.

> The repeated accusations of a "mob" or "syndicate" is a carefully created bogy, to frighten the public into supporting "reformers" who crawl out of the shadows of obscurity—bask in the bright light of the headlines, until they can manoever [*sic*] themselves into visible political position. . . .
>
> Chicago is alive with *banditti,* has a pitifully small police force

which is illy paid, and subject at all times to the blundering attacks and puerile criticisms of unthinking reformers. In spite of this, it does remarkably well [emphasis in original]. . . .

In the days of desperate conflict against Communism, and all that implies, the greatest enemies of the country are those who seek to undermine respect for law and order, as represented by the police.

Never mind about saving the country from an intangible wraith-like "syndicate," let us first try to save it from attorneys with two phones on their desks, one to conduct their normal business and the other to spark a political campaign.[11]

This document from an ethnic newspaper, so typical of its time, intimated that campaigns against organized crime amounted to treachery in the holy war against Communism. At the least, it suggested, "unthinking" anticrime crusaders were driven merely by political ambition. One of the attorneys with two presumptive phones on his desk was Aaron M. Kohn.

Kohn, a former FBI man from Philadelphia, was named special counsel for the nine. Investigator Robert Butzler, from Pittsburgh, gave Kohn and the nine a long list of figures to be subpoenaed. The nine demanded "that a list of witnesses be published in the newspapers—a procedure that would surely result in all of the fish swimming out of town. . . . Not one of the people I named was ever called before a special grand jury or indicted or prosecuted," Butzler wrote. Moreover, in a consistent pattern, "The cry of civic groups died down."[12]

The cry of civic groups died down.

Butzler went home in disgust, but the nine called him back to testify as they were winding up their task. Butzler found that under mob pressure, his wife could not get a Chicago apartment or a job. He metaphorically raised an extended middle finger and refused to testify.

In September special counsel Kohn was forced to resign. In November West Side Bloc GOP leader James J. Adduci was acquitted in a ghost-payroller trial. Charges against Cook County board president William N. Erickson were dismissed in part because Adduci refused to testify against him. Late in December, Kohn's remaining staff dumped a six-volume, 863-

page report on the city council. Chicagoans cannot complain that their city's corruption has not been documented.

Mayor Kennelly was unimpressed. The *Daily News* said he "appeared to be as excited over the fiery Kohn report as he'd be by an account of plant life in lower Australia. Kennelly said he has not seen the secret document, does not intend to see it and hasn't the slightest idea what's in it."[13]

The Independent Voters of Illinois and the Chicago Methodist Ministers Association—familiar reformist types—led a campaign to keep the Big Nine from shutting down outright. A group called the March on Crime delivered a wheelbarrow full of petitions to city hall in May 1953. The nine's chairman was Alderman Reginald Du Bois, who, amid "a two-hour uproar . . . punctuated by wild shouting between aldermen," cried out, "I don't know what the clergy wants in politics. I guess they want hanging and blood and vilification."[14] The next Sunday, many pulpits delivered denunciations of Du Bois.

On 11 June 1953, Republican state representative Celinus "Clem" Graver of the West Side Bloc was kidnapped from a garage as his wife watched from the front stoop of their home. No ransom note, suspects, or arrests ever surfaced. Graver never was seen again and is, according to rumor, encased in concrete somewhere near Springfield. Spurred by this new political killing and by continuing newspaper revelations of crooked police, the nine actually accomplished something. The number of dismissed payrollers was 127, including thirty-six Republican county workers fired as "undesirable," meaning mob-connected. In time the West Side Bloc faded away as blacks displaced Italians and Jews on the West Side. All the reformist struggles to destroy the West Side Bloc were won in the end not by political victories but by societal currents.

In July 1954, too late to matter, the Illinois Supreme Court held that Chicago indeed could compel its police to fill out Charles Bane's financial questionnaire. The nine's latest chief investigator, Downey Rice, a former FBI agent and Kefauver operative, resigned in March 1955 to return to a federal law enforcement career in Washington. He explained, "I have a reputation to maintain!"[15] The Big Nine finally sputtered to a stop in January 1956, having no more idea of who had killed Charles Gross than they had almost four years earlier. The Big Nineteen evolved into Citizens of Greater Chicago, which staged a few annual conferences on law enforcement before the City Club eventually absorbed the group.

The civic atmosphere was one of disgust and frustration when reform alderman Robert Merriam, given a turn as a figurehead chair of the Big Nine, resigned in November 1954 to seek the Republican nomination for mayor. Mayor Kennelly, meanwhile, was in a tough fight against Democratic primary challenger Richard J. Daley.

Some critics of Mayor Daley believe that he was lucky in his job of keeping the Democratic machine nailed together because white Republicans kept fleeing to the suburbs. Such flight had been spurred by a 1948 U.S. Supreme Court decision that banned racially restrictive covenants in housing deeds. This ruling permitted African Americans in Chicago at last to break out of their Bronzeville ghetto. Streets and neighborhoods turned over racially in assembly-line fashion, hastened by white real estate agents through a process called *blockbusting*. White Chicagoans today might reminisce about entering a nearly all-white kindergarten and going on to find a nearly all-black first grade. It happened that fast.

Daley's defenders counter that he dragged whites kicking and screaming into a biracial machine. Whatever the truth of the matter, it is doubtful that Daley ever regarded his racial situation as lucky. Racial disturbances in his city distressed him to a depth even now not well understood.

The flash point was the Chicago Housing Authority (CHA). Progressive and New Deal reformer Harold Ickes had decreed in the 1930s that the populations of public housing projects should reflect the racial makeup of their surrounding neighborhoods—in effect, they should be racially segregated. Later, federal courts steadily ruled that they should be integrated. The CHA and white aldermen consistently and avidly refused.

The CHA moved the first fifty-two families into the Fernwood Park development in 1947. Eight families were black. Five thousand white demonstrators greeted them. In 1949 the city council considered a nondiscrimination ordinance for publicly aided housing. The Citizens' Association, with so much history of heroic reform, displayed the increasing senescence of reformist gentility. It said the ordinance would "discourage investment of private funds, increase the threat of litigation and retard housing and slum clearance in Chicago. . . . Those groups whom the ordinance seeks to serve would be the first to suffer from a failure of the housing and slum clearance program."[16] In other words, blacks might achieve equality but only in our own good time.

In 1954 the CHA opened the Trumbull Park project with twenty-seven of 456 units rented to blacks. White housewives threw themselves in front of moving vans to try to keep them out. Black residents had to travel a mile to a bus stop at 103rd Street and Cottage Grove Avenue; closer stops effectively were closed to them. Seven families lacking cars to drive to that bus stop were ferried in a police car. Blacks also were constrained to taking police cars each Sunday to two churches just four blocks away.

City Club officers drafted a letter to Samuel Cardinal Stritch of the Roman Catholic Archdiocese of Chicago.

> Your Eminence:
> You are undoubtedly familiar with the situation at Trumbull Park in Chicago where for nine months citizens of Chicago have been guilty of violations of the law, disregard for personal rights and intolerance of fellow men.
>
> We understand that a substantial portion of the people in the area are Roman Catholic and that your Church is the only one in the area of any significant size or reputation. The people in the area must be made aware of the harm they are doing and the wrongness of their conduct. We believe that if the church publicly takes a strong position in this situation and uses its most capable men to present that position to the people involved, immeasurable harm can be avoided.

There was an anonymous, handwritten addendum: "add ¶ of good church can and has done in other somewhat similar situations."[17]

Apparently this letter, with copies assigned to the mayor, state attorney general, and chief justice of the municipal court, never was mailed. Still, it vividly expressed the snobbery of some WASP reformers. Working-class Catholics must be instructed in "the harm they are doing" while professional whites resided safely in neighborhoods and suburbs segregated de facto. Such was the snobbery that enraged Richard J. Daley. The Trumbull Park fiasco forced the ouster of liberal integrationist CHA chief Elizabeth Wood in 1954, still a dark day for Chicago liberals. There is no proof of it, but Wood's firing could not have happened without the consent of Cook County Democratic chairman Daley.

Daley was broadly attacked for his lack of sympathy for the civil rights of minorities. His critics objected that black voters got just crumbs in exchange for their obedient support. A fair conclusion might be that, as with mayors Harrison I and II, Thompson, and other predecessors, Daley's task of mediating ethnic enmities was impossible.

So it happened that Daley took office after the Kefauver, Big Nine, and Big Nineteen crime revelations and CHA race riots. Crime and racial and civil disorders would define his twenty-one-year mayoralty. During his first two terms, at least, Daley's political skills in skating over these earthquake fault lines were incomparable.

Alderman Mathias "Paddy" Bauler of the North Side's Forty-third Ward is a figure of Chicago legend alongside such as Long John, Hinky Dink, Bathhouse John, Big Bill, and Al Capone. Despite his nickname, Paddy was German, not Irish. On the night in March 1955 that Daley defeated Kennelly for the Democratic mayoral nomination, Bauler uttered his soon-classic motto, "Chicago ain't ready for reform." The last of the great saloonkeeper aldermen under the ongoing professionalization of politics, Bauler had the face of a red balloon and relished his persona as a buffoon. In fact, he had a peasant's shrewdness. As astonishingly early as 1950, he noticed that precinct captains were having trouble drawing voters away from the new television sets in their living rooms. (The machine ignored this oracular warning.) Unrepentant even at the age of eighty-seven, Bauler said, "I'll bet you one hundred bucks to any Goddamn thing you want that you will never see Chicago reformed until every son of a bitch in the town leaves the place."[18] This proffered wager was more insightful into human frailty than perhaps even Bauler realized.

Also on the night of Daley's nomination, Bauler said the other Democratic bosses "think they are gonna run things. . . . They're gonna run nothing. They ain't found it out yet, but Daley's the dog with the big nuts now that we got him elected. You wait and see; that's how it's going to be," Bauler prophesied.[19] Sure enough, no mere mortal could dislodge Daley as mayor and county Democratic chairman until death called him in 1976.

The story of Daley's plodding escalade of the party hierarchy to become undisputed boss has been told by multiple biographers. Not well understood is that he was seen, before the fiasco of the 1968 Democratic National Convention, as a rare liberal Democrat who worked well with Loop businesses and was himself an able manager of "the city that works." Even his critics concede that he was a master of governmental detail. In a *Time* magazine cover story cutely headlined, "Clouter with Conscience," Daley said, "The old bosses were not interested in what was good for the public welfare. They were only interested in what was good for themselves. . . . We're the first of the new bosses."[20] At that time, political scientists were writing elegant obituaries of urban machines. Referring specifically to Daley, one study said that he "must represent the process of collective betterment and not the process of machine greed. A new ethos of 'the good of the community' becomes dominant and shapes the administration of the mayor."[21] Daley, "the first of the new bosses," was elected with the aid of the First Ward mob and never moved to clean it up.

Initially, to be sure, some goo goos viewed Daley with furrowed brow. The *Tribune* waved red flags: "[G]rafters and fixers, the policy racketeers and others who can't do business with Mayor Kennelly and his department heads are yearning for a city administrator they can do business with. Mr. Daley is no hoodlum, but if he runs he will be the candidate of the hoodlum element." Daley, with some justice, took this as a personal affront. "I would not unleash the forces of evil. It's a lie. I will follow the training my good Irish mother gave me—and dad." Then, paraphrasing the Scripture (Micah 6:8) often quoted by Adlai Stevenson, he said, "If I am elected I will embrace mercy, love charity, and walk humbly with my God."[22] Thus did he defend his Irishness against such an Anglo organ as the *Tribune,* with grievance in his bones fathered by attacks on Irish canal diggers in 1836. Chicago in 1955 was the most Catholic big city in the nation, and parishioners hurried to his defense. Even WASP reformers were heartened by Daley's pronouncement, as the Independent Voters of Illinois, Stevenson, and other goo goos endorsed him.

Besides William Dawson's black wards, the Italian American–dominated First Ward wanted to dump Kennelly for Daley. An enthusiast for the old Progressive reform of civil service, Kennelly had reduced the number of city patronage jobs controlled by the machine from thirty thousand to eighteen thousand. That was bad enough, but then his effort to extend civil service to the sanitation crews run by the Italian arm of the machine was intolerable. Daley won a citywide plurality of 49 percent of the vote in a three-way primary while carrying a stratospheric 87 percent of the black vote and 86 percent of the First Ward. Historians, including critics of Daley, tend to stress the black vote returns and not the latter.

Daley's ensuing campaign against Republican nominee Robert Merriam reprised the reformers-versus-regulars campaigns of Medill, Harlan, Dunne, and Dever. Merriam, the son of Charles E. Merriam, was a liberal alderman from the University of Chicago precincts. Merriam filed complaints against alleged ghost voters for Daley in the Democratic primary. Predictably, the Chicago board of election commissioners censured Merriam, not the machine. Meanwhile, the Chicago Bar Association accused Daley's candidate for city clerk of accepting payoffs and kickbacks. Deftly, Daley dumped that candidate for a Polish American, thereby establishing that office as an entitlement of Chicago Poles. On 5 April 1955, Daley defeated Merriam, 708,222 votes to 581,555. Thereafter, Daley's car carried the license plate *708222*.

Daley moved swiftly and shrewdly to consolidate his power. First, he replaced the reformist chairman of the civil service commission with the head of the mob-infiltrated bakery drivers' union. Then Daley forced new rules of order through the city council as recommended by the Chicago Home Rule Commission. These rules halted much of the aldermen's traditional slouching, cigar chomping, newspaper reading, and behaving generally like oafs at their desks. Mistaking decorum for reform, the press and civic groups applauded.

Even before taking office, Daley did something more important—he persuaded the legislature to pass a bill shifting the power to write the city budget from aldermen to the mayor. The Home Rule Commission and other groups had urged this step as a management reform. Reformers tend not to appreciate how reformist institutional changes can redound to strengthen the power of bosses. State senator Daniel D. Rostenkowski, who voted for Daley's budget plan, understood.

Another Daley reform was eliminating in 1956 the city council's practice of selling driveway permits for sums that could exceed one hundred thousand dollars. The scrapping of this time-honored boodle device enhanced Daley's early reputation as a liberal reformer. Permits would be issued "strictly on the basis of good zoning and good traffic engineering," the mayor stated. Daley's floor leader, Alderman Thomas E. Keane, conveyed the message that Daley regarded this vote as a test of loyalty to him. "Gray wolves," as crooked aldermen had been called since the Progressive era, seethed but could do nothing.[23]

One of the recommendations of the Kohn report delivered to the Big Nine was the creation of a city investigative office. Accordingly, Daley did that very thing, naming Irving N. Cohen as investigative commissioner. In effect, Cohen was Daley's liaison with organized crime. State's Attorney Benjamin Adamowski, a Daley friend turned foe, began investigating the man he called "Sweep It under the Rug" Cohen. After Daley engineered Adamowski's defeat for reelection in 1960, the mayor erased the investigative office as an unnecessary nuisance and kicked Cohen upstairs to a judgeship.

The secret Chicago police intelligence unit, called "Scotland Yard," had been set up by Mayor Cermak in 1931. Its officers routinely beat confessions out of suspects, as lawsuits upheld by federal courts established. Under Kennelly, it filled five filing cabinets with data on six hundred mob leaders and thousands of their lieutenants. Well and good, but then Daley learned that it had installed electronic listening devices at Democratic headquarters in the Morrison Hotel and passed information to his political opponents. Like Thompson before him, Daley was outraged by surreptitious bugging that he did not authorize. In 1956 he padlocked the office and reassigned its officers to new regional detective bureaus. The mob-controlled First Ward nodded approvingly. Later, Daley expanded the police Red Squad, which, federal courts later confirmed, illegally spied on and sabotaged dissident groups. City hall had looked with favor on police-state tactics at least since the aftermath of the Haymarket Riot.

In 1956 county assessor Frank Keenan, a Daley opponent, was indicted for granting improper property tax exemptions and later was convicted and imprisoned. Keenan's successor as assessor was implicated in a financial scandal and saw thirteen of his aides indicted; that man's successor declined to seek reelection while under investigation. Daley remained unscathed.

In a political sideshow during this time, Roger "Terrible" Touhy finally was freed. A federal judge in 1954 gave a tongue-lashing to the Cook County criminal justice system for having framed Touhy for the bogus kidnapping of mobster Jake "the Barber" Factor way back in 1933.

Touhy had not been a model prisoner. He and his wife both had been telegraphers, and when she visited him in prison, with FBI agents standing at the ready to jot down any pertinent information, they communicated secretly by tapping Morse code via finger pressures on each other's palms. The feds never caught on to this ploy. In 1942 Touhy and six others escaped from a state prison. All were soon recaptured.

Aided by a journalist, Ray Brennan of the *Sun-Times,* who championed his cause, Touhy was released by a federal court in 1954 after spending twenty years in prison for a hoax kidnapping. However, prosecutorial maneuvers returned Touhy to jail after two days and he was not finally released until 1959.

Quickly he and Brennan wrote *The Stolen Years,* an account of his ordeal. Only a small publisher in Cleveland agreed to put it out. The alleged kidnapping victim, Jake Factor, sued for libel. The Pennington Press lacked the resources for a court fight, and *The Stolen Years* effectively was suppressed. On 16 December 1959, his twenty-third day of freedom, Touhy walked out of his sister's house and was cut down by shotguns. He personified the hold of organized crime on Chicago in the 1920s through the 1950s, persisting, to an uncertain degree, today. Meanwhile, Daley could legitimately protest that the Touhy affair, as with ongoing U.S. Senate investigations of mobbed-up Chicago labor unions, had nothing to do with his running of city hall.

Factor had been paroled in 1949 after serving six years of a ten-year sentence for mail fraud. President Kennedy pardoned him on 24 December 1962. Factor and his wife had given twenty thousand dollars to Kennedy's 1960 campaign. They gave twenty-five thousand dollars to the president's drive to buy the freedom of Cuban refugees captured in the failed, U.S.-sponsored Bay of Pigs invasion of 1961. The latter contribution was solicited by Attorney General Robert F. Kennedy at the same time that he was mobilizing the Justice Department against organized crime. Robert Kennedy had changed the rules for pardon petitions so that they would go first to the White House, then the Justice Department, not the other way around.

Traditional reformers were still seeking specific legislative and institutional changes. At first, before the Big Nineteen and Big Nine met, they favored a seemingly modest goal, a change in state law to allow Cook County grand juries to sit in terms past thirty days. The brief term precluded serious investigations of official criminality. Anticrime legislation consistently was killed by the West Side Bloc. Not until 1951 under Governor Stevenson did a bill enabling longer grand jury sessions become law. Then, after the murders that activated the nineteen and nine, an antimachine candidate for Sixth Ward alderman was shot at outside his home in 1955.

Daley shook all such scandals off, gleefully opening O'Hare International Airport and the Congress Street Superhighway (now called the Eisenhower Expressway) west from downtown. The mayor basked in his public works.

"Civic Chicago" did not grasp what was happening. A longtime reformer said recently, "When the senior Daley went in, a lot of civic clubs really sort of died, they were under the aegis of the machine. When people wanted something to happen in the city, the mayor did it. There wasn't much of an exception, maybe the BGA [Better Government Association], the Civic Federation. There wasn't much civic progressiveness."[24]

Mayors Cermak, Kelly, and Daley "reformed" city government by centralizing its operations so much that soon reformers were crying out for decentralization under what they called *participatory democracy.* This idea eventually discombobulated not just Richard J. Daley but later the nominally reformist mayors Jane M. Byrne, Eugene Sawyer, and Richard M. Daley.

In 1958 a new U.S. Senate investigative committee gave the labor arm of Daley's machine new headaches. Decorously called the Select Committee on Improper Practices in the Labor or Management Field but better known as the rackets committee, it opened hearings in Washington in July on criminal control of the Hotel and Restaurant Employees and Bartenders International Union in Chicago. Senator John Kennedy of Massachusetts sat on the panel, and its chief counsel was Robert Kennedy. One restaurant owner who resisted the union testified that he had arranged for state police protection for one of his truck runs, only to be told, "we've been called off by the Governor's office." (The governor at the time had been Stevenson, who said he knew nothing about the charge.[25]) The hearings became a sort of ritualized dance as restaurant owners explained how they were strong-armed into buying labor peace while mob leaders with funny nicknames regularly invoked the Fifth Amendment.

Led by its chairman, John L. McClellan of Arkansas, and its ferocious counsel Robert Kennedy, the committee expanded its probe into mob dominance of the jukebox industry in 1959. Kennedy outlined a shakedown racket by which tavern owners and jukebox operators in Chicago had to pay off the mob under threats of violence. Businessmen were coerced to take mob jukeboxes or face labor picketing ordered by the local electrical workers' union. These hearings also became a form of public theater as some witnesses tearfully said they were afraid to testify for fear of criminal reprisals.

These events were in far-off Washington, and Daley could protest that such matters were outside city hall jurisdiction. Then a local police scandal stunned him and even cynical Chicago. Motorists were accustomed to folding a five- or ten-dollar bill around their drivers' licenses when handing them to police during stops for traffic violations. The cash foreclosed the writ-

ing of a ticket in what was regarded as a happy local custom. The Summerdale police scandal was of a different order of magnitude.

Police officers while in uniform and on city time joined a young crook,
Richard Morrison, to burglarize retail stores. It started on 1 October 1958
at a tire store and eventually included ten major burglaries in nine months.
Arrested for a separate job, Morrison got word to State's Attorney Adamowski that he might finger crooked cops in exchange for leniency.
Adamowski had challenged Daley for the Democratic nomination in 1955
and wanted to run against him again in 1963 as a Republican. The state's
attorney set up a secret command post in a swank old goo-goo redoubt,
the Union League Club—rather as city hall was moved to a pietistic
church after the Fire of 1871.

The investigation profoundly distressed the mob: a police shakeup could
overturn its cozy relations with the police department. FBI wiretaps caught
mobsters discussing how they might keep turncoat Morrison quiet:

> *Murray "The Camel" Humphreys:* You know who this boy is that
> squealed on all these cops? Morrison? He's the brother of a little
> blonde I used to have. The one I run away with that time I
> lammed on my income tax.
> *Sam "Momo" Giancana:* Billie!
> *Humphreys:* Yeah, that's right, Billie Jean! That's Morrison's sister!
> . . . This is gonna be the biggest thing that ever hit the mayor.
> This kid has got thirty coppers, he has them all set up.
> *Frank "Strongy" Ferraro:* There is no way we can send word to the
> mayor?
> *Humphreys:* They already got recordings and everything! But I think
> you ought to send word to him not to put his head out too far.
> This will spread like wildfire. . . .
> *Ferraro:* If we could find out where they're holding this guy. But Billie
> Jean could find out.[26]

This plan and other plotted expediencies, such as having the case assigned to a crooked judge, came to nothing. Adamowski was not about
to let this spectacular case get away and successfully kept Morrison se-

creted. (As a matter of fact, Billie Jean was Morrison's aunt, not his sister.) In the end, eight officers were found guilty. Morrison, "The Babbling Burglar" to the press, entered the federal witness protection program. On 20 March 1963, he was in the criminal courts building to tell investigators about mobbed-up doctors who neglected to report to authorities the underworld gunshot wounds they treated. When Morrison walked outside, he was shotgunned, leaving his right arm mangled.

Civic groups called on Daley to name a new police commissioner from outside the ranks. He did so with the appointment of University of California criminologist Orlando W. Wilson. Avoiding blame for having tolerated police corruption, Daley won credit for cleaning it up. The machine lost some police patronage positions, amputating a branch to save its trunk.

FBI wiretap transcripts reveal that Murray "The Camel" Humphreys told his colleague, First Ward politician John D'Arco, "This mayor has been good to us." D'Arco answered, "And we've been good to him. One hand washes the other." Before long, though, Daley had consolidated his power to the extent that he could rebuff the mob if he so chose. D'Arco then complained, "We can't even get our toe on the fifth floor" (Daley's office.)[27]

Even so, not many years later, Daley's closest friend, the clerk of Cook County courts, was indicted on corruption charges, as were Daley's hand-picked governor, city council floor leader, press secretary, machine aldermen, and others. Through it all, Alderman Paddy Bauler continued to hold court at his saloon at 403 West North Avenue, where he despised the modern breed of reformers as "them new guys in black suits and white shirts and narrow ties, them Ivy League guys, them goo goos."[28]

Them goo goos.

8

Daley and Dissent

1960—69

Crime is contagious. If the government becomes a lawbreaker, it breeds
contempt for law; it invites anarchy.
—U.S. Supreme Court Justice
Louis D. Brandeis, Olmstead vs. U.S., 1928

Of all the cities I worked, Chicago is the most corrupt as far as politics
and the police are concerned. It is the only town I know of where the cops
will pick your pockets clean after a pinch [arrest]. In any other town, once
they found the needle tracks on my arm, I would be locked up for the night
with enough money to leave town the following morning. But in Chicago
they would not leave me enough money for carfare.
—junkie pickpocket "Black Sam,"
quoted by Richard C. Lindberg, "'Raising Cain'"

That Daley's machine stole votes for the Democratic ticket in 1960 has
been established beyond a reasonable doubt. However, the legend that
vote fraud in Chicago gave the presidency to John F. Kennedy is false.[1]
Certainly, Daley supported Kennedy and the president rewarded him.

In contrast to another myth that Daley never wanted any job but
mayor, he contemplated running for governor in 1960 but concluded that
the top of the Illinois ticket could not contain two Catholics. He slated a
Protestant, Otto Kerner, for governor. "I was thinking of my four sons
and I wanted John Kennedy to be their president," he said.[2] (He also had
three daughters.) The important point for understanding machine politics is that Chicago's vote fraud was directed less at electing Kennedy than

at beating State's Attorney Benjamin Adamowski. The machine could not tolerate an ambitious Republican prosecutor with subpoena powers, and so Adamowski lost. "All politics is local," as the proverb says. Extra votes for Kennedy were scooped up at the 1960 polls as an extravagant gift, so to speak, to the national party.

Senior Illinois Republicans still can cite from memory the number of disputed votes—8,858—by which Kennedy carried the state. In 1961 Roosevelt University dean George H. Watson and wealthy Republican businessman (later U.S. senator) Charles H. Percy, along with the Better Government Association, set up Operation Watchdog to monitor and expose such blatant vote fraud. A decade was needed before it spectacularly did so.

From Daley's viewpoint, scarcely had he been rid of Adamowski as state's attorney when he faced a Republican Cook County sheriff. Richard B. Ogilvie was elected sheriff in 1962. As a federal prosecutor, he had convicted mob boss Anthony "Big Tuna" Accardo of tax evasion (the conviction having been overturned on appeal). Ogilvie still is regarded as incorruptible and served from 1969 to 1973 as a great governor of Illinois.

Sheriff Ogilvie transformed the county police department from a patronage sandbox into (briefly) a respected, professional law enforcement agency. The state legislature, at Ogilvie's request and in honor of the venerable Progressive tradition of civil service, created a police merit board to protect county officers from wicked politics. Soon enough, though, the merit board became a tool of the machine. Meanwhile, Ogilvie launched eighteen hundred vice raids, including a full-scale invasion of Cicero in 1964.

Ogilvie's relationship with a crooked Chicago cop and murderer, Richard Cain, remains an enigma. Cain was yet another Chicago figure seemingly conjured by a novelist on amphetamines. Allegedly, Cain's natural father was the mobster Sam Giancana. Cain has been implicated (inconclusively) in both the training of Cuban refugees for the Central Intelligence Agency's Bay of Pigs invasion in 1961 and the mob's alleged plot to assassinate President Kennedy in 1963. Still not established is whether Cain duped Ogilvie or whether the sheriff cynically used Cain for political advantage. Not disputed is that after Ogilvie fired Cain as his chief investigator in 1964, Cain became a top aide to Giancana, then was killed by the mob in 1973.

Chicago police superintendent Orlando Wilson supposedly warned Ogilvie against hiring Cain, who had assisted Ogilvie in the investigation of Accardo. A former top state and federal investigator, Paul Newey, studied recently released FBI files on the Kennedy assassination and deduced that Ogilvie had cut a deal to hire Cain in exchange for the support of organized crime in his candidacy for sheriff. Newey also disclosed that his original source for this allegation had been J. Edgar Hoover in 1968. It is possible that Hoover was smearing Ogilvie from fear that Ogilvie might challenge him for the directorship of the FBI.[3] (All the principals are deceased; Ogilvie died in 1988 and Newey in 2001.)

Goo goos at the time did not overlook the inference that Cain had been the mob's plant in Ogilvie's office. Asked that specific question, Ogilvie told a civic group, "I rather doubt that. Cain was rather effective when he was in my office, and the documents on gambling arrests tend to prove it."[4] However, gambling shops in Cicero had reopened after the Ogilvie-Cain raids. Prevented by state law from running for a second term as sheriff—"the only reason they limited you to four years is because they figured that if you can't steal enough to last a lifetime, then you're not worth your salt," Newey said—Ogilvie won election as Cook County board president in 1966 and as governor in 1968.[5]

Meanwhile, former state's attorney Adamowski, stung by his defeat for reelection, ran against Daley as the Republican nominee for mayor in 1963. Under what was called white backlash, Daley defeated him with only 56 percent of the vote, by the machine's standards a close call. Part of the alleged deal between Ogilvie and Cain in 1962 had been that Ogilvie would suppress former Democrat Adamowski's rise in the GOP. If so, the effort was unsuccessful. Whatever Ogilvie might have done against him, Adamowski won the white vote. Daley lost it for the first and last time, while the black vote put him over the top.

Daley's victory happened after rioting by whites when the Chicago Housing Authority tried to move blacks into white neighborhoods in 1947, 1949, and 1951–54; horrific race riots in Cicero in 1951; and further riots by both races in Chicago in 1961. It also followed more testimony before the McClellan senate rackets committee about Cook County police corruption in 1962. Seemingly, African American and white reformers both would have had reason enough to oppose Daley in 1963. Yet, in testimony to his political brilliance, he carried the black wards and most white wards.

The night of the 28 February 1963 primary, the African American alderman and committeeman of the West Side's Twenty-fourth Ward, Benjamin F. Lewis, was handcuffed in his ward office and fatally shot in the head. Lewis had been among the first blacks to move into the once-Jewish Douglas Park neighborhood. Lewis sold insurance policies to ward businesses, trespassing on a white machine entitlement. He was an opponent of both Daley and U.S. Representative William Dawson. As with much of Chicago political history, the inroads Lewis might have tried to make against the Daley and Dawson machines or First Ward rackets cannot be removed from the realm of rumor. No suspects were arrested or charges filed. This was the last high-profile Chicago political murder. The cease-fire against politicians amounts to reform in Chicago.

These events and speculations have been reviewed because of the tendency to remember the early 1960s as Camelot, an American golden age before the plague of assassinations, war, and Watergate. In Chicago, corruption and violence persisted in those years, no matter Daley's mayoral skills. The truth about Ogilvie's aide Cain and the murdered Lewis probably will never be known, just as we will never know exactly why Mayor Cermak was killed in 1933.

Daley had enough on his hands with Ogilvie and Adamowski and U.S. Senate investigations of his machine's labor rackets. Then the Reverend Martin Luther King Jr. came to town.

Historians of the Daley-King fight generally conclude that the mayor outwaited and outfoxed his adversary. Whether King made a wise decision by taking his civil rights movement from the South into the North still is being sifted out by participants and scholars. King might not have appreciated that there was no tradition of black dissent in Chicago. Black bosses such as William Dawson were willing agents of the machine. King might have considered that black aldermen in Chicago were so supine before Daley that they were known as the Silent Six. Daley installed black aldermen who were respectable Catholic community leaders, not Protestant civil rights agitators such as King and those behind him. This religious division over civil rights in Chicago persisted into the 1980s if not later.

The Silent Six were no more servile to Daley than were their white aldermanic counterparts, save for a few independent Democrats and Republicans. However, the class characteristics of the city council had evolved. Aldermen typically were no longer saloonkeepers, vice lords, or morticians and other small-businessmen. Rather, with the professionalization of the political class, they were likely to be lawyers who fixed property tax assessments for their clients or insurance and real estate agents who ensured that their clients would not be bothered by city inspectors. All the while, the machine maintained its informal welfare system for compliant voters. Some social scientists hold that the national welfare state established by the New Deal eclipsed parochial urban machines. Not so in Chicago. Precinct captains handed out garbage cans, an emblem of the machine, along with jobs, "walking-around money" on election day, and other boons. Such a system had collapsed in other cities soon after World War II if not before. The political genius of Daley kept it thriving in Chicago.

Unschooled in this northern brand of feudalism, King led a protest march to city hall on 26 July 1965. On 1 August, civil rights demonstrators brazenly marched down Daley's home block in Bridgeport. The mayor's neighbors tossed vegetables and slurs at them. Police arrested marchers but no residents. Although Daley appeared complacent, he was traumatized. At the behest of U.S. Representative Dan Rostenkowski, presidential aide Larry O'Brien suggested to Lyndon Johnson that he might send Daley out of the country on some pretext until things cooled down. Daley demurred and was not sent away. All the while, Daley grew ever more fretful and isolated in his Bridgeport cocoon, even before the upheavals of 1968.

King moved into a slum apartment at 1550 South Hamlin Avenue in January 1966 to direct a Chicago crusade. King staged a massive rally in Soldier Field, then was stoned in the head during a demonstration in the white neighborhood of Marquette Park on the South Side.

In the end, King settled for little more than a face-saving, open-housing document at a 26 August 1966 summit with Daley. This pact set up a panel of goo goos, the Metropolitan Chicago Leadership Council for Open Housing, to seek an end to racial discrimination. The council mostly failed to end blockbusting or to integrate Chicago Housing Authority (CHA) projects. Of 10,256 apartment units built by the CHA from 1955 to 1971, the number outside black neighborhoods was sixty-three. This was the fact even under repeated federal court rulings mandating open housing in Chicago. Daley's city hall employed sixty black clergymen in something called Chicago United. Later it was disclosed that Daley's administration had dispatched city building inspectors to find fault with churches that had dared to join King's crusade for racial equality.

It is difficult to write about the 1960s without resorting to clichés about turmoil, passion, and blood. One focus of these phenomena was urban violence in the forms of race riots and of everyday street crime. One victim of street crime was Leon Despres, perhaps the finest alderman in Chicago history. At least he belongs in the front rank with other aldermen from the University of Chicago area, Charles and Robert Merriam and Paul Douglas. Despres led the reformist bloc of aldermen who always irritated but never could best Daley, although at least once they provoked him into a screaming tirade while presiding over the city council such that his aides feared he was inviting a stroke.

The shooting of Despres was exceptional in that it was a common mugging, not politically motivated. On 27 December 1967, he walked out of his ward office on East Fifty-fifth Street. Unable to hail a cab at night in that minatory neighborhood, he was mugged by two men and shot in the hip and ankle. Daley mourned, "We live in an age of spreading hatred and violence. We are forgetting the spirit of friendship and love."[6] The mayor pledged to put five thousand more police on the streets. Chicago had heard this before. Despres served as alderman from 1955 to 1975, then became the city council parliamentarian and a grand old man of Chicago like Abraham Lincoln Marovitz. Grand old men, however much lionized, could not reform the city.

On 27 April 1968, Chicago police attacked peaceful antiwar demonstrators at the Civic Center (now the Daley Center) across from city hall. Here was another incident that might have inoculated the public against shock at police behavior at the Democratic National Convention in August.

Daley's defenders point out that he was reelected twice again and served eight more years as mayor, contradicting the myth that he was destroyed by the 1968 convention. The case is unpersuasive. As a national spokesman for urban needs and as Democratic kingmaker, Daley was through after 1968. The convention ripped the mask of bourgeois respectability off the round Irish face of the boss of "the city that works."

He already had been condemned by the media for his shoot-to-kill order to police after King's assassination in Memphis, Tennessee, provoked riots that burned down the West Side. King was killed on 4 April 1968, and eleven days later, Daley said,

> I have conferred with the superintendent of police this morning and I gave him the following instructions, which I thought were instructions on the night of the fifth that were not carried out. I said to him very emphatically and very definitely that [he should issue an order] immediately and under his signature to shoot to kill any arsonist or anyone with a Molotov cocktail in his hand in Chicago because they're potential murderers and to issue a police order to shoot to maim or cripple any arsonists and looters—arsonists to kill and looters to maim and detain.[7]

This was the most famous thing Daley ever said. He might have claimed precedents. Police captain "Black Jack" Bonfield issued a shoot-to-kill order during a transit strike in 1885. In 1907, police chief George Shippey aimed to "strike awe to the cheap murderous thugs who think nothing of killing a man to get his money. I have told my men to shoot to kill." And as Prohibition gangsterism dawned in 1920, an alderman urged immediate promotions for "patrolmen and sergeants who kill hold up men."[8]

Further, there is some evidence that Daley's police actually had "shot to kill" the night of 5 April 1968:

Several witnesses, including a small-business owner who'd sat in his store all night and watched the looting and burning along Madison [Street], talked about a blue Chevy. They called it a "killer squad." Four white officers in the unmarked blue car, each with a shotgun, had appeared at intervals during the night, firing into stores without warning. Two of the victims had been found in the backs of stores and two in the alley just south of the stores. A store owner on that block, the 4100 block of West Madison, said there were hundreds of spent bullets on the floor of his shop the next morning.[9]

A curiosity seldom noted is that Daley's shoot-to-kill pronouncement followed the riots by more than a week. Similarly, a forgotten irony is that Daley's statement came at a news conference called to announce the naming of a commission to investigate the causes of the riots. Daley had been angered by a *Chicago Sun-Times* article that morning, STORY BEHIND RIOT TOLL: THE NINE WHO DIED. All nine fatalities were young black men; four were merchants gunned down in their stores under what Daley's blue-ribbon panel, headed by a friendly federal judge, eventually labeled "especially disturbing circumstances." The deaths officially remain caused by a person or persons unknown.

Members of the Church Federation of Greater Chicago called on Daley on 16 April, beseeching him to rescind the shoot-to-kill statement of the previous day. On 17 April, Daley said, "There wasn't any shoot to kill order. They said that I gave orders to shoot down children. I said to the superintendent, if a man has a Molotov cocktail in his hand and throws it into a building with children and women up above, he should be shot right there and if I was there I would shoot him. Everybody knows it was twisted around and they said Daley gave orders to shoot children. That wasn't true."[10] Two facts are clear: Superintendent James Conlisk never issued a shoot-to-kill directive, and public opinion polls indicated broad national support for Daley's position.

It also seems clear that Daley's identification of his ego with his city had reached heroic proportions. After surveying the destruction of the West Side from a helicopter after the assassination riots, nearly writhing in pain, he asked, "Why did they do this to me?"[11] *To me.* Daley's identity of self and city did not serve him well during the Democratic National Convention.

He was shown on television, purpled with rage on the convention floor, screaming at antiwar Senator Abraham Ribicoff of Connecticut at the podium. Ribicoff had denounced "Gestapo tactics" by Chicago police. Daley's anger was fueled by the resentment of a machine regular against a reformer. Ribicoff, by attacking a fellow Democrat, Daley, on national television yet, was blaspheming in the temple. The Irish, forever fighting their British overlords, despised informers and turncoats. Loyalty was a supreme virtue. Daley, like many Chicago mayors before and since, was upholding the institutional hierarchy against a rebel.

The fiercest battle inside the convention hall concerned a proposed Vietnam War peace plank in the party platform. In point of fact, Daley opposed the war. He never said so publicly. He would not criticize a president of the United States on the conduct of the war, not even a Republican, Richard Nixon. In 1967 Daley went to see Lyndon Johnson in the White House to argue the war's futility. The son of a close friend had been killed in combat for nothing, Daley thought. LBJ called in his military aides to spread maps over the Oval Office desk and drumbeat the rightness of his policy.

Daley was unconvinced, but soon he and Johnson connived to hold the 1968 convention in Chicago. The "long hot summers" of the mid-1960s saw race riots in cities across the country. National Democrats feared that civil rights provocateurs would disrupt the convention but figured that Daley could control his blacks in Chicago. In this respect, they were right. Civil rights activists did not trouble the 1968 convention. Daley had bought off potential black dissent in ways even now not fully revealed. Instead, the convention scene was ruined by antiwar demonstrators.

Recalling Chicago 1968 can stir passions to this day. In retrospect, perhaps the prime irony is the unequal weaponry wielded by the opposing sides. Capitalists after the Great Uprising of 1877 gave police artillery and a Gatling gun. Daley's security forces had rifles with bayonets, flame-throwers, bazookas, machine guns, tear gas, and Jeeps outfitted with barbed-wired wooden barriers on their front bumpers. These were the armaments arrayed against antiwar demonstrators who totaled ten thousand at the most. Nearly all of them were unarmed except with sticks holding placards or with devices that infuriated police and the country at large, Viet Cong flags and paper bags filled with excrement. The number of armed officers deployed against the 1894 Pullman strike was 14,186. Federal, state, and local soldiers, police, and law enforcement personnel during the 1968 convention amounted to 28,200. There were only 5,011 convention delegates and alternates. Such was the setting for the quadrennial gathering of the nation's majority party, the oldest sustained political party of a free country.[12]

Televised scenes of Chicago cops beating demonstrators along Michigan Avenue between Grant Park and the Chicago Hilton Hotel are ingrained in the national memory. The crowd of demonstrators that night might not have exceeded six thousand. Their ranks had been reduced by Daley's police-state tactics. He sent undercover agents to New York to sabotage the Radical Organizing Committee's plans to raise money and charter two hundred buses. After that, the group managed to send only sixty people in cars. Daley's illegal Red Squad, technically the security section of the police intelligence division, placed about 850 spies in organizations, including some of utmost bourgeois respectability—the League of Women Voters, Jewish War Veterans, United Auto Workers, and the Parents and Teachers Association.

Daley's cloaks-and-daggers had a ludicrous aspect. He dispatched some short-haired, clean-cut cops to infiltrate antiwar groups in Chicago that hooted at them in amusement. A sense of cynical fun and satire held by hippies and yippies colored the convention protests and the later farcical trial, pressed by the Nixon administration, of the Chicago Seven for crossing state lines to incite riots at the convention.

The convention itself, held in the old, ugly International Amphitheater near the old stockyards in Daley's neighborhood miles south of Grant Park, managed to escape disruption by demonstrators. An undercover cop broke into the Chicago Peace Council's offices to steal money and equipment and spray-paint radical slogans on the walls. Daley said, with sincere how-could-anyone-doubt-this frustration, "The police have a perfect right to spy on private citizens. How else are they going to detect possible trouble before it happens?"[13]

Forty-three news media personnel were assaulted by security forces during the convention, astounding and perhaps even radicalizing some of the national media. They would not have been so shocked were they aware of the history of Chicago police-state activity. An official study of disturbances at the 1968 convention denoted a "police riot." (The chair of the investigative commission, Chicago attorney Dan Walker, later recanted the phrase, then recanted that, was elected governor in 1972, and later went to prison for bank fraud.) Strictly speaking, the "police riot" applied only to police actions in Lincoln Park on the Sunday and Monday nights of the convention, 25 and 26 August, not the "Battle of Chicago" in Grant Park on Wednesday. That was when agitators who stayed safely behind the front ranks of protesters being clubbed and kicked by police chanted, "The whole world is watching!" So it was. Perhaps the weaponry of the protesters overpowered that of the police after all: their weapon was the media. Not until the election of Bill Clinton as president in 1992 did the Democratic party fully recover from this fiasco.

In Chicago, Daley became increasingly unhealthy physically and emotionally, although his condition was kept secret. The 1968 convention was such a convulsion that it has obscured his role as mayor during an era of middle-class flight, high crime rates, and ongoing corruption. The consensus on Daley now is that, whatever his superiority as an administrator, he totally failed to understand open and public racial and social dissent.

Certainly he did not "get" the Black Panthers. A predawn raid by police on 4 December 1969 killed two Black Panthers and wounded four others in their West Side apartment. Guns blazed for eight minutes, with but one round, possibly, fired by one of the victims. The evidence is convincing that police shot first and entered the apartment without announcing their office. This action was worse than anything police did at the 1968 convention or even, in its nakedly premeditated terrorism, the Haymarket and Republic Steel reactive assaults.

The officers were under the aegis of Edward V. Hanrahan, Daley's state's attorney. One of Lyndon Johnson's secret White House audiotapes had recorded Daley previously recommending Hanrahan for U.S. attorney: "He's a great Democrat. He ran for Congress. He was defeated. He's a graduate of Notre Dame. But more than that, Mr. President, let me say with great honor and pride, he's a precinct captain!"[14]

He's a precinct captain.

Hanrahan and thirteen officers were charged in 1971 with conspiracy to obstruct justice; all were acquitted in bench trials. Many years of subsequent civil actions ended in large damage awards for the victims and their survivors. Black voters defeated Hanrahan for reelection as state's attorney in 1972 in what was, rather than King's crusade of the 1960s, the first real uprising of black political power in Chicago.

Daley had pretty much neutered the tradition of "civic Chicago" investigations and advocacy of structural reforms. Still, reformers grew ever more inspired to challenge the secrecy and corruption of Daley's regime in ways that their revivalist, Progressive, and New Deal forefathers would not have countenanced. It is said that Franklin D. Roosevelt fathered governmental interventions in society by orders of magnitude of which FDR himself never would have dreamed. In this sense, 1960s Chicago reformers outdid their ancestors by applying new tactics at the curbside level—militant demonstrations—and at a lofty level, the federal courts. One consequence was a denigration of public authority that is continuing. Shortly before writing *If Christ Came to Chicago!*, William T. Stead abruptly put down an anarchist's call for dynamiting the established order. The late 1960s saw a vogue of respectable opinion mongers openly advocating radical, even violent, dissent.

The first powerful thrust against Daley came in the early 1960s, sprouting from the legacy of Saul Alinsky. It was championed by an unlikely radical, an Italian American housewife named Florence Scala. Daley's dream, shared by many upscale reformers, was to open in Chicago a four-year branch of the University of Illinois. The site Daley chose was an Italian residential neighborhood on the Near West Side. To prevent the uprooting of thousands of her neighbors, Scala energized the Near West Side Planning Board, the first citizens' planning board in the nation. To block Daley's moves to condemn and raze property, she led demonstrations and sit-ins at city hall. Among other outrages, from the neighborhood's viewpoint, was that Daley's plans would require the removal or destruction of Hull House (which has been preserved as a museum). Daley responded in character by viewing the contretemps as entirely political. He implied that Richard Ogilvie, Republican candidate for Cook County sheriff, was fomenting the protests.

The sit-ins and demonstrations stopped after two bombs exploded at Scala's home. The bombs caused minor damage, no injuries, and no arrests. Scala and her group then decided to "work within the system," as a slogan of the 1960s had it, and filed challenges in federal courts. Daley refused to hold off construction until the lawsuits and appeals were heard; demolition began in 1962. Ultimately, the legal challenges failed.

And yet the bitter residue from the violence and abuses of power of the 1960s has not fully eclipsed the persona of Richard J. Daley. Years after the mayor's death, Scala herself reflected,

> He had the most infectious laugh. I'd look at him on television, and I'd laugh to myself and say, 'You louse, you.' That laugh! He was just beautiful. And he was so Irish, so pure Irish. That's another thing that was charming about him.
>
> He was so articulate, but not articulate in the way the newspapers wanted him to be. They criticized his English and so on. And I rather liked that in him. I liked the strength that he had, the sense of loyalty that he had and the leadership that he showed. He did have some class, and I would attribute a lot of that to Mrs. Daley. I thought his wife was gorgeous. I still do.[15]

By the end of the 1960s, a Chicago attorney, apparently less enamored of Daley's infectious laugh, resolved to use the federal courts once again as a weapon against the mayor. Michael L. Shakman of Hyde Park ran in 1969 as an independent delegate to the Illinois constitutional convention of 1970—which finally did, after 137 years of Chicago's status as a stepchild of Springfield, write a constitution granting the city home-rule powers. After losing his race, Shakman filed a lawsuit complaining that the Democratic patronage machine had denied him the right to an open and free election. Shakman had lost by just 623 votes out of more than twenty-four thousand cast and observed that many more than 623 patronage workers lived in his district. He argued that requiring city employees to do political work and firing them at will for their political affiliation were unconstitutional. Somehow the supposedly random rotation of case assignments presented this one before Daley's pal, Judge Abraham Lincoln Marovitz, who dismissed it. "It's an obvious fact of life," Marovitz blithely opined in refusing to recuse himself, "that men in high public positions know each other. I was and am a close friend of Mayor Richard J. Daley."[16] Later, Shakman won on appeal, and in 1971 the U.S. Supreme Court declined to consider the appellate case. In 1972 Daley signed a consent decree forbidding the firing of public workers on political grounds. The machine found ways to get around this, just as it always had evaded civil service regulations, but in time successive Shakman court decrees put a serious crimp on patronage, the lifeblood of the machine.

When he accepted the Shakman decree, Daley had a bigger problem. The new U.S. attorney was taking reform, when considered a branch of law enforcement, into a dimension never contemplated by the Citizens' Association, the Secret Six, Kefauver, the Big Nineteen, or Alinsky, Scala, and Shakman. This dimension established reform as a permanent campaign against public officials and as a fixture inside government itself. The fixture was viewed as necessary because public officials presumably were always vulnerable to corruption. Reform was not the province of goo goos, street demonstrators, labor agitators, religious revivalists, or neighborhood activists so much as it was a program of three-piece-suited lawyers in the U.S. Department of Justice. President Nixon appointed as U.S. attorney for the northern district of Illinois a Chicago lawyer named James R. Thompson. Later, Nixon would come to regret the hegemony of reform in his own Justice Department.

9

Scandals and Stings

1970–82

Political scandal has proliferated. . . . The resulting culture of mistrust has made the always difficult job of governing measurably harder. The climate of sensationalism has contributed to public cynicism. . . . It is no wonder that our scandals have come to resemble little more than primitive cleansing rituals through which we declare our intention to expel the impurity of politics from public life.

—Suzanne Garment, *Scandal*

Chicago had grown used to periodic, even annual, outbreaks of political scandal for 140 years. Even so, the notion of *scandal* as a permanent presence in the national political culture was cemented in the 1970s. Since Watergate there has been much wringing of hands over public cynicism about government and the impulse to assume the worst about our leaders. Watergate spawned many subsequent national scandals suffixed with "-gate." Some writers, slighting the Progressive muckrakers, hold that journalistic eagerness to expose official wrongdoing derived from the outrage and alienation of Vietnam, Chicago 1968, and Watergate.

Maybe so. In any event, even before Watergate exploded, the U.S. attorney in Chicago was throwing the prosecutorial resources of the federal government against public officials high and low. They were jailed after prosecutors won the cooperation of their apparatchiks in one of the first instances of widespread grants of immunity in plea-bargain deals. There were precedents—for example, the Republican U.S. attorney in Boston went after Massachusetts Democratic politicians in an effort to embarrass Kennedy's 1960 presidential campaign. Still, the Chicago U.S. attorney's drive against politicians there in the early 1970s was broader even than that of the Hoover White House against Al Capone. The U.S. attorney had the entire Chicago machine on the run.

James R. "Big Jim" Thompson was the son of a West Side physician. A radio program once asked his Presbyterian Sunday school class what they wanted to be when they grew up. Unhesitatingly, nine-year-old Thompson piped up, "president of the United States."[1] Like other Chicago politicians, he never achieved that ambition. However, his success in jailing Daley's allies made him a natural Republican candidate for governor in 1976. He served in that office from 1977 to 1991, although Daley feared that he really wanted to run for the larger, in his eyes, office of mayor. A shambling, portly six-foot-six, Thompson was not initially a natural politician. Political consultants advised him to lose weight, get married, and get a dog. He followed all three instructions and eventually became a first-rate campaigner.

Daley had kicked his governor, Otto Kerner, upstairs to a federal appellate judgeship in 1968. Governor Kerner had chaired President Johnson's National Advisory Commission on Civil Disorders, which earlier in 1968 had blamed white racism for urban riots and black poverty. Thompson targeted Judge Kerner because the Illinois racing industry dispensed cut-rate racetrack stock to politicians like a gum ball machine. As governor, Kerner had gotten such a favor from racing impresario Marge Lindheimer Everett, who also had contributed large sums to his campaign. Hearing the stock offer from an intermediary, who was the chief state racetrack regulator, Kerner commented convivially, "That's awfully nice of Marge."[2] Kerner was far from alone. A racing stock scandal had smudged even the administration of goo-goo governor Adlai Stevenson. Many politicians acquired such stock, including Dan Rostenkowski, but not, with his typical prudence, Dick Daley. Thompson told his lawyers something like General George S. Patton's command to his tank officers in North Africa in 1942: "Commence firing; fire at will."

This was years before the Justice Department created a public integrity section in 1976. It might be said that Thompson's zeal exceeded in degree but was not different in kind from previous anticorruption efforts. Yet the quantum leap in degree was in itself a difference in kind. Corruption chasers became a permanent interest group inside government, working from an assumption that all public employees are at least potentially corrupt. Thompson was at the forefront of shifting the paradigm of reform from a good-government, public-administration model to a law-enforcement, scandalmongering model. Whereas anticorruption projects previously were episodic, corruption chasing became institutionalized with special prosecutors ("independent counsels"), inspectors general, public integrity units, a proliferation of regulatory agencies and ethics codes, (nominally) independent ethics and investigative commissions, and investigative reporters across the country.

When Thompson took office in 1970, the Internal Revenue Service, Chicago newspapers, and the Better Government Association already were investigating the racetrack giveaways. Another area of interest was the complex land dealings of Daley's city council floor leader, Thomas Keane. Thompson consulted with the IRS, reporters, and watchdog-group probers. He learned to cultivate the press with selective leaks and favors. When running for governor, he once permitted his traveling press corps to pen a prankish campaign speech for him at an unimportant downstate appearance. This gesture helped to earn him the fondness of the press.

The BGA, having already incorporated an old Stevenson-led group, the Legislative Voters' League, in 1946, combined with prominent Republicans and investigative reporters to form Operation Watchdog in 1961. With Operation Watchdog, reformers intended the BGA to fill a void between the Chicago Crime Commission, which focused on organized crime, and the Civic Federation, which scrutinized local governmental finances. Perhaps not recognizing the historical color, the BGA's investigative committee met regularly at the Rendezvous Room bar of a pietistic sanctum, the Union League Club. Old and new enterprises of reform bellied up to the bar.

By this time, businessmen's groups such as the Union League Club had retreated from outright reformist struggles such as those of the Big Nineteen in 1952. Daley centralized civic power so much that he marginalized reform groups. All those decades spent rationalizing and centralizing power, and this is what they got for it. Some reformers recognized the paradox at the time; Daley was a member of the City Club but the club itself was moribund. "Civic Chicago" took to providing political forums and writing occasional blue-ribbon studies of city and county operations. These were published, admired, and forgotten.

Thus the new aggressiveness of the BGA's Operation Watchdog represented a novel confederation of reform forces. It reflected ongoing professionalization. Investigative reporting was becoming a lawyers' and accountants' game. Older reporters, fond of resourceful techniques such as impersonating a police sergeant when calling crime witnesses, tended to sneer at the new type of reporters as overeducated nerds. Class divisions never escape the history of Chicago corruption and reform. *Daily News* columnist Mike Royko, for one, son of a Milwaukee Avenue saloon-keeper, was openly contemptuous of the nerds.

Another of the old-fashioned, shoe-leather reporters, George Bliss of the *Tribune,* won a 1963 Pulitzer Prize for exposing ghost payrollers, falsified time sheets, and rigged contracts in the Metropolitan Sanitary District (Mayor Kelly's old bailiwick). The BGA collaborated with Bliss to reveal more sanitary district misdeeds for the next two years. For a brief time, Bliss headed the BGA and revealed shocking abuses by private ambulance services. By the late 1960s, the BGA and reporters were investigating Alderman Thomas Keane and Judge Otto Kerner.

Initially, Thompson was unsure of exactly which federal laws Kerner might have broken. Which actions by public officials cross the line into criminal rewarding of their financial donors remains a troublesome question. Kerner did not directly steal any money from Illinois taxpayers. He merely rewarded Marge Everett Lindheimer with favorable racing dates and other matters controlled by state government. Prosecutors could not prove that gift X to politician Y produced public policy Z. When the government subsidizes and regulates almost everything, what constitutes official corruption? Revivalists such as William Stead had it easier. They were against boodle and vice. Those terms no longer are easily defined. If gambling is a vice, it now is promoted and conducted by state lotteries and franchised casinos.

And if reform is just a branch of cops-and-robbers, then two unsung Chicago heroes are Martin McGee and Matthias A. Lydon. McGee, chief inspector of the U.S. postal inspection service in Chicago in the 1960s and 1970s, helped convict Kerner and many others. Lydon, one of Thompson's attorneys, developed a theory that Kerner might be prosecuted under an umbrella charge from a nineteenth-century federal mail-fraud law of depriving citizens of his "loyal and faithful service," namely by showing favoritism toward Lindheimer. (Never charged herself, Lindheimer after the racetrack trials left Chicago for Los Angeles, where she became a close friend of Nancy Reagan.)

In the end, Kerner was convicted of conspiracy, tax evasion, perjury, and mail fraud. In 1987 the U.S. Supreme Court ruled that mail fraud applied not to intangible rights such as a public official's "loyal and faithful service" but only when victims were defrauded of property. This ruling upset some cases against crooked Chicago judges but came too late to help Kerner (or Keane).

At trial, Kerner's stiff-necked, how-dare-you-impugn-my-integrity manner did not aid his defense. The first sitting federal appellate judge to be convicted, Kerner was sentenced to three years in prison in 1973, soon released for ill health, and died of lung cancer in 1975. Perhaps reformers produce victims even as corrupt officials do. Maybe Kerner was a victim of overeager prosecution.

Some Democrats, including Kerner, believed that the Nixon White House attacked Kerner to punish Daley for having stolen the election for Kennedy in 1960. As an added spice to this supposed vengeance, Kerner was the son-in-law of Anton Cermak, founder of Daley's machine. There is a thread of truth in this argument in that the crime waves of the 1960s prompted Congress to pass anticrime spending bills. Nixon used some of this money to double the size of U.S. attorneys' offices in high-crime cities, which, as Nixon surely observed, were Democratic. But the notion that Nixon's Justice Department fingered Kerner to get back at Daley does not survive a scrutiny of the record. Further, it misunderstands the parochialism of machine politics. The imprisonment of Kerner, a mere federal judge, hardly could threaten Daley's control of his wards.

However, Thompson's prosecution of machine stalwarts did threaten it. There came a day, 9 October 1974, when Daley's city council chief was convicted in the federal courthouse as, two floors below, Daley testified at the trial of his former press secretary while, two floors above, another machine alderman was on trial.

Daley's city council floor leader, Alderman Keane of the Northwest Side, famously said that he wanted money while Daley wanted power and both got what they wanted. Keane's political biography was typical—his father had been Thirty-first Ward Democratic boss for forty years. The *Sun-Times* of 1 April 1973 said the "Keane Combine" profited on insider land deals and property tax breaks. The group included Keane's brother George, one of the two members of the Cook County board of (property tax) appeals. A county grand jury charged Thomas Keane on nine counts of conflict of interest that year, but he was acquitted in a bench trial before a machine judge. Under the "loyal and faithful service" umbrella once again, Thompson indicted Thomas Keane in May 1974 for mail fraud involving profiteering through secret land-trust deals with the city. Businesses controlled by Keane routinely bought land parcels at tax scavenger sales for as low as two hundred dollars, then sold them to city agencies for up to twenty-five hundred dollars. These sales were approved by the city council finance committee chaired by Keane. The idea of "conflict of interest" steadily was gaining currency.

Short and stocky, Keane struck the public persona of a merry leprechaun while ruthlessly running the council. He chuckled, smiled, and waved to his family and friends throughout his trial. Convicted, he was paroled in 1978 after serving twenty-two months of a five-year sentence. A BGA taxpayers' suit brought to recover $413,580 Keane made through his aldermanic salary and land deals failed because—as with Kerner—he had not directly stolen public funds. While in prison, by telephone, Keane brokered the 1977 deal that selected Daley's successor after the mayor died. Keane later became an informal advisor to Mayor Jane Byrne and died in 1996 at age ninety.

Losing Keane from the city council was bad enough for Daley, but the prosecution of Matthew J. Danaher probably was a worse personal blow.

A young pal from Bridgeport, Danaher was Daley's top aide while Daley served as Illinois revenue director, Cook County clerk, and first-term mayor. Then Danaher became Daley's Eleventh Ward alderman before taking the post of clerk of the county courts. Eventually Daley and Danaher had a falling out because of Danaher's excessive drinking and a divorce—two conditions Daley could not abide among his lieutenants.

Thompson indicted Danaher in April 1974 for his role in a dummy corporation. The firm allegedly was set up to take bribes amounting to four hundred thousand dollars from developers who needed favorable city ordinances and bank loans. In December 1974, one month before his scheduled trial, Danaher died at age forty-seven, apparently of natural causes.

Earl Bush was Daley's press secretary from 1955 to 1973. In 1974 Bush was indicted for hiding his ownership in a firm that held an exclusive city contract for advertising at O'Hare Airport from 1962 to 1973. Bush had recommended the contract to a city council committee without disclosing his own stake in it. He earned $202,000 from the franchise. Bush was convicted but never served time. Though he was sentenced to a year in prison, Thompson's refusal to place Bush in a work-release prison program angered a federal judge, who changed the sentence to two years of probation.

Thompson did not bat one thousand. For example, Charles S. Bonk, Cook County commissioner and a former alderman and state senator, was acquitted in 1975 of charges of taking payoffs for zoning cases and hiding the income from his tax returns. Bonk died the next year at age fifty-seven of an apparent heart attack. Daley said, "Through the viciousness and the actions of certain people, some people suffer immensely, even unto death."[3] That was as close as he came to accusing Thompson outright of persecuting his allies.

Forty-ninth Ward alderman Paul T. Wigoda was more direct. He said, "There's not one person in Chicago who doesn't know that I was prosecuted to help Jim Thompson get ahead in his political career."[4] Wigoda, Keane's law partner, was convicted in 1974 of tax evasion for failing to report a payoff of fifty thousand dollars to support the rezoning of a golf course. Once again, curiously, the judge presiding over Wigoda's trial happened to be Abraham Lincoln Marovitz. Wigoda, as a navy medical corpsman, had treated Marovitz's shrapnel wounds when they served in the Philippines during World War II. Marovitz did not recuse himself from the case. He sentenced Wigoda to 366 days in jail and ordered his release after six months.

The roster of other Thompson targets (a partial listing) warrants review because an ordinary political machine could not have survived such a siege:

- Joseph Jambrone, a ward sanitation superintendent and former alderman, was convicted of failing to report fifty-eight hundred dollars in zoning payoffs on his tax returns. (Recall that zoning was a reformist project of the 1920s. Daley was quoted as saying, concerning a proposed aldermanic pay raise, "What do they need a raise for? They've got zoning."⁵) Judge William J. Lynch, who had been Daley's law partner, sentenced Jambrone to two years in prison. After admitting guilt at sentencing, Jambrone appealed the conviction. He died in 1974 at age fifty-six before an appellate ruling was made.
- Edward T. Scholl, a Republican state senator and former alderman, pleaded guilty to evading taxes on $6,850 in zoning bribes and was sentenced to eighteen months in prison.
- Another Republican, Alderman Casimir Staszcuk, was convicted of taking nine thousand dollars in zoning bribes and sentenced to eighteen months in prison.
- Cook County commissioner and former county Republican chairman Floyd Fulle received more than sixty-nine thousand dollars from developers seeking zoning changes. Fulle was sentenced to five years in prison.
- Alderman Fred Hubbard pleaded guilty to embezzling nearly one hundred thousand dollars from a federally funded jobs program he had headed, but he disappeared in 1971, before he could be jailed. FBI agents tracked his gambling debts to Los Angeles, where he was seized the next year. After serving nearly all his two-year sentence, he drove a cab and worked as a substitute teacher

under an assumed name in Chicago until he was accused of propositioning a thirteen-year-old girl.

- Cook County clerk Edward J. Barrett was convicted of taking $186,000 in bribes and kickbacks from a company that sold punch-card voting machines to the county. At age seventy-two and in poor health, Barrett drew what the judge called a light sentence of three years. Under appeals, he never went to prison and died in 1977.

- State senator and former alderman Donald Swinarski pleaded guilty to taking seventy-eight hundred dollars in zoning bribes and received a one-year sentence.

- Alderman Joseph Potempa, a Republican, pleaded guilty in a bribery and tax evasion case amounting to twelve thousand dollars and was sentenced to a year and a day in prison.

- Frank Kuta, succeeding Potempa as alderman, was promptly convicted of taking a fifteen-hundred-dollar zoning bribe and was sentenced to six months in prison.

- John J. Clarke, Daley's private investigator in city hall, pleaded guilty to failing to report investigative fees on his tax returns and to trying to influence grand jury witnesses. He was paroled after serving one year of a three-year sentence.

Democrats suspected that Thompson was trying to build a case against Daley himself. Frank Sullivan, who replaced Bush as Daley's press secretary, recalled that Thompson's agents "always looked at you like you were some kind of crook because you worked for Daley."[6] Richard M. Daley said, "The federal government investigated my father thoroughly. From top to bottom. It would have been a prize plum. . . . My father knew that. But he knew his own life. He knew he wasn't a thief."[7]

All the while, the press continued to investigate the mayor. The *Tribune* found in 1972 that almost half the local budget of Model Cities, an LBJ Great Society program of urban uplift, was devoted to administrative expenses. Many such expenses were incurred by Daley's machine operatives under no-bid contracts. In 1973 *Chicago Today* reported that the city's insurance premiums of $2.9 million were switched to an Evanston firm after Daley's son John joined it. Rival papers took up the chase and revealed that Daley's lawyer sons Richard and Michael were winning lucrative receiverships from machine courts. The mayor's response was vintage Daley: "If I can't help my sons then they can kiss my ass. I make no apologies to anyone. . . . If a man can't put his arms around his sons, then what kind of world are we living in?"[8] In 1974 the *Sun-Times*, in a joint investigation with the BGA, reported that Daley and his wife Eleanor, known as "Sis," covertly owned a real estate firm with assets exceeding two hundred thousand dollars. They included the family's vacation home in Grand Beach, Michigan, the Eleventh Ward Democratic headquarters, and cash and securities worth seventy-one thousand dollars. No illegality attached to this, but it undermined Daley's stance as a common man from the old neighborhood. Journalistic ardor reached a low of pettiness with a story that Daley's daughter Patricia and her former husband had not been properly assessed for property taxes after they improved their home. All of these revelations were pinpricks, hardly the makings of a criminal case. Indeed, Daley merely was following Chicago politicians' practices honored for more than a century. How perturbed he must have been at the scandalmongers.

So Daley eluded Thompson's dragnet. However, Thompson did not confine himself to the pursuit of politicians. He also prosecuted crooked police. At one point, three federal grand juries were investigating wrongdoing in three police districts. Daley frantically tried to head off the feds by identifying and firing crooked cops before Thompson could catch them. The mayor set up a secret internal police spy network called C-5. (One of those spies was Robert Hanssen, who later joined the FBI and was revealed in 2001 to have been a secret agent for Moscow.) Daley's effort was mostly unsuccessful. For instance, Commander Clarence E. Braasch of the East Chicago Avenue district in the trendy Near North Side was considered to be a modern, clean, managerial-style cop. Along with thirty-five other officers, Braasch was convicted of extorting more than a half-million dollars from taverns in a shakedown scheme first exposed by the *Tribune* in 1969. Thompson brought charges of conspiracy, perjury, and tax evasion, but not bribery, which was merely a state crime. Braasch, at the time the highest-ranking Chicago policeman convicted of a felony, served four years of a six-year sentence. John Clarke, the cop who had suggested the C-5 operation to Daley, was jailed in 1974 for tax evasion because, he said, he refused to cooperate with Thompson. "The feds wanted me to give them the names of informants to whom I had paid $17,500. I refused to ruin their lives."[9]

Over three years, eighty-six policemen were charged with crimes. Another 407 were fired or forced to resign for illicit involvement with vice and graft. Then the *Tribune* in 1973 took up the cause of spotlighting police brutality, provoking the indictments of four officers. Daley fired his police superintendent and named another. The new chief ordered high-ranking officers to take lie detector tests on their involvement with organized crime or vice. Seven of seventy flunked outright, and nine more disturbed or "fluttered" the machine, in police parlance, on one or more questions. Also during this period, the police and fire departments were in federal court in cases charging bias against the hiring and promotion of minorities. Daley was reelected in 1971 and 1975 without much strain.

In a sense, Daley's defenders are right that he was not destroyed by the 1968 convention debacle. He survived the jailing of his political cronies, police officers, and, in still another arena of Thompson scrutiny, vote stealing. Newspapers coupled with the BGA to investigate vote fraud.

In 1968 an undercover BGA man lived in flophouses under such aliases as James Joyce, Jay Gatsby, and Henry Thoreau. He never registered to vote but somehow ended up on the voter rolls under those names. Investigators saw cash paid to flophouse residents to cast votes. The *Daily News* ran stories on Skid Row vote fraud for twenty straight days. Four political workers were convicted and three went to prison in the first convictions under the federal Voting Rights Act of 1965.

The *Tribune* won a Pulitzer Prize in 1973 for its own vote-fraud series after the primary and general elections of 1972. The newspaper covertly sent twenty reporters and the BGA ten staffers to serve as election judges and poll watchers in fourteen notorious precincts on the West and South sides in the March primary. The planted election workers noted firsthand the techniques, developed by Hinky Dink and even those before him, used to romanticize Chicago vote returns. The selected precincts had so few Republican voters that the nominal GOP election judges were ringers for the Democratic machine. Thompson indicted forty people in September 1972 for vote fraud in the primary. As with the conviction of "Chesterfield Joe" Mackin and others in 1884, the techniques were so crude that even a routinely competent Chicago board of election commissioners should have detected them.

Stamping out vote fraud was a perennial effort by reformers, and the prosecution of a few precinct workers after each election was customary. Never before the *Tribune*'s reports, however, were dirty elections so well documented. Thompson in the end indicted a total of eighty-three election officials, of whom sixty-six were convicted or pleaded guilty. In line with tradition, most of their offenses were misdemeanors drawing light sentences.

Daley's chairman of the election board was Stanley T. Kusper, who responded to the *Tribune* by saying, "They lie at the *Tribune,* and boy do they lie. Then they get the Pulitzer Prize for that lying."[10] Daley then named Kusper as county clerk to replace the indicted Edward J. Barrett. Kusper served in that office until 1990. In 1981 a top aide was convicted of delivering bribes for clouted reductions in tax assessments (a matter apart from Kusper's office). Later, Kusper gave no-bid county contracts to that former aide's business. Kusper was investigated, but never charged, for depositing county funds in non-interest-bearing accounts in banks with which he did personal business.

Despite such sorry records, by now Chicago elections are relatively clean, the weight of legend and everlasting jokes about graveyard voting aside. Still, the Democratic party controls the election machinery with the concomitant benefits of institutional dominance. The favored techniques of fraud now occur not in the polling place but in manipulations of absentee voting. The next election surely will witness Republican election judges protesting that absentee ballots were gamed, that police refused to prevent illegal Democratic electioneering outside the polling place, or some such.

Daley was old and sick; many of his best friends were indicted, jailed, sick, or dead. That he maintained a reputation and a high degree of reality as boss is a marvel. As if Thompson were not enough of a foe, the federal courts were choking off patronage, blacks-only public housing, crooked cops, and vote fraud.

Beyond these defeats, Daley was humiliated when his Chicago delegation to the 1972 Democratic National Convention in Miami Beach was unseated in favor of a rebel slate of antiwar activists led by Jesse Jackson and white lakefront liberals. The rebels adopted the old throw-the-rascals-out model of the Municipal Voters' League because Daley's slate did not meet new party rules requiring sexual and racial balance. Yet his delegates were, after all, chosen by voters in a free election. In their victory, reformers once more upheld the upper-middle-class bias for restrictive rules as against democratic preferences.

In 1974, four days after Keane was indicted, Daley suffered a stroke that required brain surgery. That was when, because he feared assassination by a power cutoff during the operation, he went under the knife a day before officially scheduled and posted police around the hospital. A machine alderman muttered, "He always had this thing about not trusting anyone, but now it looks like the old man is losing his marbles."[11]

In the 1976 Democratic primary, Daley managed to dump renegade Governor Dan Walker, who had headed the investigative commission of the notorious "police riot" in Chicago in 1968. At the 1976 Democratic National Convention in New York, which nominated Jimmy Carter, Daley was treated with the utmost deference. He had been ejected from the 1972 convention but was venerated in 1976. The latter event actually emasculated him even more, but with gentility—Daley was just an old lion to be saluted and then ignored. In the November election, Daley failed to carry Illinois for Carter or to elect Thompson's Democratic opponent for governor.

On 20 December 1976, Daley died of a heart attack. Mourners at the funeral included President-elect Carter and Vice President Nelson Rockefeller. Catholic reformer John A. McDermott reflected,

Some of the hatred of Daley was not honorable. Some of it was based on his working-class origins, and his refusal to abandon them. I think he was regarded as stupid and backward and not a modern person because he still lived in the old neighborhood. I also feel there was a certain amount of religious bigotry. I always thought this was a clue to his combativeness and defensiveness.

Daley grew up in a time when it was not fashionable to be a Catholic. You could not make it. You couldn't get into a major law firm. You couldn't get into major clubs. There were pressures to limit the number of Catholics teaching in public schools. And this is a forgotten part of our history.[12]

Sentiments such as this could have been expressed by thoughtful reformers and party regulars alike throughout Chicago's history.

Daley was far from the only fallen giant. During this period, they were toppling everywhere. Apart from the torture of the Vietnam War and before the "White House horrors" collectively called Watergate, LBJ protégé and Senate Democratic secretary Bobby Baker was convicted of influence peddling in 1963. Supreme Court justice and LBJ crony Abe Fortas resigned in 1969 for having accepted gifts from a financier. Fellow Justice William O. Douglas survived an impeachment effort in 1970 for alleged improper acts. But it was not before Thompson locally and Watergate nationally that official wrongdoing seemed *epidemic.* Vice President Spiro T. Agnew pleaded "no contest" to tax evasion for bribery and resigned in 1973. Nixon resigned on 9 August 1974. Two months later, House Ways and Means Committee chairman Wilbur D. Mills of Arkansas cavorted drunkenly with a stripper and soon was forced to retire. In 1976 "Koreagate" exposed gifts and payoffs to congressmen by South Korean agents. Even Bert Lance, budget director under the squeaky-clean Jimmy Carter, was forced to resign in 1977 for having cut corners on banking deals. Carter's chief of staff Hamilton Jordan was cleared of drug-use charges in 1979 after going broke (typically and sadly) paying defense attorneys.

Inflation was high, the economy weak, scandal rampant, and some thinkers wondered anew whether the American experiment had run its course. Such a worry now is passé, but the public contempt for politics engendered by the spectacular scandals of the 1970s and later remains a serious problem. This contempt, held by many Chicago reformers through the decades, represents a corruption of the democratic ideal perhaps as dangerous as malfeasance in office by politicians. A case can be made that the professionalization and codification of politics hammered by reformers, as in the counterproductive campaign financial reform laws provoked by Watergate, have abetted the public's alienation from politics.

Perhaps the Progressives, once again, are at center stage. Few would regret the Progressive victories, but they were dearly won. Progressives laid down the tradition of special interests exploiting the media to attain their aims. By now those interest groups include a permanent class of reformers within government and the media, layering on ever more bureaucratic hierarchies of regulation and oversight, elaborated with each new scandal, which perversely seem to create ever more vulnerabilities for corruption. The public takes a look, shakes its head, and tunes out.

Jim Thompson had anticipated and nourished the culture of scandal. In 1977 the Justice Department did a study to discover how far the epidemic of prosecuting public corruption had reached. Federal indictments of public officials rose from sixty-three in 1970 to 337 in 1976. Thompson's office led the number of federal convictions with 135. During that six-year span, 1,598 officials were indicted by local and U.S. prosecutors, of whom 1,081 were convicted.[13]

The Chicago machine, like the country at large, was demoralized. Even so, the machine, with ostrichlike obtuseness, did not believe the reelection of its hand-picked mayor, Daley's successor Michael A. Bilandic, was in jeopardy.

Harry Truman once said he would like to be president but never wanted to succeed Franklin Roosevelt. In that sense, whoever succeeded Daley was bound to be diminished by comparison. Bilandic generously gave critics opportunities for his belittlement. Daley's death provoked frantic maneuvers, as had the deaths of mayors Harrison I and Cermak. The city council president pro tem, Wilson J. Frost, had a valid claim to the mayor's seat. However, he was black. For that reason, the machine spurned him, a move that inspired more black political dissent. Eleven years later, a powerful white alderman allowed that, had Frost become mayor, "it would have prevented this racial chaos."[14]

Bilandic was the alderman from Daley's Eleventh Ward and, though Croatian and not Irish, was elected by the city council with a boost from the imprisoned Keane. In 1977 Bilandic easily won a special election to fill the remainder of Daley's term. His administration was unhappy and unlucky.

Pamela Zekman was a short, red-haired, pretty former figure skater who became a granite-tough investigative reporter. At the *Tribune,* she had been part of the newspaper's vote-fraud series and then shared another Pulitzer Prize for exposing hospital abuses in 1975. During a cold, windy walk in December 1976 across the Michigan Avenue bridge over the Chicago River with her new boss, *Sun-Times* editor James Hoge, she confessed her fantasy of running a tavern undercover to document the bribes demanded of businesses by city inspectors. Everybody knew about such shakedowns, but they remained to reformers tantalizingly unproven. Indeed, in 1969 film director Norman Jewison was so disgusted by payoff demands from cops and inspectors while trying to film *Gaily, Gaily,* based on Ben Hecht's book about Chicago, that he decamped to Milwaukee in a huff.

Amazingly, editor Hoge agreed to Zekman's scheme. Media executives normally reject elaborate investigations that require much personnel time and expense, and are not apt to increase advertising revenues or even newspaper circulations or TV audiences. With Hoge's assent, Zekman in conjunction with the BGA bought and opened a ramshackle saloon they renamed the Mirage at 731 North Wells Street on 17 August 1977. The area then was seedy but now is part of the gentrified Near North Side. The Mirage team determined the legal definition of entrapment into crimes and then devised even stricter standards.

The tavern featured awful, truly terrible wiring, plumbing, health, cleanliness, and fire-code violations. One sink behind the bar drained directly onto the floor. The basement ceiling was falling down and the basement floor was covered with human and rodent excrement. Soon the electrical, plumbing, building, fire, and liquor inspectors came calling. They had progressed past the days of the gray wolves in that they never directly asked for bribes. They merely hinted, with sinuous language and nudges, that annoying bureaucratic rules might be hurdled. There might be an understanding, a mutuality of favor. They looked approvingly on envelopes containing one hundred or fifty or even as few as ten dollars that they could deftly sweep up from the bar and place among their official papers.

Twelve city and state inspectors visited the place over four months. Six took bribes, and six were negligent for free. The Mirage never had a valid electrical, plumbing, fire, building, health, or liquor-license inspection. Meanwhile, city trash collectors pocketed fifteen dollars each to remove the tavern's refuse, although they were supposed to leave commercial establishments to private scavengers. Firefighters on duty sold tickets for a charity to aid the widows and orphans of comrades killed in the line of duty. Actually, the money supported only the fire department band.

Critics of the Mirage sting, besides charging entrapment, gibed that the bribes totaled only in the hundreds of dollars. But that was the point. Corruption was that petty and that systemic. Moreover, the evasion of sales and income taxes by saloons across the city amounted to millions of dollars. An accountant hired by the Mirage advised the tavern to cook the books so as to conceal 40 percent of its revenues. He said everybody did it. Other accountants interviewed by the Mirage team said the same thing. Pinball machine distributors skimmed cash from their collections before reporting the amount to their bosses and tax collectors. The Mirage kept six sets of phony books and a seventh upon which to pay its honest taxes.

Points raised in the inspectors' defense were that their pay was so low they felt compelled to supplement it with bribes and that the city codes were such a magpie's nest of rococo requirements, contradictions, and union featherbedding rules that they could not possibly be fully enforced. These contentions were true, but in fact the very muddle of the codes was another resource for the machine. City hall could find violations to crack down on politically uncooperative parties at will.

Zekman and her colleague Zay N. Smith, who worked as a Mirage bartender, published their stories from 8 January to 5 February 1978. They rushed into print under fear of the exposure of their sting not by city hall but by competing reporters. News writers heard rumors about the *Sun-Times* enterprise and raced to confirm them, including even fellow *Sun-Times* reporters and those at its sister *Daily News,* both owned by the Marshall Field family. There still was cutthroat Chicago journalism then.

The Mirage enterprise entered the national media culture of scandal largely because the TV program *60 Minutes* secretly filmed and later aired some of the payoffs. Talks between the TV and *Sun-Times* teams over whether an early broadcast might compromise the operation were so intense that *60 Minutes* anchor Mike Wallace threatened to throw Zekman out a window. She was not intimidated.

Any cynical regular or reformer could have written the script for Mayor Bilandic's response to the Mirage revelations. He said the grafters amounted to a few bad apples, not systemic corruption. Further, he had been contemplating reforms of inspection and licensing processes for some time and the Mirage "merely accelerated the timing of it" (the usual claim for politicians in his spot).[15] The mayor pledged to create an office of professional review to investigate complaints of shakedowns and other abuses. Chicago had heard it all before.

The city had fifty-one electrical inspectors. After the Mirage, twenty-nine were indicted and twenty-five convicted. More than a dozen city and state employees were fired. Federal and state tax collectors beefed up their investigative units in Chicago. Yet, in the end, the system once more disappointed reformers. According to Zekman and Smith, the upshot was that some city inspectors, pleading the enhanced danger of exposure, increased their payoff fees.

Bilandic had scandal problems aside from the Mirage. The newsstands and boutiques at O'Hare Airport allegedly had clouted their franchises in a reprise of the Earl Bush sweetheart ad contract scandal. More publicized was a charge from the city consumer affairs commissioner, Jane Byrne, that Bilandic had greased a taxi fare increase through the city council. Bilandic thereupon fired Byrne.

Byrne, "lace-curtain Irish," had volunteered to work for Kennedy's 1960 campaign and then was enlisted in the machine by Daley, who in time gave her the meaningless title of female cochair of Cook County Democrats. City council reformers grabbed Byrne's taxi allegations to force the creation of an investigative committee. Named as chairman was Alderman Wilson Frost, who, even though he had been denied the mayoralty because of his race, remained a machine regular. Quickly the committee decided that the fare increase was justified. On 21 April 1978, the council voted 40-3 to accept the committee's report. Three days later, Byrne declared her candidacy for mayor.

She cited the taxicab and Mirage scandals as grounds for her candidacy but made little headway until 31 December 1978. On that day, fifteen inches of snow fell, nothing catastrophic in Chicago. But by primary election day, 27 February 1979, the total accumulation was 82.3 inches, enough to drive even Chicagoans mad.

Bilandic blundered through the winter months. He awarded a lucrative snow-removal consulting contract to a machine hack whose study in due course concluded that when snow falls it has to be plowed off the streets. Bilandic also ordered rapid transit trains to speed past snowbound stations in black neighborhoods but to stop and pick up Loop commuters in closer-in white neighborhoods. Many people found fault with this directive. Under media assault, Bilandic compared the attacks on his administration to the crucifixion of Jesus, the persecution of Jews, the Soviet domination of Eastern Europe, black slavery in America, and bias against Hispanics. Voters cried few tears over the mayor's expansive catalogue of victimization. After his defeat, snow became such a political bogeyman in Chicago that public agencies would pay obscenely extravagant fees to private snowplow contractors lest the city be snowbound and voters angered again.

The local and national media compared Byrne's upset of Bilandic to all but the rising sun, the aurora borealis, the Emancipation Proclamation, and the parting of the Red Sea. Reporters wrote still more obituaries for the machine. At last the Daley machine was dead, buried with a stake through its heart. "I beat the whole goddamned machine single-handedly," Byrne crowed.[16] She had not. Her brilliant political strategist was Don Rose, who had coined the slogan "the whole world is watching" (after a Bob Dylan lyric) in 1968. Rose perceived that racial politics kept the machine glued together but that eventually a civic crisis would break the machine's control of Irish, Poles, Italians, African Americans, and others. The blizzards of 1978–79 proved to be the disaster Rose had prophesied. Rose also had an attractive candidate, a widowed five-foot-three blond with an aggressiveness that gets female candidates labeled "feisty" and "scrappy."

Byrne campaigned against the machine's "cabal of evil men." As mayor, however, she soon ran breathlessly into its fold. This decision was pragmatic, but whether it was necessary is a question that might perplex reformers even now. Her supporters tended to forget that she was a daughter of the machine, a protégé of Daley. Byrne explained, "I can't govern this city unless I cut a deal with [machine aldermen Edward R. Vrydolyak and Edward M. Burke]. I have no constituency in the council. I don't have anything in the bureaucracy. I bark orders from the fifth floor and nobody listens. If I don't have these people with me, government won't operate."[17] *Government won't operate.* That defense could have been asserted by any mayor.

The federal government, even under a Democratic president, Jimmy Carter, looked with skepticism on the operations of government as practiced by Byrne, Vrdolyak, and Burke. Michael Shakman kept pressing lawsuits against patronage, and in 1979 a federal court banned public hirings as well as firings based on political affiliation. This ruling badly wounded the machine but did not deter Byrne from employing a city officer whose portfolio explicitly was patronage.

Besides Vrydolyak and Burke, another member of the "evil cabal" was Charles R. Swibel. A Polish refugee from Nazi Europe, Swibel grew rich in Chicago real estate and was named by Daley to chair the Chicago Housing Authority (CHA) in 1963. In 1975 the *Sun-Times* disclosed that Swibel gave the CHA security contract to a firm that had installed a sixty-five-hundred-dollar burglar alarm for free at his home. Swibel also deposited CHA funds in no-interest accounts at a local bank that gave him multimillion-dollar lines of credit for his personal real estate deals. In 1980 the BGA and *Chicago* magazine said the CHA's elevators were in such horrible disrepair that seventeen deaths and four hundred injuries had occurred in the past ten years. (This and other mechanical problems persisted for fifteen more years until the federal government decided that the only solution was to take over the CHA and demolish its high-rises.) In 1981 the CHA was broke, prompting an audit by the U.S. Department of Housing and Urban Development (HUD). HUD under President Reagan was itself so corrupt that it warranted a special prosecutor, admittedly not a high hurdle in the Washington of the 1980s and 1990s. Anyway, HUD's audit of the CHA was damning. It said the agency's purpose apparently was the "acquisition of as many Federal . . . dollars as possible for the creation of patronage jobs and financial opportunities."[18]

Patronage jobs and financial opportunities.

Byrne had promised to implement any reforms sought by HUD. The department said it would bail out CHA only on condition of certain reforms, including the ouster of Swibel. At that, Byrne balked. What happened next was predictable: the secret HUD study was leaked to the media. The Illinois legislature stepped in, mandating that the CHA chairmanship be a full-time, professional job. Under fire, Byrne accepted Swibel's resignation, reluctantly, she said. He remained a personal adviser.

The centuries-old conflict between pietists and ritualists reached its logical extreme with newspaper, criminal, and even Vatican City investigations of the head of the Roman Catholic archdiocese of Chicago. The *Sun-Times* still was owned by a descendant of Marshall Field. The U.S. attorney had been appointed by the Southern Baptist Jimmy Carter. To view the case of John Cardinal Cody in this historical framework is to say nothing about any possible anti-Catholic bias among personnel at the *Sun-Times* or the U.S. attorney's office. Instead, the legacy of different cultural attitudes toward probity merged with the modern culture of scandal to place under criminal jeopardy even an ecclesiastical worthy who normally would have been above suspicion. The antiauthoritarianism of the Great Awakenings had attained this plane. Over many years, Protestant reformers unwittingly had contributed to a general disrespect for authority that undermined the WASPs' own status.

Whatever one thinks of the press or the church, the *Sun-Times* took a heavy risk in assaulting the leader of the archdiocese, which comprised 2.4 million members of its potential readership. Three reporters spent eighteen months on the project, an amazing expenditure of time and manpower. One of the reporters was a Catholic who endured obloquy from his local parish and soon after died, his son said, in part because of the stress of the Cody case.

The paper broke its five-day series of Cody stories, again under time pressure from competing media, on 10 September 1981. The resulting uproar was typically Chicagoan in fomenting reports and rumors of double-dealing, hidden agendas, conspiracies, and bad faith.

John Patrick Cody (1908–82) was the son of an Irish immigrant, a firefighter in St. Louis. Cody served as a priest for fifty years, during which he fought for racial integration in New Orleans before assignment to Chicago in 1965. There he closed black inner-city parochial schools, not because they were black but because they had too many non-Catholic pupils. Even his defenders allowed that he was autocratic and imperious. He also was the target of a grand jury under U.S. Attorney Thomas P. Sullivan (a Catholic).

The *Sun-Times* revealed that Sullivan's grand jury had subpoenaed church and bank records in January 1981 to investigate whether Cody had diverted up to $1 million in church funds to a childhood friend and cousin by marriage, Helen Dolan Wilson. Detractors charged that the newspaper first approached Sullivan with the allegations, not the other way around. By citing official action, the paper would have a peg on which to hang its stories, a defense against a possible libel action.

Helen Wilson, a policeman's daughter, after retiring from a modestly paid office manager's job in St. Louis in 1969, had residences in a St. Louis suburb, in Boca Raton, Florida, and at Lake Point Tower in Chicago. It was the symbolism of Lake Point Towers, a deluxe, curvilinear trefoil of a high-rise on the downtown lakefront, that seemed to drive the story home. The paper also stated that Wilson, seventy-four years old, divorced since

1939 and the mother of two adult children, drew a small but secret salary as an office worker for the Chicago church from 1969 to 1975, although she was a retiree who spent winters in Florida. Further, the *Sun-Times* reported that Cody steered archdiocesan insurance contracts to Wilson's son and that Wilson was the owner and beneficiary of Cody's life insurance policy worth one hundred thousand dollars.

Reactions from different quarters followed pietistic and ritualistic lines. Cody, Wilson, and the archdiocese denied everything. U.S. Attorney Dan K. Webb, who had replaced Sullivan under President Reagan, would confirm only that his office was looking into whether Cody had violated federal laws. Cody embraced the modern media culture in 1980 when he hired a public relations consultant who spun the story that the *Sun-Times* wanted to smear the cardinal because of his conservative stances on abortion, divorce, and other church doctrines. The *Tribune* eyed a circulation gain among Catholics and tried to knock down the *Sun-Times* investigation. The *Tribune* had spent the 1970s moving to the center to overcome its reputation, dating from Colonel McCormick and earlier, as a Republican reactionary rag.

The *Chicago Catholic,* reacting to rumors of the *Sun-Times* probe a year before it was printed, editorialized on 22 August 1980:

> The Chicago Sun-Times appears to see circulation profit in anti-Catholicism. The hostility of the Sun-Times toward the Catholic Church threatens the right of Catholics to worship as they choose and to conduct their religious affairs as they choose. By its own choice, the Sun-Times is a major opponent of the Catholic Church and of individual Catholics who wish to practice their faith prayerfully and without hindrance of government or press.

This editorial carried a touch of hysteria, especially considering that the *Chicago Catholic*'s editor privately had remarked that Cody was "the only truly evil man that I have ever known. He is a perfect monster."[19] The *Chicago Catholic* did not explain how the *Sun-Times* could gain circulation by alienating Catholics.

Frankly but only off the record, U.S. attorney's officers and anti-Cody priests expressed the morbid hope that the ailing Cody would die before the government had to do anything as drastic as indicting him. The Vatican had been looking into reports of Cody's malfeasance in office since the 1970s. Like any bureaucracy, private or public, the church wished to keep its dirty laundry in-house. Cody deflected efforts by the pope himself to kick him upstairs to a sinecure in Rome. After the *Sun-Times* went public, talk in Chicago speculated on who had fingered Cody and what forced the *Sun-Times* into print sooner than it planned. The culture of scandal melded with the culture of celebrity. Local and national reporters had been trying to scoop the *Sun-Times*. A prevailing rumor was that Andrew M. Greeley, a priest, sociologist, newspaper columnist, and novelist, had schemed for years to oust Cody for his conservatism.

The mining and countermining of media positions will take some patience to sort out. Greeley's critics said he never had an unwritten thought. At the least, that prickly priest never left a critic comfortably unanswered. He protested indignantly that he had many unwritten thoughts. In any case, he spoke his thoughts into tape recorders from 1975 to 1978. While the *Sun-Times* was investigating Cody, Greeley was writing *The Makings of the Popes 1978*, an account of the successions of John Paul I and John Paul II. The *Chicago Lawyer* got hold of Greeley's book galleys and reported that by his telling, Cody would be destroyed by a plot to enlist investigative reporters against him. Further, the scheme would replace Cody with Archbishop Joseph Bernardin of Cincinnati. Still further, Bernardin was behind a plot to elect a new pope of liberal persuasion. The *Tribune* headlined the *Chicago Lawyer*'s findings on 27 September 1981, just two weeks after the *Sun-Times* revelations. Greeley's alleged machinations were confirmed at least to the extent that the church sent Bernardin to Chicago to succeed Cody after his death in 1982.

Now the plot grows even thicker. The *Tribune* said the *Chicago Lawyer* story was based in part on Greeley's letters and 1975–78 personal audiotapes housed in his archives at Rosary College in west suburban River Forest. In turn, this material allegedly had been taken without Greeley's permission by the managing editor of *Notre Dame Magazine*. This editor had approached the *Sun-Times* with his information but was spurned because it was irrelevant to the Cody probe and unverified besides. The *Notre Dame Magazine* editor then knocked on the door of the *Tribune,* where he tried to cut a deal to be hired in case Notre Dame should fire him. *Tribune* executives turned him away. The Cincinnati archdiocese and Greeley both called the Notre Dame editor's allegations fantasies. Greeley denied he was behind any plot to "get" Cody. Later he wrote that Cody suffered from a clinical case of "antisocial character defect," not a contemporary psychiatric term.

Cody died on 25 April 1982, leaving a farewell letter that said, "I have forgiven my enemies. I yield up resentment, forego rage and anger and will not seek retributive justice or gross vengeance. . . . But God will not so forgive."[20]

It was all too, too Chicagoan in its class, ethnic, religious, political, Byzantine, Machiavellian, media, and Daleyesque pathways. Imagine the consternation of Dan Webb when, on being briefed by Thomas Sullivan's U.S. attorney's office before taking it over in 1981, he was informed that it not only was investigating the Catholic cardinal of Chicago but setting up elaborate stings for a scandal even bigger than the Mirage or Cody: the thorough corruption of Cook County courts. Here was the young lawyer Webb, thrilled to win such a federal plum, suddenly told that he would be responsible for prosecuting not just the highest Catholic official in the city but the entire court operations of the Democratic machine. "Sullivan, you sonofabitch," Webb thought. "But I wasn't frightened. I was fascinated."[21]

The Justice Department, armed with the technology of electronic surveillance, grew institutionally fond of sting operations. They seemed to yield easier cases than the technique perfected by Jim Thompson and Watergate prosecutors of pressuring wrongdoers to "flip," to testify against higher-ups in exchange for plea bargains. Courts largely ruled that government stings, inventing crimes for the opportunity to nab politicians predisposed to corruption, did not constitute legal entrapment. Nonetheless, the judicial and ethical argument still is waged.

The FBI was making local cases with stings in Louisiana, Massachusetts, Ohio, and Oklahoma. In Chicago, Teamsters Union president Roy

L. Williams and mobster Joseph "Joey the Clown" Lombardo were convicted of conspiring to bribe a U.S. senator from Nevada who influenced gambling in Las Vegas. Chicago's U.S. attorney Sullivan saw stings caught by electronic surveillance as the only way to cleanse Cook County courts of their historical and pandemic corruption. On 26 November 1980, FBI agents bugged the chambers of circuit court judge Wayne W. Olson. This date was a milestone both in the annals of corruption and reform and in the eternal struggle of individual privacy against governmental intromission. It was the first legal bugging of a sitting judge's office.

By the time of Sullivan's Operation Greylord, illegal bugging and spying by government agencies were coming to light. A Senate investigative committee and a presidential commission in the 1970s had revealed illegal domestic spying and other abuses, such as drugging unsuspecting subjects with LSD, by the Central Intelligence Agency (CIA). In Chicago, the *Daily News* in 1975 broke the story of Daley's police Red Squad, which spied on and disrupted dissident groups. Reformers filed a class-action, civil-rights lawsuit against city and federal law enforcement agencies. The discovery phase of the case put startling facts on the record that seemed to make little splash. Perhaps the public was growing inured to scandal. The FBI conceded that it had 837 informants in Chicago reporting only on dissident groups' lawful activities, not criminal conduct. The bureau had committed more than five hundred break-ins in the city. Late in 1980, the FBI and CIA signed consent decrees to settle the lawsuit, admitting no wrongdoing but agreeing to strict limits on surveillance of activities protected under the First Amendment. Mayor Byrne at first refused to accept a similar consent decree for the city but relented in 1981.

Attendant negative publicity did not deter the Justice Department from pursuing stings against criminality. The department had picked up from the Pentagon the public relations device of tagging its operations with catchy code names. Sullivan's investigation was labeled Greylord, which the press took for a sardonic allusion to bewigged judges in British courts but in fact was named for a racehorse.

Corruption as revealed by Greylord had much of its basis in reform legislation, one more example of iatrogenic corruption. In 1959 there was a scandal of abuses in the bail-bonding business, which Mayor Ed Dunne had tried to clean up a half-century earlier. In 1963 the state legislature eliminated bail bondsmen who charged a fee of 10 percent of the bond. Instead, defendants could be freed upon posting themselves a mere 10 percent of the amount of the bond. Reformers exchanged congratulations. In 1969 the legislature amended the law to permit defendants to sign over their bond refunds to their attorneys. Ostensibly, this was a reform measure to provide private legal counsel to defendants who otherwise could not afford it. Lawyers started loitering about courtrooms, offering to represent defendants facing traffic offenses or misdemeanors for no fee, just the bond refund. Many lawyers fixed cases with judges by kicking back part of the refunds. Unlike the inspector bribes in the Mirage case, these were not small-time payoffs in the aggregate. Hustling lawyers and judges both grew wealthy under the volume of cases.

The *Sun-Times* broke the Greylord story on 5 August 1983. It provided sensational news copy for the next seven years. Wayne Olson, the first to have his chambers bugged, said, "I love people that take dough because you know exactly where they stand."[22] That became a reformist battle cry. Two persons in particular enchanted the media and the public. Attorney "White Knight" Terrence Hake agreed to wear a secret recording device under his suit jacket to catch judges on the take. "Hillbilly Judge" Brockton Lockwood, serving a visiting stint in Chicago from a bench in Marion, Illinois, hid a microphone in his cowboy boot. The final tally listed convictions of or guilty pleas from fifteen judges (two were acquitted), forty-seven lawyers, and twenty-four court, sheriff's, and police personnel. Greylord stands without even a close second in exposing crooked court proceedings in America. The human cost of the investigation, meanwhile, expressed a historical constant. A potential witness, police sergeant Roger D. Murphy, committed suicide early on the day, 14 December 1983, that Webb held a news conference to announce the first Greylord indictments. A crooked divorce court judge, Allen F. Rosin, killed himself on 21 June 1987.

Governor Thompson had won the U.S. attorney's appointment for Webb, his director of state law enforcement, to succeed Sullivan. In 1988 Webb, who by then had entered private practice, said, "In terms of convictions, Greylord is the most successful undercover operation in the history of undercover operations. But in terms of institutional impact, Greylord has been a miserable failure."[23] The Mirage had not rid the city of fake inspections, and Greylord did not yield the reform Webb expected: a merit system to select judges instead of the spoils system that endures today.

In hindsight, though, Webb might have been too pessimistic. Former U.S. attorney Scott R. Lassar, who began his federal career on Greylord cases, said in 2001 that Greylord had a positive outcome. He said it forced Cook County courts to professionalize operations, monitor the performance of judges more closely, and transfer or dump judges of dubious qualifications or ethics.

A panel of blue-ribbon reformers had been set up in the 1980s, urging the usual steps to rationalize, regulate, and codify procedures, many of which were adopted, although not, or course, merit selection. The chairman of the panel opined that two-thirds of Cook County judges, crookedness aside, were incompetent. Lyndon Johnson, on being told by a colleague that politics is the art of accepting half a loaf, legendarily offered the gruff reply, "slice of goddamned bread, even." Greylord gave reformers at least a slice of bread, maybe even half a loaf.

Even the most ardent businessmen reformers, evangelists, settlement-house liberals, Progressives, muckrakers, and Saul Alinsky–style radicals might not have imagined widespread, official bugging of judges, let alone a federal investigation of the Catholic cardinal of Chicago. The new mayor as Greylord escalated, Harold Washington, regarded it with interest but not personal involvement. Machine judges, after all, hardly were his pals. Washington, a reform genius of a type not seen before or since, soon had reasons of his own to dread federal stings.

10

"Harold!" and More Scandals and Stings

1983–89

My election was made possible by thousands and thousands of people who demanded that the burdens of mismanagement, unfairness and inequity be lifted so the city could be saved. One of the ideas that held us all together said that neighborhood involvement has to take the place of the ancient, decrepit and creaking machine.
　　　　—Mayor Harold L. Washington, inaugural address, 1983

The Niagara of African American enthusiasm for Harold Washington in the Chicago mayoral election of 1983 is becoming lost to memory. In degree it exceeded even, by the author's observations, black support for Maynard H. Jackson Jr. of Atlanta, the first African American mayor of a major southern city, in 1973. By now the election of blacks or, more pointedly, their subsequent defeat by white challengers as mayors of big cities has become commonplace. In 1983 black mayors were novelties, while it seemed everyone, black and white, was hurt by the social and political traumas of the 1960s and 1970s. Some thinkers opined during the recession of 1982–83 that Rust Belt industrial cities were dying or dead. Vietnam, Chicago 1968, Watergate, and the general crookedness of government at all levels were fresh in people's minds.

In this context, the optimism of Chicago blacks was superlative. Their high hopes, like those of white Progressives earlier, in time were disappointed. But after the indignities of the Daley, Bilandic, and Byrne administrations, blacks were as one in wearing blue Washington campaign buttons with a rays-of-the-rising-sun motif. One could see them on the winter coats of every black passenger on Chicago Transit Authority trains to the South and West sides—grandmotherly maids, Loop attorneys, ward heelers, punch-press operators, McDonald's burger flippers, the homeless, little kids, everybody. White media executives, going home to the North Side or to the suburbs, did not notice. They thought Mayor Byrne or State's Attorney Richard M. Daley would win the Democratic primary.

Harold Washington's victory was a historic event but perhaps nobody's finest hour. The campaign was racially charged on both sides. Some black clergy, reversing a time-honored courtesy extended to all mayors, refused to allow Byrne to make campaign appearances in their churches. During her four years, Byrne had gone through three police chiefs, three chiefs of staff, and three press secretaries. She displayed still more apparent inscrutability by replacing blacks with whites on school board and housing authority seats. These seemingly foolish acts were intended to entice a black challenger into the Democratic primary against her and Daley. By dividing the opposition, Byrne calculated, she would win by a plurality. Bilandic's 49 percent of the vote in 1979, heralded as the demise of the machine, actually approximated the machine's historical showing in multicandidate mayoral primaries. Byrne had defeated Bilandic in a one-on-one race in 1979 but was not about to subject herself to another.

Be careful what you wish for. At the time, blacks and whites were roughly equal in voting-age population but whites had a substantial lead in the number of registered voters. Congressman Washington, who held William Dawson's former seat in the Near South Side, the oldest locus of black political power in America, was reluctant to run for mayor. He required that activists first register at least fifty thousand new black voters. A campaign led, at least in publicity, by Jesse Jackson accomplished this and more—140,000. In the February primary, Byrne and Daley split the white vote, allowing Washington to win with a plurality of the citywide vote.

Like previous and later reform mayors, Washington was an imperfect model. He had spent thirty-six days in jail in 1972 under a two-year suspended sentence for failure to file income tax returns for four years in the 1960s. Actually, the prosecution alleged, he had not filed a return since 1952 (taxes were withheld from his paychecks; he just didn't bother with tax forms). From 1970 until 1976, Washington's law license was suspended on five counts of taking legal fees without performing legal services for his clients and two counts of failing to appear at bar association hearings to answer the allegations. Washington's fees hardly had been clout-heavy— four clients had sought divorces and the fifth wanted to void a traffic ticket. In petitioning the state Supreme Court to regain his law license, Washington swore he had not been a defendant in a civil or criminal case during its suspension. In fact, he was a defendant in five civil actions, two filed by the city and three "forcible detainer actions" trying to remove him from his apartment at 4948 South Martin Luther King Drive.[1] These minor misdeeds are recited in some detail because they formed the basis for Washington's white opponents to assert that he was unfit to serve as mayor, having nothing to do with race. However, similar baggage carried by white politicians somehow did not trouble them so. In any case, Washington's habitual inattention to detail hobbled his administration.

Washington (1922–87) was as much a son of the machine as Byrne its daughter. Washington's father Roy was a Protestant minister, attorney, and Third Ward precinct captain. In 1954 Roy got his son a ghost payroller job as an inspector for the city corporation counsel. Washington would drop by the office every two weeks to pick up his paycheck, then once a month to get two checks, and then, when even that became too burdensome, he asked to have the checks mailed to him. Twenty years later, as a state legislator after Daley died, Washington challenged Mayor Bilandic in the 1979 special election to express black anger over the machine's exclusion of Wilson Frost from the mayoralty. Washington won just 11 percent of the vote and did not fully break with the machine until 1980.

After winning his 1983 mayoral nomination, Washington ran against an obscure Republican attorney, Bernard Epton. Irish, Italian, and Polish Democratic ward bosses secretly or sometimes openly supported the Jewish Republican over the black Democrat. The campaign was ugly. Epton's slogan called on Chicago to elect him "Before It's Too Late." Washington was the victim of a poison-pen effort alleging he was a closet homosexual and pedophile. Former vice president Walter F. Mondale was at Washington's elbow at a Northwest Side church where they encountered a jeering, hateful crowd and a spray-painted slogan on the church wall: "nigger die."[2] Inevitably, the rumor surfaced that this demonstration was staged by Washington's forces to galvanize black voter turnout. Maybe Chicago politics could have floated such a rumor at any time in its history. Then again, maybe it could have followed only the cynicism begot by Chicago 1968, Vietnam, and Watergate. On 5 April, Washington defeated Epton, 52 percent to 48 percent of the vote.

The ensuing, nationally notorious Council Wars, named by a comedian riffing on the movie *Star Wars*, pitted Washington's twenty-one aldermen (seventeen blacks, two whites, and two Latinos) against twenty-nine white aldermen. The conflict was never subtle. White aldermen proudly wore lapel buttons bearing the number *29.* The origin of Council Wars is little known. Two days before the new mayor's 29 April inauguration, machine aldermen Edward R. Vrdolyak and Edward M. Burke went to Washington, D.C., to attend the unveiling of Rostenkowski's official portrait as House Ways and Means Committee chairman. Another Chicago congressman there, William O. Lipinski, informed them that Alderman Wilson Frost secretly was assembling a coalition of pro-Washington and pro-Daley aldermen to dump pro-Byrne loyalists from their city council committee chairs. The "two Eddies" flew back to Chicago with what one ally called "a coach-like enthusiasm" to prevent this misfortune.

At Washington's first council meeting on 2 May, Vrdolyak and Burke's twenty-nine seized every position of leadership. Daley, at such critical proceedings, always had packed the galleries overlooking the council floor with what were humorously called "ruly crowds." When Vrdolyak and Burke triumphed, black supporters of Washington in the galleries pounded on the glass wall and screamed in frustration.

The twenty-nine's obstructionism was not just racial and political but also cultural and stylistic. Washington was hard to figure out. Crowds chanted, "Harold! Harold!" and he would reply with a huge grin and twinkling eyes, "You want Harold? You've got him!" Gifted with spectacular charm and eloquence, plus toughness, Washington was at heart a brooding, solitary, bookish sort who stayed up late many nights reading weighty volumes. At the least, the twenty-nine did not understand black political folkways or Washington's disdain for the white machine's folk-ways of old boys' favor trading. Washington had attended the machine's traditional postprimary, peacemaking breakfast. He gathered white aldermen's private phone numbers and promised to call them but did not, puzzling politicians who had grown up under the administrative genius of Dick Daley. And yet this was the mayor who crammed the city's first ethics ordinance down aldermen's throats.

The federal government continued to prosecute aldermen, judges, county officials, state legislators, and contractors, including some allies of Washington, during the epidemic of indicting public officials. For all that, Washington reformed municipal government. The difference is that he did not hold the traditional idea of rationalistic, managerial, white bourgeois reform. To him, reform meant that minorities and women got their fair share of public jobs and contracts. Further, all wards, regardless of ethnic composition, received roughly equal shares of public services. His successors, one black and one white, took pains to uphold these principles. In this sense, Washington was the city's most successful reformer ever.

Mayor Washington was untouched by Greylord. But his nearly five years in office were marked by constant investigations and scandals. The first was uncomfortably personal. He fired his closest aide Clarence McClain in October 1983 amid press revelations that McClain was a convicted pimp. Throughout his tenure as mayor, Washington remained highly sensitive to criticism linking him and McClain. In 1986, interviewed by the FBI, Washington insisted he had severed all ties to McClain upon his dismissal, despite McClain's claims to the contrary. In 1989 McClain was convicted of taking thirty-five thousand dollars in bribes to help a New York firm seek a city contract. At his sentencing hearing, McClain said federal agents had threatened to expose Washington's alleged homosexuality if he testified in his own defense at trial. "They said they were going to beat me with Harold's masculinity, and they beat me with it. I let them beat me with that sexual garbage."[3] The judge called him an inveterate liar and sentenced him to eight years in prison. That did not end the whispering campaign about Washington's sexuality. If indeed the government made any such threat against McClain, it would have been in keeping with the odor of modern epidemic scandal, the removal of any curtain of modesty across the lives of public figures.

McClain's conviction was part of Operation Incubator. Like Greylord, it offered a colorful mole and dramatic, secretly recorded bribery. Operation Incubator's casualties included black, junior aldermen from low-income wards who supported Washington. They were unsophisticated politically and lacked the means to retain top-drawer defense lawyers. All recent U.S. attorneys in Chicago have winced at criticism that they fingered small-fry minority politicians instead of bigger fish. Former U.S. attorney Scott R. Lassar said, "As new people come into power, some of them have the attitude, 'Now it's our turn to make some money.'" Lassar said minorities actually were underrepresented in all cases brought by his office, although not, he allowed, in the number of public corruption cases.[4] In any event, black anger against Operation Incubator contributed to Washington's reelection in 1987.

Michael Raymond, also known as Michael Burnett, a fat, oily hoodlum and con man, was arrested in Tennessee for attempted robbery in July 1984. To gain leniency, he consented to become a government mole, wearing a hidden microphone for eighteen months to record bribe-seeking politicians and bribe-paying contractors in Chicago and New York. In New York, Raymond's work led to the suicide of Queens borough president Donald R. Manes in 1986.

In Chicago, the FBI placed Raymond in a suite in the deluxe Lake Point Towers, 505 North Lake Shore Drive. There he entertained any and all politicians dumb enough to listen to him. Raymond doled out $255,600, much of it captured on a hidden video camera, in cash, cars, trips, and lodging to politicians and businessmen while seeking a city contract to collect overdue parking fines. At least by a reasonable doubt, Washington was innocent of all this. Convictions were won against McClain, Cook County circuit court clerk Morgan Finley, African American aldermen Wallace Davis, Marian Humes, Perry Hutchinson, and Clifford Kelley, and nine other public officials and businessmen. The firm in question, Systematic Recovery Service of New York, lost the parking-ticket contract but managed to win another to collect overdue water bills. Informant Raymond died in 1996 at age sixty-seven in federal prison, where he was serving time for plotting a New York murder.

Mayor Washington reacted to Operation Incubator as a conventional politician. He rejected advice from white reformers such as Leon Despres, the grand old man of reform, to publicly denounce McClain. However, he signed the city's first executive order for ethics. Also, he named former U.S. attorney Thomas P. Sullivan as his special counsel to get to the bottom of the scandal. On a trivial level, Sullivan's appointment provoked hard feelings, accusations of bad faith, and religious sensitivities, as had the Cardinal Cody affair.

Sullivan soon quit in a turf struggle over the degree of his independence from city hall. As his replacement, the mayor named thirty-one-year-old private lawyer Michael Dockterman. Gossip columnists soon fingered Dockterman as the Christ figure in a recent photographic poster, "The Last Yupper," a wickedly funny parody of da Vinci's *The Last Supper*. The poster had been designed and marketed by one of Dockterman's former law partners and featured Dockterman and his friends in various styles of yuppie apparel and attitudes. Conservative Christians objected on radio talk shows and in letters to editors. Dockterman's problems deepened when Alderman Ed Burke alleged that he could not be independent because he had counseled the city in protecting a clouted contract for a "people mover" at O'Hare Airport. Within days, Sullivan was back in the job with promises of independence. Dockterman departed without a cross word.

When it came, Sullivan's study damned the Washington administration. The mayor promised to release the report and then said the law prevented him from doing so. At a press conference in New York with Mayor Edward Koch in 1986, Washington suggested the FBI was setting people up for prosecution. Pointedly, though, he declined to endorse Incubator targets Humes and Hutchinson for reelection in 1987. They were leaning to enticements to join Vrdolyak's twenty-nine and moreover were apt to flip for the government against Washington administration figures. In a little understood phenomenon, some black aldermen resented Washington's clean-government reforms.

Of course Sullivan's report swiftly was leaked to the press. Besides chiding the Washington administration for ethical laxity, it contained the usual goo-goo recommendations for codifying and consolidating operations. In January 1987, Washington won the passage of an ethics ordinance, with aldermen reluctant to vote against ethics shortly before a primary election, by a vote of 49-0. Judged on the public record, it has been ineffective.

U.S. Attorney Dan K. Webb indicted ten officers of the West Side's Marquette police district for taking bribes to protect two heroin rings. Relations between Chicago and federal law enforcement agencies, normally strained as in every city by mutual suspicions and jealousy over jurisdiction, were embittered by this episode. The federal operation did not lack examples of bungling. The FBI staged a bogus theft from a screeching car on North Michigan Avenue of a briefcase supposedly containing cocaine. The agents' intent was to present a sting before a corrupt judge to test whether he would solicit or accept a bribe. Chicago police raced to the scene, and the sting fell apart when they found FBI identification on the alleged perpetrators.

Webb's "Marquette Ten" protested that they did not take bribes, merely made curbside accommodations with drug-dealing informants as part of their job. Federal agents tailed, wiretapped, and audited them. Their working-class lifestyles, in contrast to the high-living Summerdale burglars of Daley's grand police scandal of 1960, seemingly would have aided their defense. They had no luxury cars or vacation homes.

Webb was less interested in the ten cops than in the prospect that one or more might flip and lead him to crooked judges under the ongoing Greylord probe. This did not happen. A class division defined Greylord. Judges were easily convicted in the lowly traffic and divorce courts, but making cases against judges in the higher felony courts was more problematic. Presumably there was less corruption there. Yet again, class separations described corruption and reform.

Although government audiotapes of the alleged Marquette Ten bribes were muddy and unclear, all ten were convicted on 30 June 1982. They were given harsh sentences of at least ten years without parole. The last to be released greeted a welcome-home party in 1995 of five hundred police, defense lawyers, and their families. The department still believes the ten got a bum rap. Webb was unapologetic. "Nobody turns a jury off more than dope peddlers. . . . The Marquette 10 case was the most difficult I ever tried. Here we had 60 or 70 dope peddlers testifying against members of the Chicago Police Department. That's not an easy case. . . . I could be criticized for a lot of things, but not for that."[5] His position is understandable in that one of his witnesses mumbled incoherently on the stand, high on drugs. In any event, the law of unintended consequences, forever applied to reformers, visited the case. Drug dealers accosted by police soon took to threatening, "You mess with us and we'll go down and see Dan Webb in the morning."[6]

In October 1988, twelve officers in the Wentworth police district were indicted for taking bribes from drug dealers, gamblers, and prostitutes. As that case hit the headlines, a jury was being selected in a separate case charging eight officers with taking bribes to grease liquor license approvals. In December, that jury acquitted all eight defendants. The verdict stunned the government, which called its investigation of city licensing practices Operation Phocus. The eleven-week trial featured many hours of secret government tape recordings. Perhaps to view the acquittals as a consequence of public skepticism about prosecutorial excesses under the epidemic of indictments would be facile. Originally, eleven officers were indicted and three had pleaded guilty. This was hardly the end of prosecutions of Chicago police. In 1990 ten officers were convicted of taking bribes to protect South Side gambling and narcotics. More cases could be cited.

Greylord, Incubator, Safebet, Phocus, Lantern, Gambat, Silver Shovel, Haunted Hall, Hedgeclipper, Sourmash . . . Justice Department investigations with these code names sent Chicago and Cook County politicians and businessmen to prison throughout the 1980s and 1990s. (Hedgeclipper and Sourmash exposed fraud among Chicago commodities traders.) After decades of religious and secular campaigns for moral, political, and social reform, reform in the traditional, not the radical, Saul Alinsky, sense pretty much came down to assigning federal lawyers and accountants to find prosecutable offenses by public officials. This outcome was part of the ever-escalating dominance of the federal over state and local governments since the New Deal.

In Chicago, local government had not seen a real crime-busting official since Sheriff Richard B. Ogilvie (of the curious association with mobster Richard Cain) in the early 1960s. There was a practical reason for this gap beyond the historical coziness of the Cook County state's attorney with the Chicago machine. The Justice Department could wire an undercover agent without a court order, whereas state's attorneys had to obtain a judge's approval under Illinois law. Even so, this difference is an excuse. Democratic and Republican state's attorneys from the 1970s through the 1990s did not much alarm the machine. Newly elected Republican state's attorney Jack O'Malley said in 1990 he might set up a public corruption strike force to complement the feds', remarking that there was enough corruption in the county to go around. Running for reelection six years later, he said he had made few such cases because they were the U.S. attorney's job, not his. (On the state level, Illinois attorneys general have made similar disclaimers.)

Operation Safebet convicted sixty-eight people in the Chicago suburbs, part of the state's attorney's realm, on vice and racketeering charges during the 1980s. They included two high-ranking sheriff's officers and a lieutenant and sergeant who had commanded the intelligence unit. Safebet also offered examples of dubious federal practices. In effect, FBI agents were pimps. The government ran a prostitution sting, called National Credit Service, which rang up its customers' bills on credit cards. The defense lawyer for a strip club in suburban Lyons objected, "For 18 to 20 years, [his client] did not use credit cards. Then the FBI and NCS [National Credit Service] told them they were the only club not accepting credit cards, and they could increase their business 20 percent if they did." The defense lawyer said federal agents spent six months persuading the club to use credit cards, which back then entailed phone calls to confirm a customer's creditworthiness: "Use that phone, we want you to commit a federal crime [wire fraud]."[7]

The media consumed the corruption stories eagerly, sometimes with bemusement. Chicago's naughty pride in its reputation for criminality was expressed in a *Tribune* editorial of 21 August 1987.

> As an example of Chicago-style corruption, the case of former State Sen. Edward Nedza is a classic. It should put to rest reports that official bribery is worse in New York state than here. . . . Mr. Nedza skimmed off profits from a flea market in the 31st Ward, where he was Democratic committeeman. Those indicted with him are Chester Kuta, former alderman of the ward; the late Benedict (Sparky) Garmisa, a former state senator, and Leonard Kraus, owner of the Buyer's Flea Market. . . .
>
> The state's case was that the three elected officials secretly obtained a 50 percent interest in the flea market that netted them a total of $60,000. Mr. Kraus agreed to this to get the zoning changes and licenses that he needed to operate. . . .
>
> The Nedza case arose out of Operation Phocus, a federal investigation into Chicago's licensing and enforcement system. So far it has led to the convictions of 31 people including a former alderman, a city department head, and more indictments are expected. Mr. Nedza, incidentally, was a political protégé of former Ald. Thomas Keane. . . .
>
> Compare this to the outcry in New York and New Jersey over the arrests of 44 present and former municipal officials for bribery. The most startling statistic there came from an FBI agent who posed as a company representative selling steel products: Of 106 bribes he offered to local officials, 105 were accepted, and the 106th was refused because it was too small.
>
> Granted, that is an impressive score. On the other hand, the FBI undercover agent paid out only $40,000 in bribes over 2 years of his operation. Under Chicago standards, that wouldn't last him a month.

So there, New York.

Operation Phocus convicted sixteen sewer inspectors of bribery in the mid-1980s. Chicago's extravagant appetite for corruption even in the face of reformist crackdowns was expressed during the sewer inspectors' trials. While the press reported on the trials, the feds continued to bug other city inspectors. Incredibly, "tapes of these consumer services inspectors reveal that while taking bribes they would often discuss the trial of the sewer inspectors taking place in federal court."[8]

A separate, three-year investigation into purchasing practices called Operation Lantern had indicted forty-two businesses and persons, many of them government or corporate purchasing officials, by June 1988. The public officials gave work to private suppliers in exchange for kickbacks, vacation trips, and campaign contributions. Mayor Washington's response was, again, conventionally political. Noting that the cases dated to the Byrne administration, he said, "Based on what we do know, the people involved, in the main, are people who were in the government and left before we got here, or people we inherited."[9]

Aside from the dominance of federal prosecutors, a collaboration of the Better Government Association and reporters generated an old-fashioned local scandal. George W. Dunne was tall, dignified, and handsome, far from the caricature of a stout, fedora-adorned, pinky-ringed, cigar-chomping ward boss. He was a rare public official in that he answered his own phone without screening calls through layers of secretaries. Democratic committeeman since 1961 of the Forty-second Ward—which then bordered the First Ward on the north and had a similar, though less legendary, history of criminality—he was asked by Richard J. Daley in 1975 to consider replacing him as mayor. Of course Dunne told Daley that the city clamored for his reelection, no matter his questionable health. After Daley's death, Dunne succeeded him as Democratic county chairman. In 1982 Mayor Byrne, Richard M. Daley, and Edward R. Vyrdolyak deposed him as chairman, but he regained the seat in 1987.

The easy-going Dunne was everybody's friend. With other machine worthies, he ran an insurance firm that won many business clients needing political help. During the Washington mayoralty, he was praised as one of the few white committeemen willing to play ball with the black mayor.

As chairman of the Cook County board of commissioners, Dunne ran the county's Forest Preserve District, including its patronage police force. Nearly half the officers were temporary appointees, a time-honored machine technique to evade civil service procedures. After the BGA and a television station exposed this practice in 1986, civil service exams were given to the "temps" and nearly half of them failed.

Two years later, a forest preserve policewoman called the BGA to complain of sexual harassment. A meeting was arranged. The BGA investigator asked facetiously, "I suppose next you're going to tell me you've slept with George Dunne?" Unflinchingly, she replied, "Yes."[10]

At least two women obtained forest preserve police jobs after having sex with Dunne, and another, the original accuser, said she was coerced into having sex with him after acquiring her job. One woman was arrested for speeding and having an open container of liquor in her car. She called Dunne from the Hebron, Illinois, police station; he gallantly came to bail her out. Dunne, seventy-five years old and a widower, had group sex with two lesbian county employees at his Hebron farm. One of them won a job for her lover as a forest preserve laborer.

A news-radio station broke the story on 28 April 1988. Three days later, Dunne held a news conference, admitting to the sex but denying trading jobs for sex. Then he lost his cool. "The jobs had nothing to do with sex, and you know it." Leaving the podium, he told reporters, "You're the scum of the Earth, and so's the BGA."[11] He shoved a newsman away from his office door. Besides Dunne's anguish, the human toll taken by the scandal was the usual. One of Dunne's paramours attempted suicide and was fired from her county job on the ground that she was emotionally unstable.

Reflexively, much of the respectable establishment rallied to Dunne's defense. As with the scandal of Bill Clinton and Monica Lewinsky nine years later, the sexual aspect of the story overwhelmed the issue of abuse of power. To be sure, the *Tribune* and *Sun-Times* editorially scolded Dunne. But when he walked into Eli's steak house, a downtown hangout of politicians and journalists, a standing ovation greeted him. The *Sun-Times* political columnist sneered that Dunne was more popular than, and a superior public servant to, BGA head Terrence J. Brunner. True, Brunner was an abrasive reformer in the Chicago style. *Newsweek* wondered, "In any other city such a saucy scandal would outrage the populace. But the saga of 75-year-old 'Gentleman George' Dunne . . . has drawn not censure, but support from a Chicago electorate so inured to influence-peddling and other political shenanigans that good government types are derided as 'goo-goos.'"[12]

Chicago was showing the scandal fatigue that pundits noted during the national political scandals of the 1990s. The miasma of constant prosecutorial pursuit of the lives, public or private, of elected officials was soiling the commonweal. It seems the electorate by now is scandal-hardened. Throughout his impeachment by the House and trial by the Senate in 1998–99, President Clinton scored consistently high in public approval ratings.

All of this—federal and state prosecutions of public officials and media exposure of their wrongdoings—did not seem to strike at pervasive, endemic corruption. The difference was that some practices regarded as corrupt had become legal under the codification of political behavior as constantly pressed by reformers.

One of the last outbursts of the Great Society was a 1968 law to allow state and local governments to issue tax-exempt bonds to subsidize residential mortgages. The idea was to help the working class realize the American dream of home ownership. Some state housing authorities floated such bonds, but cities took little interest. Charles Swibel, then chairman of the Chicago Housing Authority, saw an opportunity being missed. In 1974 he personally bought property at Madison and Canal Streets at an urban-renewal land price set in 1968. The land multiplied in value under the inflation of the 1970s and under President Reagan's tax-cut laws favoring commercial real estate in the early 1980s. During this process, Swibel neglected to pay property taxes on the land.

Now standing at that site just west of the Loop, a former Skid Row, are four forty-nine-story upscale residential high-rises called Presidential Towers. The free market adored by Republicans, or so they say, could not have built them. If the developers had had a sense or humor, they would have called them Clout Towers. Under the presidencies of Carter, Reagan,

Bush, and Clinton, Presidential Towers consumed almost $200 million in federal subsidies, tax breaks, and defaulted loans. Governor and judge Otto Kerner, jailed for a mere stock swap of $150,000, might have looked with envy on such perfectly legal churning of cash.

In 1978 under Mayor Bilandic, city hall floated $100 million in five-year, tax-exempt construction bonds to develop CHA chief Swibel's land west of the Loop. Swibel sold it to three businessmen including Daniel J. Shannon. Swibel, slapping his forehead in remembrance, paid up the back property taxes so that he could legally convey the title. Shannon meanwhile operated U.S. Representative Dan Rostenkowski's nominally blind trust of investments. Shannon's development company employed a Rostenkowski son-in-law. Shannon also had headed the Teamsters Union Central States Pension Fund, under constant federal investigation for bank fraud.

U.S. House Ways and Means Committee chairman Al Ullman of Oregon perceived that the Great Society housing-bond program had become a scam to make urban developers rich rather than to provide home mortgages for the working class. In 1980 Congress voted to phase out the program in three years. In the meantime, new projects had to set aside at least 20 percent of their apartments for low- to moderate-income tenants. Rostenkowski quietly slipped into the bill an amendment favoring Shannon and others by exempting Presidential Towers from the 20-percent rule.

Even with that waiver, the Reagan tax laws spawned so much overbuilding of urban commercial real estate that Presidential Towers did not make money. By 1990, nine luxury housing projects in Chicago had defaulted on Federal Housing Authority loans. Presidential Towers developers fired every arrow from their clout quiver to stave off default.

U.S. Representative Frank Annunzio of Chicago passed an amendment exempting Presidential Towers from certain fees attached to federal mortgage bonds. This exemption was worth $3 million. Rostenkowski, by then chairman of Ways and Means, inserted into a tax bill a depreciation rule relieving the 590 investors in Presidential Towers of $7 million in income taxes.

The developers also won a forty-year, low-interest mortgage of $159 million from the Government National Mortgage Association. It was the largest mortgage "Ginny Mae" had ever made. Mayor Washington increased the city's construction bonds from $100 million to $180 million. The finance chairman for his 1987 reelection campaign was a proposed underwriter for the bonds. Mayor Washington's price for the bonds was that the developers fund a new low-income housing trust. It did not materialize.

Others who went to bat for Presidential Towers included Governor Thompson; senators Charles Percy and Alan Dixon; mayors Byrne, Sawyer, and Daley; U.S. representative and later labor secretary Lynn Martin; Housing and Urban Development (HUD) secretaries under Presidents Bush and Clinton; aldermen Edward Vrydolyak and his brother Victor, and more. Developer Daniel E. Levin testified before a city council committee, "I want no sympathy. I am not a poor man. But building residential buildings is a risky business. Presidential Towers could not have been built conventionally."[13]

There was the voice of the modern high-stakes entrepreneur, exploiting government's power to condemn private property, hold it, sell it cheap, and subsidize development on it. Old-style reformers wanted Christians to put down vice and petty graft. Presidential Towers was in a different realm. Getting rich depended on a sophisticated mastery of bureaucratic processes under the constant expansion of governmental subventions and regulations of business.

Rostenkowski was indignant. "Anything I did for Presidential Towers, I did for the city. I guess I use my leverage for any kind of project that benefits the city."[14] Later he added, "I had Jim Thompson in here begging me to do it. . . . [Governor Thompson and Senator Percy] didn't do much. I did a heck of a lot more. When all the accolades were pointed out they were in the front row. When all the criticism comes out I don't see them anymore."[15] This defense—*I used my political power to seek economic growth for my constituents*—could have been voiced by the original mayor, William Ogden, and indeed was raised by politicians charged with financial misdeeds throughout the 1980s and 1990s.

Doors opened in 1985 for 2,346 Presidential Towers apartments featuring access to a health club, satellite television, concierge, maids, restaurants, a florist, drugstore, and bank on the premises. Young professionals did not flock to the units, located in a then-disreputable neighborhood. Presidential Towers appealed its property tax assessments, hiring the law firm of Michael J. Madigan, a Southwest Side Democrat and Speaker of the Illinois House, to do the job. Thompson's personal lawyer, Anton R. Valukas (later a U.S. attorney), was retained to lobby the governor. Alderman Victor Vrdolyak's security firm handled security for the Towers.

Despite all its friends in high places, Presidential Towers, leaking money, was compelled to ask HUD for a bailout loan of $16 million in August 1989. Six months later, the Towers missed its first monthly mortgage payment of $1.5 million. In April 1990, the trustee of the bonds filed with the Federal Housing Authority a notice of election to assign. That is how lawyers spell default. By then the amount of the defaulted mortgage was $171 million.

For the next four years, HUD tried to avoid acquiring title to four residential apartment towers it did not want to own and operate. Not until April 1994 under HUD Secretary Henry Cisneros (himself the target of a special counsel's unrelated prosecution) was the deal finally struck. HUD agreed not to foreclose on the property, and the owners promised to reserve 165 apartments—7 percent of the units—for tenants with low to moderate incomes. That is what a Great Society program to help working people own homes amounted to: 165 apartments after nearly $200 million in subsidies, tax breaks, and defaulted loans. For that money, the government could have built 165 mansions for $1.2 million each and given them away.

The argument is made that Presidential Towers anchored the economic revival of the Near West Side during the prosperity of the 1990s and thus represented, all things considered, a sound public investment. Free-market advocates would dispute that, but in either case, the Presidential Towers affair did not pass what politicians call "the smell test." The impression was underscored that government is an insiders' game for the wealthy and well connected. It was a long, large scandal that convened no grand juries but promoted the public's belief that all politics is corrupt.

On 1 November 1987, soon after Washington finally won "Council Wars" and was launching his second term with relish, the U.S. Justice Department emplaced a scarcely noticed milestone in the politics of corruption and reform. "Soft-on-crime" liberal judges had provoked congressmen to enact minimum sentencing standards. Seemingly a technical change— section 5K1.1 in sentencing guidelines—a new Justice Department rule allowed judges to ignore mandatory prison terms if prosecutors vouched that the defendant had provided substantial help in investigating or prosecuting someone else. Not only could defendants escape stiff sentences by turning informant, they also could be rewarded with 25 percent of the assets seized from criminals under asset-forfeiture laws. These rewards could amount to $250,000 per case. Not surprising is that many criminal defendants were motivated to flip and some to lie.

In 1989 after a seven-year investigation by federal agents and Chicago police, the Justice Department indicted sixty-five reputed members of the El Rukns criminal gang. The El Rukns cases represented the informant system run amok. After some El Rukns agreed to testify against others, prosecutors covered up favors given them by federal agents including sex and drugs while in federal custody. Eventually, the convictions of six El Rukns "generals" were thrown out, although five, plus an affiliated businessman, were retried and convicted again. The feds agreed to reduced sentences for twenty-four convicted of lesser crimes and dismissed charges against four others. Not until 1998 were efforts to punish the lead investigator for misconduct finally resolved.

El Rukns were murderous drug dealers. The gang was founded from prison by Jeff Fort, a leader of the Black P Stone Nation in the late 1960s. That was the gang that had won nearly $1 million in federal antipoverty grants from the Nixon administration. Fort used the funds to buy drugs and weapons. After going to prison in 1972, he converted to Islam and established the El Rukns.

The chief investigator of the El Rukns was William Hogan Jr., a Midwestern-poor-boy-who-clawed-his-way-up-through-law-school FBI type. "Public corruption was a problem," Hogan said, "but it paled in comparison to the mayhem that was going on in the streets."[16] Hogan used thousands of hours of taped conversations from the original Jeff Fort case to pursue El Rukns.

In June 1993, two federal judges overturned the convictions of six El Rukns leaders because prosecutors had concealed favors given informants. One judge issued a forty-four-page philippic against law enforcement, reprising the official condemnations of the Haymarket and Roger Touhy prosecutions. And so the U.S. attorney's office in Chicago, exposer of so many corruption scandals, was itself scourged by scandal. The Justice Department, facing a public relations fiasco, placed Hogan on paid administrative leave until its Office of Professional Responsibility fired him in 1996. Hogan appealed to the U.S. Merit Systems Protection Board, which reinstated him with back pay in 1998. At that point, the Attorney Registration and Disciplinary Commission of Illinois dropped its case against Hogan. Whoever was right or wrong, this episode illustrated the proliferation of due process under the steadily accreting layers of official oversight in the anticorruption enterprise.

Earlier, smaller scandals continued to beset Washington's administration even as he entered a triumphant second term. Council Wars had lasted three years, 1983–86. In 1986 a federal court ordered special aldermanic elections in seven wards because the ward redistricting map drawn by Byrne, Vrdolyak, and others after the 1980 census illegally discriminated against minorities. When Washington's forces narrowly won the final runoff contest in a hard fight in a Latino ward, the council was split 25–25. Washington was enabled to cast tie-breaking votes. The media wrote obituaries for the old machine once again. Dead, dead, the witch is dead! Quickly, Washington broke a tie to reduce the number of council committees—the council had more standing committees than the U.S. House—from thirty-seven to twenty-eight. Also, Washington at last was able to pass his nominations for city boards and commissions through the council. The twenty-nine had blocked scores of them, even Washington's own ex officio seat on the Public Building Commission.

To prevent its two-whites-one-black debacle of Byrne, Daley, and Washington in 1983, the machine contrived a solitary challenge by Byrne against Washington in the February 1987 primary. The incumbent won 53 percent of the vote. In the general election, Vrdolyak ran on a third-party platform. Washington beat him as well as the Republican nominee, again taking 53 percent. The mayor's job became more enjoyable. He deposed machine aldermen from their committee chairs and planned to spur his long-stalled programs.

The dogs did not stop snapping at the mayor's ankles. The BGA and the press reported that Washington disguised the size of his personal and public relations staffs by assigning their paychecks to other city departments. This report was accurate but trivial. Presidents, governors, and mayors normally do this. A footnote is that the 1986 budget ordinance had stipulated that "no employee whose title appears herein under one department shall work for another department, except upon the order of the City Council."[17] In the 1987 budget, Washington craftily dropped this provision. Such tricks enhance the public disgust with politics. At the same time, even some reformers wonder whether the assault on authority has gone too far.

Another miniscandal involved the Chicago Transit Authority, one more nominally independent agency actually controlled by the mayor, in January 1987. A private bus company providing rides to handicapped CTA passengers allegedly falsified documents to evade penalties for poor service. The head of the bus company was a Washington campaign contributor appointed by the mayor to the police board. The mother-in-law of a CTA official was on the bus company's payroll at the same time she worked for the CTA approving applications for service from the disabled.

More serious charges that Chicago remained Chicago, even under a reform mayor, emerged after Washington's death. Federal agents had investigated the Chicago Housing Authority's minority business office for allegedly asking CHA vendors to contribute to Washington's reelection in exchange for obtaining CHA business. Private consultants hired by Mayor Richard M. Daley said that during the 1980s, the city housing department dispensed money to political favorites in violation of federal regulations and kept such sloppy books that many transactions could not be reconstructed. Among abuses in other areas, the city health insurance plan blithely paid fraudulent claims without checking them.

Washington died on 25 November 1987. At age sixty-five, the man who had vowed to be mayor for twenty years suffered a fatal heart attack. The biracial citywide grief for an indisputably great mayor, despite his flaws, matched that for Daley in 1976.

On 1 December, the city council held a 10 A.M. memorial service, the mayoral chair draped in black. At 5:30 P.M., the council convened to elect one of its own as the next mayor. The following ten hours and sixteen minutes were a Chicago summit of political acrimony and farce.

Washington's forces supported the cerebral attorney and alderman Timothy C. Evans of the low-income Fourth Ward. White aldermen favored Alderman Eugene Sawyer of the middle-class Sixth Ward. Both candidates were black and from the South Side. Sawyer was a get-along, go-along sort who spoke in a soft mumble from his Mississippi upbringing. The media touted Evans as the next mayor except that the *Sun-Times* discovered that white aldermen had cut deals to elect Sawyer.

Black demonstrators packed city hall and the bordering streets to chant, "no deal, no deal!" This was like shouting at a zebra, "no stripes, no stripes!" The Evans forces bused many demonstrators to city hall in city buses at taxpayer expense. At one point, Sawyer offered Evans his own vote for mayor if Evans could put together twenty-five others for a majority. Evans never came close. Sawyer retreated to his upstairs office with his pastor while the council fell into pandemonium. Sawyer pleaded to go home, to delay the vote for a couple of days, but his white backers would not permit it.

On the chaotic council floor, a couple of white aldermen each came within one vote of assembling a majority. Behind the scenes, Democratic boss George Dunne understood the venom that would spill if a white mayor replaced Washington and blocked these moves. Evans told the media that Sawyer's claim of holding a majority was a lie. That made Sawyer mad. He returned to the council and took his seat at 12:07 A.M., guarded by police. The roll call ended at 3:59 A.M. with twenty-nine votes, including those of six blacks, for Sawyer. In his brief inaugural speech, he claimed to be a disciple of Washington. Rightfully, Washington might have seen the machine as "ancient, decrepit and creaking," yet the machine had beaten the reformers once again.

Sawyer was an unsuccessful, indecisive mayor. In the special mayoral election of 1989, his black supporters sloganeered, "He took the heat to keep the seat." But the black political unity created by Washington fell to pieces upon his death and never revived. Evans stayed out of the Democratic primary, which Sawyer lost to Richard M. Daley, to run as a third-party candidate in the general election. Daley saw that the city was weary of racial polarization and campaigned as a healer. He dispatched a parade of black challengers with assembly-line efficiency in the elections of 1989, 1991, 1995, 1999, and 2003. The word in city hall, which Daley will not confirm, is that he intends to serve in the office longer than his father did.

11

Daley and Dissent Redux

1990–2003

Corruption seems to persist and even flourish despite threats, scores of arrests, administrative sanctions, prosecutions, organizational reshuffling, stings, undercover operations, intensive monitoring, and operational initiatives to strengthen central authority and the chain of command.
—Frank Anechiarico and James B. Jacobs,
The Pursuit of Absolute Integrity

The period 1990–2003 saw corruption exposed in and scandals broadcast from these public agencies: Chicago's city hall, city council, parks district, police department, and public schools; Chicago's housing and transit authorities; the Cook County board of commissioners, forest preserve district, hospital, judiciary, parks district, sheriff's office, and suburban city halls; the Metropolitan Water Reclamation District (the old Metropolitan Sanitary District); the Cook County delegation to the Illinois House and Senate, and the Cook County delegation to the U.S. House. This catalogue does not even consider corruption in Illinois state government, which merits a book of its own.

Chicago's original reformer, Jeremiah L. Porter, stepped off a skiff in 1833 on fire to eliminate drinking, gambling, and whoring in the frontier settlement. His enterprise was private and sectarian. By 1990 it seemed the effort to stamp out the human capacity for error was a permanent project of governmental prosecutors and their confederates in the scandalmongering mass media. Previously, reform struggles were episodic;

now, reformers are just another special-interest group. They have their own entrenched apparatus of investigation, oversight, and publicity.

A major historical shift is that the religious division between upscale Protestant reformers and working-class Catholic machine regulars has mostly withered away under the secularization of society and the sickliness of the political machine. Richard J. Daley polarized the electorate. His son, Mayor Richard M. Daley, does the opposite. He combines whites, blacks, Hispanics, and Asians in support of a bland, managerial style of government. In political science jargon, he has moved city hall from a *machine regime* to a *managerial regime* after the city flirted with different *progressive regimes.* Under Daley the Chicago tradition of vigorous dissent dating from "People's Tickets" and businessmen rebels of the nineteenth century has wafted away. Even lakefront liberals and black and Hispanic aldermen see Daley as at least a satisfactory mayor and in some respects a good or excellent one.

Still, problems of corruption and of ethnic-group politics have dogged his mayoralty from the start. The politics of corruption nettled Daley during his first race for reelection in 1991. His running mate, city clerk Walter Kozubowski, was under federal investigation for ghost payrolling. Daley decided not to choose a new running mate and ran again with Kozubowski. In 1992 Kozubowski was indicted. In 1993 he pleaded guilty to fraud and tax evasion in running a ghost payroll operation. He admitted operating a crooked clerk's office since taking it in 1979, upholding the machine value of consistency. Kozubowski was sentenced to five years in prison. Daley replaced him with another Pole, James Laski. He soon came under investigation for ghost payrolling in his office but was never charged.

Daley had named Miriam Santos as city treasurer, the first Hispanic to hold citywide office, in 1989. Soon she got on his bad side in a turf battle over the management of city pension funds, but he did not dump her from his 1995 ticket. She ran for Illinois attorney general in 1998, using city employees for campaign work on city time and ending a brokerage firm's city contract because it refused to contribute ten thousand dollars to the state Democratic party on her behalf. A federal jury convicted her of these campaign-law violations, but an appeals court overturned the conviction. Santos returned from prison in 2000 to assume her old job as city treasurer. Daley would not have it. To avoid a retrial, Santos pleaded guilty to a single count of mail fraud with the sentence reduced to the fifteen weeks already served. Daley appointed a black woman as the new city treasurer.

As these incidents suggest, one thing that has not changed, for all the erosion of the Protestant-Catholic division in public life, is the enduring importance of ethnicity and class in the politics of corruption and reform. Democratic and Republican U.S. attorneys in Chicago have protested vigorously that they do not target ethnic minorities. The fact remains that African American and Hispanic American politicians have gone to jail while some of their Anglo- and Irish American colleagues remained comfortably emplaced. Nonwhite, junior aldermen seemed especially vulnerable.

In 1989, Dick Simpson, a professor at the University of Illinois at Chicago and a lakefront-liberal former alderman, published a study of what was wrong with the city council. This was the final outburst of the privately funded, investigation-publication-condemnation tradition of Progressive, muckraking, and businessmen's civic-group outrage. Simpson's study was financed by WASP businessmen via a grant from the Amoco Foundation. He wrote (emphasis in original),

> *Did you know that neither citizens nor aldermen know what legislation is pending and that no record of City Council debate is kept?*
>
> *Did you know that aldermen spend more than $8 million a year without accounting for the expenditures?*
>
> *Did you know that they don't have to disclose that they have an interest in property that they are rezoning?*
>
> *Did you know that there is no simple, usable voting record to inform citizens how their aldermen voted? . . .*
>
> *Did you know that the Chicago City Council has more committees and spends more money than any other city council in the United States?*
>
> *Did you know that the committees are solely controlled by the council faction in power and do not provide information for all aldermen and citizens? . . .*

While many units of local government need reforming, the most backward and destructive is the Chicago City Council. Bound by secrecy, it vacillates between being a useless rubber stamp and an anarchy of "gray wolves" dividing the spoils under weak mayors.[1]

The first city council session under Rich Daley in May 1989, the fourth reorganization of the council in three years under mayors Washington, Sawyer, and Daley, reduced the number of council committees by one to twenty-six. Later, addressing the complaints of reformers such as Simpson, Daley forced more reforms through the council. He created the post of city inspector general to root out corruption. (Naturally, aldermen refused to grant that new public servant subpoena powers over the city council's own doings.) In 1991 the inspector general found that thirty-seven street sweepers in the First Ward's office of the Department of Streets and Sanitation received paychecks even though they did not show up for work. They spent their time running private businesses, patronizing racetracks, and even, in one case, committing a jewelry robbery in Wisconsin.

Daley reacted professionally. He tried to fire the ghost payrollers but mostly was stayed by opposition from the laborers' union. Then, following the Progressive model, he centralized and codified operations: a new First Ward sanitation office to exorcise the ghosts. In 1993 it was revealed that a First Ward "streets 'n' san'" employee was paid thirty dollars an hour on city time to chauffeur mobster Joseph "Joey the Clown" Lombardo. The driver even filed for overtime. Daley, in character, promptly closed the First Ward sanitation office and named to take over its operations a former aide to a reform alderman. Yet with all this reform, indictments of public officials under Daley continued.

Greylord, Gambat, Haunted Hall, Lantern, Phocus, Safebet, Silver Shovel: the code names warrant listing again because the relentless procession of politicians to prison, the astonishing range of corruption, strain credulity.

Gambat is short for "gambling attorney." In 1986 attorney Robert J. Cooley turned himself in to the feds. He said he was sick and tired of court corruption, having bribed dozens of judges and politicians. He became, like the Greylord and Incubator moles, an undercover agent who intrigued the press and the public upon his emergence. With his secret taping of conversations with judges and politicians, he brought down much of the First Ward's political union with organized crime, at least its older generation. In any case, there is no longer a First Ward of legend. One First Ward alderman had resigned his seat in 1968 on the ground that serving in that particular office was smearing his reputation. Daley cannily redistricted the ward in 1991 as the Forty-second so that *First Ward* is no longer a metonymy for organized crime.

The First Ward alderman had been Fred B. Roti. His father, Bruno "the Bomber" Roti, had been a small-time hoodlum under Al Capone. Fred Roti at one time had seventeen family members in city jobs. He and an aldermanic pal, Bernard Stone of the Fiftieth Ward, almost daily visited the city hall pressroom, often joking about Roti's reputed ties to organized crime. A reporter's suggested campaign slogan, "Vote for Roti and nobody gets hurt," drew laughs for years. When one of Roti's nominal Republican campaign opponents failed to show up at ward forums, Roti feigned alarm because the disappearance of somebody from the First Ward invited invidious inferences.

The U.S. attorney bugged Roti's customary booth at the Counselors Row restaurant across LaSalle Street from city hall. Roti and his cronies lunched there almost daily, hunching over the table and speaking softly. FBI mole Cooley met there with Roti to seek a zoning change in Roti's ward. Tapes played in court had Cooley asking, innocently enough, "Tell me what the procedure is now."

Roti reached for Cooley's notebook, slid it across to his seat at the booth, wrote "75" on a corner of the page, underlined it, and pushed the notebook back.

"Hmm. Okay," Cooley said.

"You know what I'm talking about?" Roti inquired.

"Yeah, little ones, not big ones," Cooley joshed, referring to denominations of bills.

"Nooooo," Roti laughed.

"Okay."

"Seventy-five hundred."

"Hmm?"

"Seventy-five hundred."[2]

With that coquettish "Hmm?" Cooley made sure the amount was audible on tape. In due time, the payoff was made at the back of the restaurant. Roti never seemed to notice that Cooley always made a point of clearly specifying the numbers aloud. The Counselors Row phase of the feds' Operation Gambat ended when a busboy accidentally discovered the government's secret bugs.

On 15 January 1993, Roti was convicted of taking $17,500 in bribes to fix a civil court case and a zoning matter. He was acquitted of fixing a 1981 murder trial. Sentenced to four years in prison, he died in 1999 at age seventy-eight.

Indicted along with Roti on 19 December 1990 were state senator John A. D'Arco Jr. and his law partner, Pasqual "Pat" Frank De Leo; First Ward Democratic secretary Pat Marcy; and David Shields, presiding judge of chancery court. After Wayne W. Olson, Shields was the second judge to have his chambers legally wiretapped. As always, the political and family kinships were braided: D'Arco was the son and De Leo the son-in-law of a former First Ward committeeman. Marcy, accused of fixing a mob hit man's murder case, buying an associate judgeship, and bribing a judge to acquit a man charged with the savage beating of a policewoman, died in 1993 before his trial was completed. Shields, D'Arco, and De Leo were convicted of taking bribes from Cooley, and each was sentenced to three years.

In a separate case, Alderman William C. Henry was indicted in 1990 for using his office to collect cars, cash, and a diamond ring. Henry was a flamboyant politician in the Chicago tradition who ran an old-fashioned machine ward and once tried to market "Soul Cola" to his constituents. With a television station, the Better Government Association reported in 1988 that Henry profited from a putative charity he ran. Henry's trial on unrelated federal charges was suspended owing to ill health, and he died in 1993.

The most prominent aldermanic scandals of the 1990s after Gambat were operations Haunted Hall and Silver Shovel. The investigation of ghost payrolling at city hall—hence, Haunted Hall—indicted thirty-eight people, of whom thirty-five were convicted. Former alderman Anthony Laurino, who bragged of having learned his trade at the feet of Hinky Dink and Bathhouse John, was indicted in 1995, but the trial was delayed because of his poor health; he died in 1999 at age eighty-eight. Those who fell included Cook County treasurer Edward J. Rosewell, who pleaded guilty but died before sentencing; state senator Bruce Farley; and aldermen John S. Madryzk, Joseph Martinez, and Ambrosio Medrano. The last technically was convicted in a Silver Shovel case but admitted hiring two ghosts.

Silver Shovel featured another unsavory mole, John S. Christopher, a career criminal. Christopher had served prison time for bank fraud, having refused to cooperate with the government. Therefore, when he flipped to wear a secret recording device for the feds in 1992, politicians did not suspect him as a mole. The feds recruited him with a strong argument: Christopher would be charged with conspiracy to murder a colleague who had flipped unless he also cooperated in turn.

Silver Shovel was an ironic allusion to Christopher's front business as a waste hauler and dumper. His stings differed from others in that they produced actual, tangible harm to low-income wards by illegally dumping tons of debris in them. U.S. attorneys insisted that this price had to be paid to cleanse corruption. Reformers were not so sure. Christopher gave out more than $150,000 in bribes for political favors, including a bogus minority certification for a phony firm he set up. (Contract set-asides for minorities were yet another reformist imposition that provided added vulnerabilities for corruption.) Unwisely, Christopher refrained from paying taxes on the money the government paid him for undercover work. In 2000 he received one of the harshest sentences in Silver Shovel, thirty-nine months for bankruptcy fraud and tax fraud. The operation ended anticlimactically in February 2001 when the former town collector of Cicero was spared a prison term because of poor health.

Eighteen people were convicted, including six Chicago aldermen. The only Silver Shovel target to win an acquittal was Alderman Rafael Frias, charged with a single bribe of five hundred dollars. Prosecutors speculated that a Chicago jury judged those potatoes too small to warrant a conviction. The aldermanic casualties were Lawrence S. Bloom, Jesse Evans, Percy Giles, Virgil Jones, Ambrosio Medrano, and Allan Streeter.

Streeter consented to wear a government wire while talking with aldermen. When news of this came out, some aldermen denounced him as a turncoat, stool pigeon, traitor, snitch, and Judas with no apparent embarrassment at being quoted on the record. At the least, word that an alderman had flipped made politicians suddenly much more circumspect. Ralph W. Conner, an African American businessman who later became mayor of west suburban Maywood, and two business associates paid a call to an alderman concerning a "brownfield" environmental project. They were surprised when that alderman would scarcely speak.

"It was funny because I didn't know at the time there was [the Silver Shovel] investigation going on," Conner said. "They threw us out. The alderman was very evasive. Well, he was friendly last week. So then here comes a Chinese guy, a black guy, an Irish guy [from Conner's engineering firm]. The alderman must have thought, 'If this ain't the FBI! These guys have got to be wearing wires!'"[3]

The commissioner of the Metropolitan Water Reclamation District, Joseph Gardner, a reputed reformer and one of the string of black mayoral challengers easily beaten by Daley, died in 1996 at age fifty before he could be indicted for allegedly taking bribes from Christopher. Reclamation district president Thomas Fuller was convicted. Former city water commissioner John Bolden was acquitted of extorting a two-thousand-dollar bribe but was convicted by the same jury of failing to pay taxes on that bribe.

In 1995 Daley and the city council responded to Operation Haunted Hall by passing an ethics ordinance requiring council committee chairmen to keep attendance records of their employees and make the records public. The inadequacy of this measure was exposed within two years. Daley's council floor leader from his ancestral Eleventh Ward was Alderman Patrick Huels. He liked to live well. On 17 October 1997, the *Sun-Times* exposed Huels's insider deals, as nested and mutually rewarding as a political satirist might imagine.

Along with Southwest Side alderman Edward M. Burke, Huels operated a security firm. Huels's and Burke's council committees paid $633,731 in city consulting fees to a lawyer who served as president of the firm, SDI Security. SDI owed $1.32 million in federal tax liens. SDI was bailed out with a $1.25 million loan from a company headed by Michael Tadin. Tadin was a Bridgeport boyhood friend of Daley. Huels helped Tadin get a $1.1 million city redevelopment contract as well as Cook County property tax breaks worth ten thousand dollars a year over eight years. Daley said he was disappointed in Huels and called on him to repay the loan from Tadin. Soon, on 21 October, Huels resigned as alderman.

In December a federal grand jury subpoenaed the financial records of Huels and Burke. Former alderman Joseph A. Martinez had pleaded guilty in January under Haunted Hall to holding ghost jobs with three city council committees, including Burke's finance committee, while working full-time in Burke's law firm. Burke denied that Martinez had been a ghost. Burke also was under fire because his law firm represented businesses seeking property tax reductions and city subsidies.

Burke and Huels reacted conventionally by hiring a former U.S. attorney, Anton Valukas, as defense counsel. Prosecutorial foxes seem to turn naturally to guarding the henhouse. The city council also behaved conventionally by yielding to Daley's pressure for incremental and piecemeal reform. A 1997 ordinance granted the city ethics board powers to subpoena aldermen and levy small fines for wrongdoing. However, the board could move only upon receiving a signed complaint, not anonymous allegations. After the Huels and Burke news surfaced, the council in December tightened the ethics ordinance a little more, broadening disclosure rules for lobbyists. In 1998 the *Sun-Times* reported that Burke helped a developer get a $1.2 million city subsidy without disclosing that Burke and his wife, a state appellate judge, took three hundred thousand dollars in legal fees from the developer. No indictments followed. In the modern pattern of manipulations of governmental process, federal investigators might have found that Burke's and Huels's actions, however unsavory, were legal.

Comparing the relative power of different mayors in different eras is an indoor sport with no rules and no final buzzer. Still, a strong case can be made that the bossism of Richard M. Daley and his highly placed brothers over Chicago, Cook County, and Illinois governments exceeds even that of Richard J. Daley.

In one field, at least, Richard M. Daley is bolder than his father. He willingly took direct, personal command of Chicago's disastrous and scandalous public schools. The senior Daley would not have dreamed of such a move. Richard J. Daley regarded public schools as a political hiring hall, while his base constituency sent their children to parochial schools anyway. John J. Hoellen, who in 1975 was Daley's last Republican election opponent, said recently, "Nobody got on the school board unless the old man OK'd it. He had to OK almost every principal, or at least his henchmen did, and every [building] engineer [janitor]. It was just a cesspool of political activity. That's why it was teeming with incompetence. . . . Rich [Daley, the incumbent mayor] has a much broader sensitivity toward his responsibility."[4]

The political history of Chicago public schools, again, would require its own book. In recent decades, the schools steadily have turned out quarter-literate graduates, chewed up superintendents, and produced scandals. The modern reform effort dates to 1979, when the system failed to meet its payroll and required a state bailout. As its price, Springfield imposed the Chicago School Finance Authority to approve budgets, yet another ineffective hierarchy of reformist overview—the authority was scrapped by a 1995 reform law.

A minor scandal will be cited because it was typical, even trite. A twenty-dollar bill was clasped in a handshake to the school official who awarded school-bus contracts. Then, ten hundred-dollar bills were delivered in an unmarked envelope to a school board auditor. In the end, more than seventy thousand dollars passed in bribes, federal prosecutors said in 1989. The man who oversaw bus contracts and a former bus company owner each was sentenced to forty-two months in prison.

Recent massive reforms were launched in 1986 by Mayor Washington, whose contribution is forgotten. He convened an education summit that devised a model school reform law based on academic studies of effective schools. Here again was the Progressive model of modern, scientific public administration in the conviction that rational administration by itself will reduce the opportunities and incentives for corruption. The vogue concepts of the time were decentralization and site-based management. In 1988 the legislature passed the Chicago School Reform Act. It established local school councils of parents, community members, teachers, the principal, and a student representative with powers to hire and fire principals, approve the local school budget, and write a school improvement plan. On 1 October 1989, the first councils were elected—5,420 members at 542 schools.

Before long, some councils got into trouble. Whatever the reformist motives of council members, the elected councils were political animals. Chicago, accustomed to ghost payrollers, now discovered ghost classrooms. At one high school, phantom classes were used to rig overtime pay for teachers and an assistant principal. A newly empowered board of education dissolved that council and ordered new elections in 1995.

After a state "academic decathlon" test-cheating scandal at another high school in 1995, school board president D. Sharon Grant said, "What it does is show me how far we've come in our society. When I was in school, cheating was a monumental offense. Honor was held in high esteem."[5] Later that year, Grant was sentenced to twenty-one months in prison for failing to file income tax returns for seventeen years. In 1996 the former director of school facilities, James P. Harney, pleaded guilty to taking $337,000 in cash and goods to steer contracts to private bidders. Such high-profile cases obscured endemic, systemic corruption.

Disgusted with gamed Chicago school budgets that persisted even after saddling the system with the school finance authority, the state created an office of inspector general in 1993. School board rules required that a school engineer be on site whenever the school was open. Often, community groups met in schools on weekends. Engineers and school maintenance assistants filed for overtime, not just per weekend day but for each of several group meetings. The scam was so lucrative that the new inspector general wondered "why droves of potential applicants are not standing in line outside the Department of Facilities waiting in line to apply for the position of school engineer. . . . Approximately $1.1 million was expended in overtime payments to school engineers in instances when more than one engineer was working at the same school, on the same weekend day, at the same time."[6] Another $374,000 was paid in overtime to school maintenance assistants to watch over heating systems that were fully automated. Although the inspector general had subpoena powers, he found that the school system resisted him at every turn. His request (not a subpoena) for overtime records was bounced from the law department to an assistant superintendent to the payroll department, which finally produced three sets of records, incomplete and inaccurate. During that same year, 1994, an outside auditor retained by the school board discovered, for instance, that the system routinely paid seventy-five dollars for an eighty-cent electrical wall plate.

Such was the nature of the public schools when Republican leaders of the Illinois legislature assigned their management to Daley in 1995. As they had in 1988, businessmen reform groups such as Chicago United and the civic committee of the Commercial Club took corporate jets to Springfield to lobby for the new law. Daley understood viscerally that the sorry state of the schools drove the middle class to flee the city. "Every city in this country is seeing families move out for one reason: the schools," he said. "You have to take responsibility for that. Of all the things I'm doing, this is the most important."[7]

The school decentralization reform had not worked, so the next reform centralized with a vengeance. Far beyond a political event, this was a historic experiment for America's urban centers. New York City followed suit in 2001.

Amendments to the Chicago School Reform Act, although they maintained local school councils, called for the adoption of the corporate management model. Daley would appoint a boss explicitly called the chief executive officer, not superintendent. The existing school board, board nominating committee, and district council superintendents were trashcanned. Powers of the teachers' union, including the power to strike, were strictly limited. The CEO was given broad authority to identify failing schools and enforce accountability with sanctions, including closing such schools. Daley named his aide Paul G. Vallas as CEO.

In 1980 the schools had entered a voluntary desegregation plan with the U.S. Justice Department. In 1995 the Monitoring Commission for

Desegregation Implementation spent nine thousand dollars on food, liquor, theater tickets, massages, and other amenities during a weekend at
a suburban resort. That was nothing. The commission had paid $219,000
to about twenty-five consultants who did not document their work. One
of Vallas's first actions was to put a stop to such practices, although critics said he delivered his own sweetheart contracts.

In a speech to the National Press Club in Washington in 1997, Daley
said,

> The system was plagued by failing schools and nine [teachers'] strikes
> between 1972 and 1995. . . .
>
> Instead of bailing out the schools, the Republican State Govern-
> ment decided to turn over responsibility to the City of Chicago.
> Many people said they weren't doing this as a favor to Chicago.
>
> But I wanted this new responsibility—because I knew it was the
> only way to change society and move our city forward. . . .
>
> We ended the policy of social promotions [advancing students
> through the grades regardless of their scholastic failure]. . . . A man-
> datory homework rule was passed. . . . And the Chicago Public
> schools also took a bold and needed step by putting schools on aca-
> demic probation.[8]

City hall has touted gains made by public school students in standard-
ized achievement tests since 1995. In fact, these reported gains are mar-
ginal, inconsistent, and open to question. For instance, a University of
Chicago economist, Steven D. Levitt, conducted a computer study in 2001
demonstrating that teachers in 4 to 5 percent of Chicago elementary school
classrooms had cheated in reporting their students' scores on the Iowa Test
of Basic Skills from 1993 to 1999. As a result, Levitt calculated, about 10
percent of a claimed four-year increase in mean Iowa Test scores was bogus.[9] Meanwhile, the high school dropout rate has held steady at about
16 percent a year.

Roti, D'Arco, De Leo, Marcy, Shields, Henry, Laurino, Rosewell, Farley,
Madryzk, Martinez, Medrano, Bloom, Evans, Giles, Jones, Streeter,

Gardner, Fuller, Bolden, Huels, Burke, Grant, Harvey . . . was there *nothing* clean in Chicago and Cook County governments? With political skills equaling if not surpassing his father's, Daley has avoided personal accountability for such endemic and widespread corruption. Even so, recent years have seen escalating allegations of the mayor's supposed largesse in steering public contracts to cronies, including some figures of organized crime.

The Democratic sheriff of Cook County had been Richard J. Elrod, son of a former county Democratic chairman. Elrod was partly paralyzed after having tried to tackle a demonstrator during the radical Days of Rage protests in 1969. Scandals in Elrod's office led to his election defeat in 1986 by Republican James O'Grady, who promised a clean administration. O'Grady was touted as a potential mayor or governor. His undersheriff was James E. Dvorak, chairman of the Cook County GOP. In 1993 Dvorak pleaded guilty to taking payoffs to protect organized crime, putting seventeen ghosts on the payroll, and falsifying test results for politically connected job applicants. He was sentenced to nearly eight years in prison. Twelve other sheriff's employees also pleaded guilty.

The Dvorak case was not out of the ordinary except in offering a clear example of prosecutorial excess. At a bond hearing for mobster Ernest Rocco Infelice and four others in February 1990, the government played what became the notorious "Dvorak tape." It captured Infelice telling a bookmaker who was a secret government informant that his gambling branch of organized crime paid thirty-five thousand dollars a month to law enforcement officials and imprisoned mobsters.

> "Between you and I, the sheriff [O'Grady] gets ten," Infelice said.
> "Yeah, with the Bohemian [Dvorak]?"
> "Yeah. Five goes to another guy . . ."
> "I got no right to ask you the question, what . . . do you get for 10 thousand a month."
> "Sheriff never bothers us, then we got a guy at the state's attorney's office. We got another guy downtown."[10]

Infelice also asserted on the tape that the mob had aided Daley's mayoral election in 1989 by muscling a major contributor to abandon chal-

lenger Ed Vrdolyak. Further, he claimed that when Daley was state's attorney in the early 1980s, Daley blocked the subpoena of a mobster as a
favor to the mob. All of this was played in open court at a mere bond
hearing, not a trial. Dvorak and Daley rightly cried foul. Daley called the
allegations bullshit, strong language in public for him. Without corrobo-
rating evidence, the tape might have shown Infelice only as a blowhard
braggart, dropping names. Dvorak objected that publicity from the defa-
matory tape might prejudice a potential jury. A month later, the Justice
Department disciplined the lawyer who played the tape. He was suspended for two weeks without pay. In 1992, during an Operation Gambat
trial, the tape was played anew and Daley had to deny it all again.

The senior Mayor Daley claimed in 1976 that organized crime had been
driven out of the city and was occupying the suburbs—foreign territory,
in his eyes. Apparently he overlooked the First Ward. However, Operation Safebet in the 1990s made his case that some suburbs were mob-rid-
den. In 1993 Chicago Heights mayor Charles Panici was convicted of
extorting more than six hundred thousand dollars in bribes from contractors. Two city council members and seven other officials were convicted
as well. In 1994 the deputy police chief was convicted. Officials in the
townships of Addison and Bloom were found guilty of ghost payrolling
and bribery. The mayor of Lyons died before facing indictment for taking bribes to protect prostitution. Poor Cicero, headquarters of Al Capone
in the 1920s, witnessed indictments of thirteen town officials and employees extending into 2000. In 2002 town president Betty Loren-Maltese and
six others were convicted in federal court in a scheme to steal $12 million
through a fake insurance company. Loren-Maltese was sentenced in 2003
to eight years in prison. All of this is by way of saying that organized crime,
however much reduced after decades of rackets busting, has not gone away.

The question before the house is: Richard M. Daley, reformer or regular?
There is no definitive answer, just as there is no final interpretation of the
tenures of previous reform mayors or, indeed, the entire history of Chicago corruption and reform. Mayors Harrison I and II, Dunne, Dever,
Kennelly, Byrne, Washington, and even Richard J. Daley in his early years

all were reformers and regulars at once. Richard M. Daley is of that ilk. For instance, a federal judge threatened to hold the city in contempt of court for violating a Shakman decree against patronage. Daley responded in 2002 by moving to vacate Shakman. At the same time, he insisted that he indulged in no political hiring at all.

Although he was state's attorney during the Greylord investigation of the 1980s, Daley has shown no interest in devising a merit system for the local judiciary. It remains stabled in machine politics. Retired judge Thomas J. Maloney, who cultivated a reputation as a tough-on-crime hanging judge, was convicted in 1993 of taking bribes to fix three murder trials and a fourth felony case—not even Greylord had convicted a Cook County judge of rigging a murder case. In 2002, Judge George J. W. Smith was sentenced to twenty-seven months in prison for paying bribes to obtain his seat on the bench. Smith had been among numerous judicial occupants of "Camp Muni," a holding pen on the thirteenth floor of the Richard J. Daley Center for judges awaiting resolution of charges against them. There they perform administrative tasks such as reviewing "paupers' petitions" for waivers of court costs.

In the park district, workers were convicted of ghost payrolling and of drawing fraudulent unemployment checks. In the Chicago Transit Authority, chairman Robert Belcaster, a Daley appointee, was forced to resign in 1996 for having bought stock in a company that won a transit contract. Former Chicago Housing Authority chairman Vincent Lane, another reputed reformer once touted for mayor, was convicted in 2001 of defrauding banks in his private businesses.

Daley's police department showed worse corruption. In 1997, the "Austin Seven" (officers from the Austin district on the West Side) were indicted for robbing drug dealers, actually moles. Two pleaded guilty, and five were convicted. Daley's response was conventional. He forced the resignation of the police superintendent because of his longstanding friendship with a convicted felon. What came next? Daley named a commission on police integrity, chaired by former U.S. attorney Dan K. Webb, to review police operations.

On another front, Daley won a federal appellate court decree in 2001 that relaxed rules against police spying imposed in 1981 in a settlement of the Red Squad case against surveillance and sabotage of dissenters. Daley asserted the enhanced threat of violence from terrorists and hate groups. Still, police scandals did not cease. Former gang crimes investigator Joseph Miedzianowski and fourteen others were charged in 1998 with running a drug distribution ring. Miedzianowski was sentenced in 2003 to life in prison. Former deputy superintendent William Hanhardt, the highest-ranking Chicago officer ever convicted of corruption, was sentenced in 2002 to nearly sixteen years for taking payoffs from the mob and running a jewelry theft ring. His sentencing followed a suicide attempt. Currently, a special state prosecutor is investigating charges of cover-ups of police brutality, including torture, in some police districts that date to the 1980s. As recently as 2002, a federal judge accused Chicago police and Cook County prosecutors of routinely violating the rights of witnesses by putting them in small, windowless, locked interrogation rooms for a day or more to coerce confessions. Police claimed they were witnesses, not suspects, and therefore not immediately entitled to lawyers. In 2003 a federal jury fined the city $1 million because it failed to discipline off-duty police who beat up civilians.

Daley mostly has refused to endorse candidates personally, at least up until the elections of 2002, lest he be given the horrific title *Boss*. In one case, Daley did stick close to a friend who fell to investigators—but only to a point. Dan Rostenkowski, a protégé of the senior Daley, went to Congress in 1959 and rose to become chairman of the tax-writing Ways and Means Committee in 1981. Rostenkowski had a cavalier disregard of reform laws and congressional ethics rules that strictly separated public, campaign, and personal funds. His attitude atavistically followed that of nineteenth-century Chicago: *The pickings are easy and nobody except a few goo goos cares anyway.* He totally misunderstood the post-Watergate culture of scandal. In the 1994 Democratic primary, "Rosty" was in serious political trouble. He had not yet been indicted, but charges from a Washington grand jury obviously were forthcoming. He faced four challengers, including Dick Simpson, author of the critical study of the city council. Daley's machine went throttle-to-the-fire-wall for Rosty, deploying as many as eight hundred precinct workers. The congressman was renominated with 50 percent of the vote.

Two months later, Rostenkowski was indicted on seventeen counts of effectively stealing $724,267 through various schemes including ghost payrolling. At that point, Daley dumped him. In the November general election, which Rosty lost to an unknown Republican, the machine strangely slept. Daley, self-protective above all, would not hug an indicted felon.

In 1996, Rosty pleaded guilty to two minor mail-fraud counts and later served 451 days in federal custody. The grief expressed by the Chicago establishment and Washington pundits over the downfall of a giant such as Rostenkowski could scarcely be exaggerated. They believed he was victimized by media scandalmongers and an overzealous Justice Department. The punditry did not acknowledge that this was where post-Watergate reforms, codifying political behavior and institutionalizing permanent prosecutions, had taken them. Rostenkowski, unrepentant to this day, developed a consulting business and in 2000 was pardoned by his friend Bill Clinton.

Another congressman allied with Daley was Mel Reynolds, who represented the Far South Side and some southern suburbs. He had tried twice unsuccessfully to unseat Representative Gus Savage, whom critics called a black racist and who was accused of sexually harassing a Peace Corps volunteer during a congressional junket to Africa. Savage's opponent Reynolds was young, articulate, well educated, and rags-to-riches, and boasted of ties to the Kennedy family. In fact, Reynolds was a fraud. In his successful 1992 campaign against Savage, he staged a press conference with a large bandage on his forehead, claiming he was wounded by shattered glass in his car during a drive-by shooting incited by Savage. With this melodrama, Reynolds at least honored the lapsed Chicago tradition of gunfire at politicians. But police could not confirm that the alleged assault had actually happened. Reynolds won that election and was rewarded by Rostenkowski with a coveted freshman seat on Ways and Means.

When the sexual scandal hit in 1995, the details were squalid. Reynolds, who was married, cruised by South Side high schools to pick up girls. A campaign volunteer went to Chicago police to say she had a sexual relationship with the congressman at age sixteen. At once, Daley divorced himself from Reynolds. Reynolds was convicted of sexual misconduct, child pornography, and obstruction of justice. After steady population losses since 1950, Chicago was down to seven congressmen and two of them were in jail. While serving his five-year state sentence, Reynolds also was convicted in federal court in 1997 of campaign financial violations and sentenced to an additional six and one-half years. President Clinton, on his last day in office, pardoned Reynolds.

Like his father, Daley might have claimed that the convictions of a county undersheriff, a school board president, a city clerk, a city treasurer, suburban crooks, congressmen, and even police officers had nothing directly to do with him. But other scandals knocked right on the door of the fifth floor of city hall.

In 1993 John Duff III was arrested in Miami Beach for soliciting prostitutes. The arresting officer reported that Duff "stated that if I did not remove his handcuffs immediately and let him go, he was going to find this officer and my family and kill them one by one while this officer watched. [Duff] stated to officer that I better listen to what he was saying because he has connections with organized crime in Chicago."[11] The last statement, at least, was true. A special monitor appointed by the Justice Department to root organized crime out of the Hotel Employees and Restaurant Employees International Union accused Duff in 2000 of looting $172,000 from the union and banned him from it. The union had been headed by Edward T. Hanley, who gave lucrative consulting contracts to Rostenkowski and other politicians.

Duff III is a son of John Duff Jr., the head of a family whose companies won $100 million in government contracts under Daley. Duff Jr. (formerly a city investigator) served seventeen months in prison in the 1980s for embezzling union funds in Chicago and Detroit. Shortly after Daley's 1989 election, Duff Jr. formed Windy City Maintenance, a janitorial firm. Daley allegedly suggested that his director of special events include the Duffs in her department's business. Daley denied it, but in any case,

Windy City soon won a no-bid contract to clean up after the summer Taste of Chicago festivals. Windy City won the award under affirmative-action policies because it was run by a woman. However, this was a scam, as revealed by the *Tribune* in 1999. Duff companies also received contracts to clean O'Hare Airport, the McCormick Place convention center, and the new police 911 emergency-call center. In 2000 Daley said, "I have no financial or political ties to them [the Duffs]," but two years later said, "I've taken it [campaign funds] from them. You know that. We acknowledged everything."[12] Between 1991 and 1998, the Duffs and their corporations donated $8,875 to Daley campaigns. The family also staged fundraisers for the mayor and provided campaign workers for candidates backed by Daley.

One of Daley's civic-improvement programs was to place wrought-iron fences around city parks. GF Structures, a Daley campaign contributor, got the contract to dig up old fences and erect new ones. The firm bought its insurance from the mayor's brother, John, a Cook County commissioner who also was a friend of the city purchasing agent. GF Structures charged much more than provided by contracts over eight years and lost its city work to lower bidders in 2000.

It was O'Hare Airport contracting that finally soured some of the goo-goo element against Daley. A no-bid airport concession contract was gained by a firm headed by two friends of Daley's wife. Daley's friend Oscar D'Angelo negotiated the contract for a fee of $480,000, although he had not properly registered as a lobbyist. D'Angelo privately had lent $10,500 to a mayoral aide who was forced to resign because of that loan. The aide's brother was the deputy aviation commissioner. This scandal was exposed by the Better Government Association. Result: Daley ostracized D'Angelo and amended the ethics ordinance to forbid letting contracts to firms whose lobbyists had not registered. Considering Huels, Burke, Tadin, Duff, D'Angelo, and the rest, Daley also wrote an executive order to list the names of everyone involved with new city contracts and leases on the city's Internet site—the first such endeavor in the country.

In March 2001, the largest contract in city history, $1 billion for a new

O'Hare terminal, was awarded to a development consortium whose lobbyist was Daley's recently retired political enforcer, Victor Reyes (formally, his intergovernmental affairs director). This contract was approved by the city council at lightning speed with no discussion. Back in the 1890s, the council at least would take the trouble to debate streetcar franchise giveaways to Charles Yerkes. The *Tribune* reported later in March 2001 that another Daley political strategist, former state senator Jeremiah Joyce, earned $1.8 million as a lobbyist for an O'Hare concession deal that yielded less than half the revenue that the city expected.

Daley insisted that he had no direct involvement in or even knowledge of his aviation department's contract awards. "I'm not here to turn anyone into millionaires. I resent that." Throughout the contracting scandals, Daley has been consistent: "I don't know what part of the action he [Joyce] has. I don't know and I don't care. . . . I have billions of dollars of work going out. None of it can be clouted. They cannot be clouted! . . . I know them [the Duffs] but I don't know them personally. . . . [Tadin is] not my friend. I mean I know him. I know him, but he's not my friend."[13]

Such is the record of a modern, managerial, postmachine mayor. Some have called Daley a "stealth boss." In retrospect, the old urban machine of small-time vice, boodle, patronage, and vote fraud might not look so bad. At least these pathologies, in their rough and crude ways, were small-*d* democratic. The legal gaming of the system in such as the Presidential Towers and O'Hare Airport developments is plutocratic. Daley's administration has exacerbated the cynical view that government is an insiders' game for the wealthy and well connected, manipulating bureaucratic processes, despite— even at times by way of—all the encrustations of reformist oversight.

Richard J. Daley took his political funds from labor unions, organized crime, and industrialists. When donors extended cash across his desk, the elder Daley would arise from his throne, walk to the front of the desk, and shake hands heartily. If the donor handed over a check, Daley would issue a grumpy thank-you and remain seated. Richard M. Daley, under penalty of law, must spread all his contributions above a certain amount on the public record. The junior Daley's funds tend to flow not from

unions, organized crime, and industrialists so much as from lawyers, lobbyists, and entrepreneurs of the new cybernetic economy, all, at least on
the public record, perfectly legally.[14]

However, no alderman, committeeman, or candidate since 1964 has
been shot, pistol-whipped, kidnapped, dumped in the Sanitary and Ship
Canal, or encased in concrete. This is progress.

CONCLUSION

> Corruption! Good Lord! Was it invented here? . . . In some ways the city
> is so much better and in some ways it has only changed a little bit.
> —Thomas J. Kneir, FBI special agent in charge, Chicago bureau,
> remarks to local public-agency inspectors general, March 2002

> If somebody's not from Chicago, he can never understand Chicago.
> Chicago's a very complex place, and the politics are almost medieval. . . .
> I know Chicago politics and I feel it, it's a part of me, in a way that other
> people can't.
> —developer Tom Rosenberg, *Chicago* magazine, April 1992

A cigar-chomping city fire inspector silently and critically appraised the interior of Catherine O'Leary's barn behind her house at 137 DeKoven Street on 8 October 1871. Nervously, timorously, Mrs. O'Leary paused from milking her cow to ask whether a mutual understanding could be reached. The officious inspector puffed his cigar and allowed that it just might be possible. She slipped him an envelope containing cash, whereupon he marked his form *Approved* and left. A relieved Mrs. O'Leary sat on a stool to resume her milking. Then the cow kicked over a kerosene lantern on the floor and ignited the Chicago Fire.

On election day of 1960, with the presidential candidacy of John F. Kennedy and the office of state's attorney at stake, a Northwest Side precinct captain patriotically roused his troops thus:

Don't let the federal marshals and FBI agents stop us from doing what has to be done. Getting out the vote. Like Mrs. Smoliniski, the old lady who ran the grocery on Ashland [Avenue] and died last weekend. She always voted straight Democrat, and you know she would have today. So somebody please tell me why, just because she's six feet under up in Rosehill [Cemetery], her vote has to die with her?

Both of these incidents are fictional. The first was a skit by Chicago's Second City comedy troupe in 1978 after the *Sun-Times* Mirage series. The role of inspector, by the way, was played by the actor James Belushi. The second is part of the dialogue of a play, *Early and Often,* entitled after the Chicago vernacular slogan, "vote early and often." It was written by Barbara Wallace and Thomas R. Wolfe and played at Chicago's Famous Door Theatre in 2000–2001.

These tales are repeated here not just for amusement but to underline the folkloric and even comedic aspects of Chicago's history of corruption. Psychologists tell us that behind every joke is an unspoken truth or at least what the joke teller regards as true. Mrs. O'Leary and Mrs. Smoliniski are civic archetypes of ethnicity and the political matrix of coercions and favors. Chicago's comedic folklore recognizes the ubiquity and persistence of corruption in a room in which reform is always entering and exiting.

The parades in and out of this room have been persistent ever since Protestant evangelists tried to cauterize vice 170 years ago; since good citizens nominated People's Tickets in the 1860s; since the Citizens' Association strived to put local government on a sound business footing in the 1870s; since the Civic Federation labored for general social uplift in the 1890s; since the Municipal Voters' League kicked crooked aldermen out of office at the turn of the century; since settlement-house reformers, Progressives, and muckrakers marched toward their vision of a New Jerusalem; since wealthy businessmen employed extralegal means to ease the scourge of 1920s gangsterism; since abolitionists, socialists, anarchists, and Saul Alinsky launched the traditions of radical dissent; since sober civic groups and fiery neighborhood activists advanced their concepts of the common weal; since Richard J. Daley stifled dissent from 1955 to 1976; throughout the population explosion of special prosecutors, inspectors general, review boards, ethics codes, disclosure laws, and watchdog groups; and since Richard M. Daley has consolidated his power even in the face of the media ethos of permanent scandal. Surely corruption would not have endured through so many whirlwinds of change unless it served some societal functions and values.

In fact, there is something of a case *for* public corruption. The liabilities of corruption seem obvious—"Systematic corruption generates economic costs by distorting incentives, political costs by undermining institutions, and social costs by redistributing power toward the undeserving," as one study noted.[1] Even so, some studies of corruption have argued that it supports the values of stability and of mediation among competing class and economic interests, hardly unimportant values in an America of constant social mobility and cultural transformation.

Few except colorful rascals from the past such as Hinky Dink, Bathhouse John, and Paddy Bauler have openly supported what their comrade in arms George Washington Plunkitt of Tammany Hall once called "honest graft," public business awarded private parties through the spoils system. Plunkitt scorned politicians who stole because so much money could be made legally through manipulations of governmental process. In this, like many other old rascals, Plunkitt was prophetic. Those growing wealthy now on O'Hare Airport contracts might recognize the theory while disdaining its authors. Still, the O'Hare contractors might be supporting a partially beneficent tradition. As the noted political scientist Samuel P. Huntington wrote,

> Like machine politics or clientelistic politics in general, corruption provides immediate, specific, and concrete benefits to groups which might otherwise be thoroughly alienated from society. Corruption may thus be functional to the maintenance of a political system in the same way that reform is. Corruption itself may be a substitute for reform and both corruption and reform may be substitutes for revolution.[2]

In other words, but not for boodle and graft, farmers with pitchforks and canal diggers with pickaxes might have stormed the Bastille. Anyone who has participated in the underground economy by taking cash payments for moonlighting jobs, or in a black market by brokering ration stamps in wartime, or who has lobbied for subsidies or tax breaks might understand this concept. Though Huntington wrote in 1968, the apologia is an old one. Some writers expressed it even during the Progressive era.

More recent studies, however, have superseded the Huntington theory.

> Some literature on corruption in the 1960s tended to excuse corruption as something like a market price when markets weren't allowed or something like an expression of interest when more democratic markets were closed. Since then, both empirical and theoretical studies have persuaded most people that most types of corrupt behavior are economically and politically costly, even if they sometimes benefit the group in power.[3]

Political scientists have long tried to identify the functions and values of corruption and reform but have arrived at no general theory, no central organizing principle. This book has reviewed the history of corruption and reform in Chicago largely as an outgrowth of class and ethnic antagonisms. Certain groups held a reformist ethos that placed a high value on rectitude and efficiency and a lower value on the private exchange of favors, loyalties, and personal gains. Other groups held a reverse scale of values. On this basis, considering that corruption and reform are ambiguous and inconstant concepts, corruption could be less of a moral or legal problem than a reflection of conflict between opposing social groups. This viewpoint might be labeled the *societal* or *functional* theory of corruption.

The major schools of thought are the *functionality* and *utility* ideas of corruption. The functionality view holds that corruption serves social ends, else it would not be sustained. The utility theory examines ethical and moral decisions on the basis of cost-benefit, reward-punishment calculations. Reductively, these might be labeled the macroeconomic or microeconomic schools of thought. Corruption can be conceived as a governmental market in which the public tolerates precisely the level of corruption that will clear the market, while any stealing beyond that invites eventual eradication. Such a dynamic has been found in many recent studies of corruption in developing Third World governments. The analogy to Chicago is obvious. For much of its history, it was a developing market economy struggling to find its way with newly invented institutions.

Whatever the merit of this analysis, the question remains: Why Chicago? Why did this frontier parvenu become the epicenter of public corruption in America, at least in national folklore? The superb Chicago reformer and political scientist Charles E. Merriam favored a *structural* theory under, in modern jargon, the *functional* school. The original ward-politics underpinning of the city proliferated such a menagerie of overlapping and competing public jurisdictions that none but grafters, or at least professionals, could navigate them.

But Chicago is not singular in this regard. Writers have applied that same theory to other cities and the federal government. The specific American political arrangements of separated powers, federalism, and aggressive localism—carrying such a broad range of autonomous actors—all but cry out for cutting corners, making deals, applying a matrix of coercions and favors. "What the Founders have put asunder, the politicians must join together if anything is to be accomplished," the renowned scholar James Q. Wilson wrote.[4] The census bureau has counted roughly eighty thousand units of local government and 526,000 federal, state, and local elective offices. No other country has anything close to these immense and diverse ballots, this huge magpie's nest in the public square. Meanwhile, the public is kept appeased with public works and government benefit checks.

Reformers are given to "if only" thinking under the structural rubric: absent a moral revolution of the people as sought by evangelists, if only we could rationalize, consolidate, and unify governmental operations, then enticements for corruption would fade away. Thus the obsession of reformers with procedures and methods. Today's headline about some politician assailed for some ethical misstep might not assert that he or she did anything inherently wrong, only that some obscure rule, regulation, canon, norm, code, or statute was transgressed. The accretion of reformist laws and bureaucracies has produced all the familiar pathologies of bureaucracy—red tape, delay, obfuscation, vitiation of accountability. At the same time, the new bureaucracies create new vulnerabilities for corruption, such as in contracting set-asides for minorities. In the apothegm of Carl J. Friedrich, "Corruption is kept functional by the efforts to get rid of it."[5] Corruption and reform set up a reciprocal, even mutually generating relationship. For instance, the legal hustling that animated the Greylord investigation derived from reform laws against the bail-bonding racket. Such is the dark side of reform, which this book has endeavored to review along with the depredations of crooked politicians.

Yet again, why Chicago? Since the nineteenth century, writers have labeled it the most typically American city, and as Dick Simpson recently observed, Chicago is "an extreme example of American politics that magnifies its virtues and defects."[6] Or as the Reverend Jesse L. Jackson frequently remarked, "Chicago is the Super Bowl of politics." We might do well to remember that a multiethnic democracy is a new idea. The world had never seen one before America created it. In Chicago all these ethnicities and their aspirations came together in all their roaring magnificence, with all their inspiriting successes and heartbreaking failures.

Someone has said that the only real reformers left in Chicago are the agents of the U.S. attorney. The past thirty years have seen a spectacular number of federal indictments and convictions of politicians and their clients. Reformers of all stripes might agree that too great an emphasis on jailing dishonest politicians, however gratifying to a citizen's soul, has not on its own cleaned up government. A stable and enduring pattern of corruption such as Chicago has displayed indicates that, no matter how many greedy politicians hear jailhouse doors clanging behind them, something is wrong with our laws and institutions.

This book has sought to identify the constants in corruption and reform. Surely a dominant constant is the steady expansion of governmental intervention in the economy and everyday life. The problem, *corruption in government,* always has galvanized reformers to reduce the amount of corruption with stricter laws and regulations. By now the true remedy might lie in addressing the other side of the equation: reduce the amount of government.

Notes
Chicago Political Glossary
Selected Bibliography
Index

Notes

The following abbreviations are used for frequently cited sources in the notes:

BGA   Better Government Association
CAC   Citizens' Association of Chicago
CCC   City Club of Chicago
CDN   *Chicago Daily News*
CHS   Chicago Historical Society
CST   *Chicago Sun-Times*
CT   *Chicago Tribune*
MRL   Municipal Reference Library

Introduction

1. William M. Beavers, in "Quotables," *CT,* 5 May 1999.
2. Fremon, *Chicago Politics,* 48.
3. Steve Neal column, *CST,* 11 July 1997.
4. Scott R. Lassar, interview by the author, 12 September 1999.
5. "Public Career Had Its Twists and Turns," *CST,* 9 July 1997.
6. "Reckoning the Cost of Silver Shovel," *CT,* 18 March 1999.
7. "Mr. Clean Falls: Bloom Cops Plea," *CST,* 6 December 1998.
8. "Bloom Joins Long, Sad List," *CT,* 6 December 1998.
9. Michael Sneed column, *CST,* 10 November 1999.

1. Frontier, Finances, and Fire: 1833–71

1. Porter, "Earliest Religious History," 6.
2. Porter, "Earliest Religious History," 5.
3. Asbury, *Gem of the Prairie,* 33.
4. For the political and social importance of the first two Great Awakenings, see Armstrong, *Battle for God,* 78–80, and P. Johnson, *History of the American People,* 109–17, 296–307.
5. Miller, *City of the Century,* 74–76.
6. Balestier, "Annals of Chicago," 25.
7. Balestier, "Annals of Chicago," 26.
8. Balestier, "Annals of Chicago," 33.
9. Merriner, *Mr. Chairman,* 52.
10. Porter, "Earliest Religious History," 62–63.

11. Many scholars have explored this theme; for discussion of its political implications, see Kleppner, *Cross of Culture,* 69–91, and Tarr, *Study of Boss Politics,* 18–21.

12. Algren quoted in John D. Buenker, "Chicago's Ethnics and the Politics of Accommodation," in *Wild Kind of Boldness,* ed. Adams, 126.

13. Downard, "William Butler Ogden," 47.

14. Asbury, *Gem of the Prairie,* 24.

15. Cleaver, "Early-Chicago Reminiscences," 36–39.

16. Pierce, *History of Chicago,* 1:379.

17. Miller, *City of the Century,* 135.

18. Levi Boone, "Inaugural Addresses of the Mayors of Chicago," MRL, 9–10.

19. Dedmon, *Fabulous Chicago,* 26.

20. Manufacturing and employment figures cited by Peterson, *Barbarians in Our Midst,* 36, 375.

21. David L. Protess, "Joseph Medill," in *Mayors,* ed. Green and Holli, 13, 220–21 n. 31.

22. Flanagan, *Charter Reform in Chicago,* 167 n. 21.

23. Miller, *City of the Century,* 138.

24. Miller develops this argument at 165–66.

25. Editorial, *CT,* 11 October 1871.

26. "Chicago and the Tribune Ride Waves of Change Together," *CT,* 18 March 2001.

27. Andreas, *History of Cook County,* 51.

28. Hirsch and Goler, *City Comes of Age,* 71.

2. Businessmen Rebels: 1872–93

1. William L. Chenery, "Works Long of Interest in Chicago," *Chicago Herald,* 15 November 1914.

2. Roberts, "Ousting the Bummers," Roberts Papers, folder 1, file 3.

3. Graham Taylor, "Will Chicago Repeat Its Best History?" *CDN,* 21 January 1925.

4. Roberts, "Ousting the Bummers," folder 2, file 1.

5. CAC, executive committee minutes, CAC Collection, 1:115.

6. In 1880 the *CT* and twenty-five other tenants signed fifty-year leases on School Fund property with a clause requiring periodic revaluations of the rents. In 1895 the board of education gave the *CT* and *CDN* fixed-rent leases omitting revaluations, good until 1985.

7. Banfield analyzed the crucial housing-price factor, as new immigrants sought the cheapest rents close to inner-city jobs while residents there saved to buy dwellings in more respectable outlying areas, in *Unheavenly City Revisited,* 25–51.

8. Peterson, *Barbarians in Our Midst,* 49.

9. Dedmon, *Fabulous Chicago,* 151–52.

10. Richard Schneirov, "Chicago's Great Upheaval of 1877," in *Wild Kind of Boldness,* ed. Adams, 87.

11. CAC, minutes, 1:133.

12. Miller, *City of the Century,* 438.

13. Lindberg reviewed police repression in *To Serve and Collect,* 63–72, and *Return to the Scene,* 274–76.

14. Miller, *City of the Century,* 236.

15. John Kinsley, "Tells How Ring of Boodlers Was Smashed in 1887," *CT,* 20 April 1930.

16. Kinsley, "Ring of Boodlers," *CT,* 20 April 1930.

17. Roberts, "Businessmen in Revolt," 84.

18. Roberts, "Businessmen in Revolt," 93.

19. Kinsley, "Ring of Boodlers," *CT,* 20 April 1930.

20. Rex, *Mayors of Chicago,* 86.

21. Rex, *Mayors of Chicago,* 66–67.

22. Dedmon, *Fabulous Chicago,* 127.

23. *Traveler* clipping, n.d., in CAC minutes, 1:127.

24. CAC, secretary's report of 6 February 1892, in minutes, 2:44–45.

25. CAC, secretary's report of 7 May 1892, in minutes, 2:51.

26. CAC, secretary's report of 7 May 1892, in minutes, 2:52.

27. Roberts, "Ousting the Bummers," folder 4, file 8.

28. Clayton, "Scourge of Sinners," 77.

29. In 1898, for example, the effective ceiling on Chicago property tax levies was 1 percent of the total amount of assessed valuation. In 1904 the per-capita property tax in Chicago was $9.32, the least of the nation's ten largest cities. See W. L. Sullivan, *Dunne,* 247.

30. Merriner, *Mr. Chairman,* 126.

31. Merriam, *Chicago,* 191.

3. Progressives and Muckrakers: 1894–1909

1. Besides Yerkes's four thousand dollars, Philip D. Armour's personal real estate was assessed at five thousand dollars; George M. Pullman's, twelve thousand dollars; Potter Palmer's, fifteen thousand dollars, and Marshall Field's, twenty thousand dollars. Stead, *If Christ Came,* 214.

2. Stead, "My First Visit to America," in *As Others See Chicago,* ed. Pierce, 363.

3. *CT,* 29 December 1893, quoted in Baylen, "Victorian's 'Crusade' in Chicago," 429.

4. See Holli, "Varieties of Urban Reform," 217–19.

5. Stead, *If Christ Came,* 298, 300.

6. Stead, *If Christ Came,* 237.

7. Roberts, "Municipal Voters' League," 133.

8. Harrison, *Stormy Years,* 157.

9. Dedmon, *Fabulous Chicago,* 262.

10. Ginger, *Altgeld's America,* 92–93.

11. Merriam, *Chicago,* 146.

12. Roberts, "Municipal Voters' League," 171.

13. "Kup's Column," *CST,* 24 March 1954.

14. Gould, "Walter L. Fisher," 162.

15. Roberts, "Businessmen in Revolt," 171.

16. Merriam, *Chicago,* 20.

17. C. Johnson, *Wicked City,* 3–4.

18. See Teaford, *Unheralded Triumph.*

19. Merriam, *Chicago,* 105.

20. Roberts, "Businessmen in Revolt," 158.

21. McCarthy, "Businessmen and Professionals," 132.

22. Hirsch and Goler, *City Comes of Age,* 42.

23. Miller, "Politics of Municipal Reform," 28.

24. CCC, board of governors' minutes, 23 March 1904, CCC Collection.

25. Stead, *If Christ Came,* 111–13.

26. See Harrison, *Stormy Years,* 113, 141.

27. Steffens, *Autobiography,* 365.

28. Steffens, "Chicago," 563.

29. Steffens, "Chicago," 575.

30. Harrison, *Stormy Years,* 129, 162.

31. Addams, *Democracy and Social Ethics,* 243.

32. Addams, *Democracy and Social Ethics,* 222.

33. Skerrett, "Irish of Chicago's Hull-House Neighborhood," 35.

34. Theodore Roosevelt, "The Man with the Muckrake," *New York Tribune,* 15 April 1906.

35. CAC, "What It Has Done in a Third of a Century of Civic Work 1874–1908," in "Miscellaneous Pamphlets" folder, CAC Collection.

36. Merriam, *Chicago,* 14.

37. Flanagan, *Charter Reform in Chicago,* 136.

38. Harrison, *Stormy Years,* 253.

39. Piper, *Report on Police,* 39.

40. Piper, *Report on Police,* 5.

41. Simpson, *Rogues, Rebels,* 65.

42. Lindberg, *To Serve and Collect,* 105–6.

43. Merriam, *Report on Municipal Revenues,* xi.

44. *Eagle,* 27 February 1909, in box 11, Sikes Collection.

45. Maureen A. Flanagan, "Fred A. Busse," in *Mayors,* ed. Green and Holli, 229 n. 13.

46. "'Grey Wolf' Pack Beaten to Finish," *CT,* n.d. but by inference 1909, in box 11, Sikes Collection.

4. Progressive to Prohibitionist: 1910–20

1. McCarthy, "Prelude to Armageddon," 516.

2. C. E. Merriam, "An Analysis of Some Political Personalities I Have Known," Charles E. Merriam Papers, 6:2.

3. Ickes, *Autobiography*, 131.

4. Merriam, *Chicago*, 286–87.

5. Griffin, "Sin-Drenched Revels," 56.

6. Griffin, "Sin-Drenched Revels," 56.

7. Graham Taylor, "Facts Best Undermine Public Evils," *CDN*, 11 September 1926.

8. Graham Taylor to Victor F. Lawson, 31 October 1912, "Outgoing," box 1, Taylor Collection.

9. Rex, *Mayors of Chicago*, 91.

10. Edward R. Kantowicz, "Carter Harrison II," in *Mayors*, ed. Green and Holli, 32.

11. CCC, minutes, 1 February 1905.

12. Werner, *Julius Rosenwald*, 91–92.

13. McCarthy, "Businessmen and Professionals," 177.

14. Morris Markey, "Chicago's Dramatic Approach," in *As Others See Chicago*, ed. Pierce, 506.

15. Simpson, *Rogues, Rebels*, 70.

16. Tarr, *Study in Boss Politics*, 303.

17. Nowlan, *Glory, Darkness, Light*, forthcoming.

18. Bukowski, *Big Bill Thompson*, 43–44.

19. Sawyers, *Chicago Portraits*, 251.

20. Bukowski, *Big Bill Thompson*, 186.

21. "'I Am Weary'—Dr. Sachs' Last Message," *CT*, 3 April 1916.

22. "'I Am Weary,'" *CT*, 3 April 1916.

23. See Armstrong, *Battle for God*, 172–73.

24. Thompson's remark, variously quoted, was that he would hit King George V "on the snoot." Bukowski, *Big Bill Thompson*, 6.

25. Bukowski, *Big Bill Thompson*, 66.

26. CCC, minutes, 12 and 15 January, 1919.

5. "Big Bill" and Bootleggers: 1921–33

1. Bukowski, *Big Bill Thompson*, 3, 218–21; see also Barra, "Most Overrated Gangster." The unsubstantiated stories about Capone's lavish funding of Thompson's 1927 campaign and about Capone's office portrait of the mayor were retold as recently as 2002 in Russo, *Outfit*, 38.

2. Peterson, *Barbarians in Our Midst*, 117.

3. Russo, *Outfit*, 198.

4. Bukowski, *Big Bill Thompson*, 131–32, 242; and R. N. Smith, *Colonel*, 201–10, 240–45.

5. Sikes, "What's the Matter," 287.

6. C. E. Merriam, "An Analysis of Some Political Personalities I Have Known," Charles E. Merriam Papers, 6:12.

7. Lombardo, "Genesis of Organized Crime," 13.

8. The title of Schmidt's fine biography.

9. St. John, *This Was My World,* 185–86. As with many incidents of the Capone saga, the details are disputed. St. John's book does not say that Frank Capone appeared, and whether he did is uncertain. The author has been unable to locate any extant copies of the *Cicero Tribune.*

10. St. John, *This Was My World,* 186.

11. C. Johnson, *Wicked City,* 200.

12. Some sources state that Weiss ordered the fire set after a transaction with the committee, but St. John said only that a minister leading the committee "never revealed how they located a willing arsonist," 187. The origin of the fire is officially unknown.

13. St. John, *This Was My World,* 192–93.

14. St. John, *This Was My World,* 195.

15. "Mr. Chesterton Looks Us Over," in *As Others See Chicago,* ed. Pierce, 501–3.

16. CAC, "Bulletin No. 72," September 29, 1927, 3–4.

17. "Decide Mann Killed Himself While Insane," *CT,* 10 October 1930.

18. Women's Civic Council, "Dishonest Elections," no. 2, 14.

19. Hoover, *Memoirs,* 276–77.

20. Lindberg, *To Serve and Collect,* 197.

21. Editorial, *CT,* 16 February 1929.

22. R. N. Smith, *Colonel,* 277–78; C. Johnson, *Wicked City,* 298.

23. Williams, *Fix-It Boys,* 22.

24. This phenomenon is nearly unexamined. Bukowski glances at it in *Big Bill Thompson,* 28. Concerning Daley, see Merriner, *Mr. Chairman,* 144–45.

25. For McCormick's letter, see Smith, *Colonel,* 421–23; McCormick's mother was quoted, 522 n. 58.

26. Smith, *Colonel,* 296.

27. Smith, *Colonel,* 299.

28. Editorial, *CT,* 9 April 1931.

29. Hoffman, *Scarface Al,* 145.

30. Wendt, *Chicago Tribune,* 527. Various sources identify the six as Robert Isham Randolph, Frank Loesch, Samuel Insull, Julius Rosenwald, Edward E. Gore, and George A. Paddock. However, the membership might have fluctuated in number and persons.

31. Grant, *Fight for a City,* 235–36.

32. At least that was the judgment of Allswang in *House for All Peoples,* 105.

33. Anton Cermak, "Inaugural Addresses of the Mayors of Chicago," MRL, 4.

34. *CT* columnist John Kass retailed this story anew in an article welcoming visitors to the Democratic National Convention in Chicago, 25 August 1996.

35. For Cermak, see Cohen and Taylor, *American Pharaoh,* 51; for Thompson's posthumous cache of $1.84 million, see Bukowski, *Big Bill Thompson,* 254. For a recent argument that Cermak and not FDR was the assassin's target, see Russo, *Outfit,* 93–96.

36. Irv Kupcinet, "1900: A City Full of Newcomers," in *20th Century Chicago,* ed. Drell, 13.

37. Simpson, *Rogues, Rebels,* 95.

38. Williams, *Fix-it Boys,* 22.

39. Williams was an anti-Democratic party polemicist but apparently took pains to be factually accurate. By his account, a second grand jury, after the first was dissolved, declined to reindict Kelly by a single dissenting vote. It was cast by the jury foreman, an officer of a company that had sold supplies to the sanitary district while Kelly was its engineer. See *Fix-it Boys,* 25.

6. Depression and War: 1934–45

1. Studs Terkel, "1929: Crash Brings on Hard Times," in *20th Century Chicago,* ed. Drell, 71.

2. Dennis E. Hoffman, "Watchdog on Crime," in *Wild Kind of Boldness,* ed. Adams, 6.

3. Harold Ickes, *The Secret Diary of Harold L. Ickes III: The Lowering Clouds* (New York: Simon & Schuster, 1954), 94.

4. John Gunther, "How 'Tom' Courtney Fights Crime and Rackets," *CDN,* 7 and 8 November 1934.

5. Merriner, "Political Hits," 22–23.

6. Roger Biles, "Edward J. Kelly," in *Mayors,* ed. Green and Holli, 114.

7. CCCs, "Bulletin," 2 June 1930, 110, CCC Collection.

8. Dan Haar, "1933: Awe-Inspiring Fair," in *20th Century Chicago,* ed. Drell, 79.

9. Royko, *Boss,* 48, 51.

10. Douglas, *In the Fullness,* 93.

11. Ickes, *Autobiography,* 38.

12. Douglas, *In the Fullness,* 94.

13. CCC, minutes, 30 March 1937.

14. CCC, "Report of Elections Committee," in minutes, n.d., 1927.

15. Women's Civic Council, "Dishonest Elections," no. 1, 1–2, 35, CHS.

16. CCC, "Rebuilding Chicago," 1939, Holli collection.

17. CCC, "Your Job," 1938, Holli collection.

18. "Alinsky, 63, Self-Styled Professional Radical, Dies," *CT,* 13 June 1972.

19. *CT,* quoted in CCC, minutes, 9 September 1952.

20. Peterson, *Barbarians in Our Midst,* 225.

21. CCC, "Bulletin," 3 June 1944.

22. Peterson, *Barbarians in Our Midst,* 215.

23. CCC, "Public Works as an Element in Full Employment after the War," 7 June 1944, 12.

24. CCC, "Public Works," 1.

25. CCC, "Public Works," 2, 11–12.

7. Big Nineteen, Big Nine: 1946–59

1. See "The Contrasting Lives of Sidney I. Korshak," *New York Times,* 27 June 1976, and a rebuttal by Fontenay, *Estes Kefauver,* 178. Russo recently developed the allegation against Kefauver in *Outfit,* 258–60, but likewise used blind sources.

2. Joseph S. Nye Jr., Philip D. Zelikow, and David C. King, eds., *Why People Don't Trust Government* (Cambridge: Harvard University Press, 1997).

3. Peterson, *Barbarians in Our Midst,* 260.

4. *CST,* 2 November 1950.

5. "Kennelly Tells Own Story of His Life," *CDN,* 23 January 1947.

6. Arnold Hirsch, "Martin F. Kennelly," in *Mayors,* ed. Green and Holli, 140.

7. "Civic Group Fights to Rid Chicago of Gangs," *CDN,* 12 February 1952.

8. Merriner, *Mr. Chairman,* 128. Such denials of the existence of organized crime, however self-serving, might not be so ludicrous as they appear. Some scholars maintain that organized crime is far less organized, disciplined, and influential than the popular imagination believes. See Morris and Hawkins, *Honest Politician's Guide,* 202–10.

9. CCC, *Bulletin,* 3 March 1952.

10. "10,000 in Religious Rally at Amphitheatre," *CDN,* 28 July 1952.

11. Editorial, *Guardian,* 10 October 1952, in box 9, Robert E. Merriam Papers.

12. Robert Butzler, as told to A. E. Hotchner, "I Spied for the Chicago Crime Committee," n.d., n.p., in box 6, file 8, Robert E. Merriam Papers.

13. "Kennelly Calm about Crime Report," *CDN,* 10 January 1953.

14. "Petition Mayor in Crime Fight," *CDN,* 14 May 1953.

15. Lindberg, *To Serve and Collect,* 285.

16. (Headline illegible on microfilm), *CDN,* 21 January 1953.

17. CCC, minutes, 22 April 1954.

18. Bob Greene column, *CST,* 24 March 1977.

19. Biles, *Richard J. Daley,* 43.

20. *Time,* 15 March 1963, 35.

21. Bradley and Zald, "From Commercial Elite," 167.

22. Merriner, *Mr. Chairman,* 67.

23. "Driveway Permits Taken from Aldermen," *CDN,* 29 April 1956.

24. Thomas F. Roeser, interview by the author, 30 March 2001.

25. "Crime Tie-In Seen in Waiter Unions," *New York Times,* 9 July 1958.

26. Roemer, *Roemer,* 114–15.

27. Roemer, *Roemer,* 115, 118.

28. Merriner, *Mr. Chairman,* 65.

Check Out Receipt

Beverly

Thursday, June 1, 2017
12:05:14 PM

Item: R0401079292
Title: Grafters and Goo
Goos : corruption and
reform in Chicago,
1833-2003
Due: 06/22/2017

Total items: 1

Thank You!

76

also, Cohen and Taylor, *Ameri-
nan,* 83–89.

idberg later expanded on the case
Police and Sheriffs' News website,

k," *CDN,* 29 December 1967.

ense. Statistics regarding 1968 are
wam, 243–72.
463.

December 1986.
518.

Aagic," in *20th Century Chicago,* ed.

l Criminals," *CT,* 7 February 1980.
:uary 1980.
The Culture Club," *Chicago Reader,*
25 April 2003.
6. Frank Sullivan, interview by the author, 17 April 1995.
7. "Mayor Daley Remembered," *CST,* 10 December 1986.
8. Cohen and Taylor, *American Pharaoh,* 526.
9. Michael Sneed column, *CST,* 22 February 2001.
10. "Kusper Assails Tribune on Prize," *CT,* 10 May 1973.
11. Edward R. Vrydolyak, quoted in O'Connor, *Requiem,* 132.
12. "Mayor Daley Remembered," *CST,* 10 December 1986.
13. "Indictments on Rise for Public Officials," *New York Times,* 11 February 1977.
14. Richard Mell, quoted in CCC *Briefings,* May 1988, p. 2, Horist collection.
15. Z. Smith and Zekman, *Mirage,* 241.
16. Merriner, *Mr. Chairman,* 164.
17. Simpson, *Rogues, Rebels,* 188–89.
18. Biles, *Richard J. Daley,* 231.

19. Greeley, *Confessions,* 406.
20. "Cardinal's Last Letter: I Forgive My Enemies," *CT,* 26 April 1982.
21. "Days in Court," *CT,* 13 January 1985.
22. Tuohy and Warden, *Greylord,* 31.
23. Tuohy and Warden, *Greylord,* 257.

10. "Harold!" and More Scandals and Stings: 1983–89

1. Citizens for Epton, "The Case Against Harold Washington," 21 March 1983, MRL.
2. Merriner, *Mr. Chairman,* 190.
3. "McClain Gets 8 Years for Taking Bribe," *CT,* 12 September 1989.
4. Scott R. Lassar, interview by the author, 12 September 1999.
5. "Days in Court," *CT,* 13 January 1985.
6. Tuohy and Warden, *Greylord,* 122.
7. Louis Carbonaro, quoted in "FBI Tactics Attacked at Prostitution Trial," *CT,* 20 July 1988.
8. Anton Valukas, "We Must Take a Stand Against Public Corruption," *CT,* 2 August 1988.
9. "City Aides Indicted in Bribe Plot," *CT,* 11 November 1987.
10. BGA, "Annual Report 1988/1989," 6.
11. "Dunne Fights Back," *CT,* 2 May 1988.
12. *Newsweek,* 16 May 1988, 27.
13. "Council Panel Stalls Funds for Presidential Towers," *CST,* 30 January 1987.
14. "Rostenkowski Bill Saves Pal Millions," *CST,* 20 November 1983.
15. "Rosty Defends Tax Breaks for Towers," *CST,* 23 May 1990.
16. "Too Close for Comfort?" *CT,* 21 August 1994. William Hogan Jr. should not be confused with the Teamsters Local 174 official of the same name.
17. BGA, "Annual Report 1986," 15.

11. Daley and Dissent Redux: 1990–2003

1. Simpson, *Chicago City Council Reform,* 2, 7.
2. "Roti Told He'll Stand Trial Alone," *CT,* 24 December 1992.
3. Ralph W. Conner, interview by the author, 9 August 2001.
4. Merriner, "Stealth Boss," 16.
5. "Grant Gets Prison Term for Failing to Pay Taxes," *CT,* 20 October 1995.
6. Chicago School Finance Authority, Office of the Inspector General, "First Annual Report," 29 December 1994, 27, MRL.
7. "Corporate-Style Board Backs the CEO," *Catalyst,* December 1996, 3.
8. "Mayor Daley's National Press Club Address on Chicago Public Schools," Office of the Mayor, 5 June 1997, 2–3.
9. Merriner, "Running Up the Scores," 62.
10. "Organized Crime Caught in 3-Way Squeeze," *CT,* 11 February 1990.
11. John Kass column, *CT,* 12 February 2000.

12. "Grand Jury Seeks City Contract Files," *CST,* 19 March 2002, and "Daley Mum on Duff Ties, Undecided on Fifth Term," *CST,* 8 August 2002.

13. These and other Daley quotations were compiled in a stinging *CT* editorial of 25 March 2001.

14. For Richard J. Daley, see Merriner, *Mr. Chairman,* 88. For an analysis of Richard M. Daley's campaign contributions, see Simpson, *Rogues, Rebels,* 247–49.

Conclusion

1. Klitgaard, MacLean-Abaroa, and Parris, *Corrupt Cities,* 4.

2. Samuel P. Huntington, "Modernization and Corruption," in *Political Corruption: A Handbook,* ed. Heidenheimer, Johnston, and Levine, 381.

3. Klitgaard, MacLean-Abaroa, and Parris, *Corrupt Cities,* 151 n. 3.

4. James Q. Wilson, "The United States," in *Political Corruption,* ed. Heidenheimer, Johnston, and Levine, 300.

5. Friedrich, *Pathology of Politics,* 230.

6. Simpson, *Rogues, Rebels,* 322.

Chicago Political Glossary

blind pig (archaic). An unlicensed saloon, as distinct from **speakeasy,** an illegal saloon during Prohibition (1920–33).

boodle. Originally, the private use of public funds, a corrupt legislative fund, or the practice of selling one's legislative vote; now a generic term for graft, bribery, gratuities, or just ordinary pork-barrel benefits.

bummers (archaic). Men hired to disrupt, by brawling if necessary, a gathering of the political opposition.

Camp Beverly. An office where Chicago public schools employees accused of misconduct perform menial administrative tasks while awaiting resolution of the charges; named for the supervisor.

Camp Muni. A room in the Richard J. Daley Center where municipal and Cook County judges accused of misconduct await resolution of the charges while performing only menial judicial tasks.

captain's man (archaic). A police officer selected by his captain to collect the police district's illegal payoffs from businesses and vice operations.

chain voting. A vote-fraud practice by which a precinct captain outside the polling place fills out a ballot and gives it to a voter, who drops it in the ballot box and then is given a fresh ballot. Upon exiting the polling place, the voter hands the new ballot to the precinct captain, who marks it in advance, and so on.

Chinaman. A political sponsor or patron.

clout. Originally, a noun meaning improper political influence or the bearer of it or a verb meaning to exercise such influence; now a national generic synonym for power.

collection (archaic). The practice of taking bribes, kickbacks, gratuities, or boodle.

fetcher bill. A legislative measure contrary to corporate interests introduced merely to solicit, or "fetch," payoffs or at least campaign contributions to kill it.

floaters. Transients rounded up on election day and transported from precinct to precinct to cast multiple ballots, as distinct from **repeaters,** voters who cast multiple ballots under various names in the same precinct.

four-legged voter (archaic). A vote-fraud practice in which an election judge (a machine worker at the polling place) accompanied a voter into the polling booth, allegedly for assistance, which is legal, but actually to ensure that the correct machine votes are cast.

ghosts. See **payroller.**

goo goos. Derisive term for reformers, short for "good government." Attributed to Charles A. Dana, editor of the *New York Sun* in the late nineteenth century. *Goo goo* originally might have been applied to members of the Good Government Association of Boston, energized by Harvard reformers in suburban Cambridge.

gray wolves. Crooked and powerful aldermen. Coined in 1895 by reform alderman William Kent and in use at least into the 1950s. The term also has been attributed to Chicago reformer Walter L. Fisher, muckraker Lincoln Steffens, and newspaper writers.

handbook (archaic). A bookie carrying racing forms who took illegal bets on the street; later, a room, usually behind a saloon or poolroom, for illegal off-track betting.

juice. A modern term for **Chinaman, clout,** or **rabbi** (political sponsor or patron).

kink. An unethical politician or judge, especially one with a contrary reputation.

kinky. Corrupt.

lakefront liberals. Reformers, mostly independent Democrats, residing in the Gold Coast, Near North, or Lincoln Park on the North Side or in Hyde Park on the South Side. Some strays reside on the Far North Side or in landlocked Chatham in the African American Sixth Ward of the South Side. A nearly extinct species.

man on five. The mayor, from the fifth-floor suite of his city hall offices; mainly an epithet for Mayor Richard J. Daley (1955–76).

outfit, the. The Chicago branch of organized crime; dating to the 1930s but of unknown lineage.

palm cards. Printed cards listing the machine's endorsed candidates, handed to voters on or just before election day.

panel house (archaic). Rooms for prostitution containing only a bed and chair; the pocket of the customer's pants placed over the chair was picked by an outstretched arm from a hidden closet. The pickpocket was called a **dip** and the closet a **dipping room.**

patronage. The awarding of public jobs to politically deserving people.

payroller. Short for "ghost payroller," a holder of a patronage job who does little or no governmental work but is expected to perform political tasks such as helping to turn out machine voters.

rabbi. Like **Chinaman,** a political sponsor or patron.

reformer. The opposite of **regular;** anyone who opposes the prevailing political system on moral, political, or religious grounds.

regular. A politician or voter who always supports his party's organization. **Reform** and **regular** formerly were spoken without a preceding article, as "I am **regular**" or "I am **reform.**"

river wards. Inner-city, white-ethnic wards along the Chicago River notorious for vote fraud; legendarily, nonmachine ballot boxes were tossed into the river. Now an expression of "local color" for general political mischief.

round-tabling. The practice of falsifying a candidate's ballot-access petitions by passing them around a table where **regulars** forge voters' signatures in turn, using different pens but sometimes not even bothering with that expedient.

short pencil (archaic). A pencil secretly used by election judges to deface and thus invalidate nonmachine ballots. Adepts employed a piece of pencil lead secured under the thumbnail with sealing wax. Others palmed a pencil stub. The term also denoted a pencil given to nonmachine voters that was either too stubby to hold or attached to a string so short that the entire paper ballot could not be marked, encouraging a simple straight-ticket vote.

temps. Government patronage workers nominally hired for temporary jobs to evade civil service regulations; their temporary status is renewed indefinitely.

trimming. Suppression of votes for a candidate who is nominally endorsed by his party organization but actually is intended for defeat. Techniques include failing to stimulate turnout in the candidate's strongest precincts, omitting the candidate's name from **palm cards** while claiming that the cards did not come back from the printer in time, and betraying promises of personal and financial support. Also known as **knifing.**

vised. Ousted from a machine office or job.

wine room (archaic). Euphemism for a private room in a hotel or tavern for drinks and prostitution.

Selected Bibliography

Manuscript Collections

Better Government Association of Chicago. Annual reports, 1968–98.
Citizens' Association of Chicago. Collection. Chicago Historical Society.
City Club of Chicago. Collection. Chicago Historical Society.
City Club of Chicago. Personal collection of Melvin G. Holli.
City Club of Chicago. Personal collection of Larry P. Horist.
Merriam, Charles E. Papers. Chicago Historical Society.
Merriam, Robert E. Papers. Chicago Historical Society.
Municipal Reference Library. Harold Washington Library Center. Chicago.
Municipal Voters' League. Papers. Chicago Historical Society.
Roberts, Sidney I. Papers. Chicago Historical Society.
Sikes, Madeleine Wallin. Collection. Chicago Historical Society.
Taylor, Graham. Papers. Newberry Library. Chicago.

Books

Adams, Rosemary K., ed. *A Wild Kind of Boldness: The Chicago Historical Reader.* Grand Rapids, MI: William B. Eerdmans, 1998.
Addams, Jane. *Democracy and Social Ethics.* New York: Macmillan, 1907.
Allswang, John M. *A House for All Peoples: Ethnic Politics in Chicago 1890–1936.* Lexington: University Press of Kentucky, 1971.
Andreas, A. T. *History of Cook County, Illinois.* Chicago: A. T. Andreas, 1884.
Anechiarico, Frank, and James B. Jacobs. *The Pursuit of Absolute Integrity: How Corruption Control Makes Government Ineffective.* Chicago: University of Chicago Press, 1996.
Armstrong, Karen. *The Battle for God.* New York: Alfred A. Knopf, 2000.
Asbury, Herbert. *Gem of the Prairie: An Informal History of the Chicago Underworld.* 1940. Reprint, De Kalb: Northern Illinois University Press, 1986.
Banfield, Edward C. *The Unheavenly City Revisited.* Boston: Little, Brown, 1974.
Biles, Roger. *Big City Boss in Depression and War: Mayor Edward J. Kelly of Chicago.* De Kalb: Northern Illinois University Press, 1984.
———. *Richard J. Daley: Politics, Race, and the Governing of Chicago.* De Kalb: Northern Illinois University Press, 1995.
Bukowski, Douglas. *Big Bill Thompson, Chicago, and the Politics of Image.* Urbana: University of Illinois Press, 1998.
Cohen, Adam, and Elizabeth Taylor. *American Pharaoh: Mayor Richard J. Daley.* Boston: Little, Brown, 2000.

Dedmon, Emmett. *Fabulous Chicago: A Great City's History and People*. New York: Atheneum, 1981.

Douglas, Paul H. *In the Fullness of Time: The Memoirs of Paul H. Douglas*. New York: Harcourt, 1972.

Drell, Adrienne, ed. *20th Century Chicago: 100 Years, 100 Voices*. Champaign, IL: Sports Publishing, 2000.

Flanagan, Maureen A. *Charter Reform in Chicago*. Carbondale: Southern Illinois University Press, 1987.

Fontenay, Charles L. *Estes Kefauver: A Biography*. Knoxville: University of Tennessee Press, 1980.

Fremon, David K. *Chicago Politics Ward by Ward*. Bloomington: Indiana University Press, 1988.

Friedrich, Carl J. *The Pathology of Politics: Violence, Betrayal, Corruption, Secrecy, and Propaganda*. New York: Harper and Row, 1972.

Gardiner, John A., and Theodore R. Lyman. *Decisions for Sale: Corruption and Reform in Land-Use and Building Regulation*. New York: Praeger Publishers, 1978.

Garment, Suzanne. *Scandal: The Culture of Mistrust in American Politics*. New York: Times Books, 1991.

Ginger, Ray. *Altgeld's America: The Lincoln Ideal Versus Changing Realities*. New York: Funk and Wagnalls, 1958.

Grant, Bruce. *Fight for a City: The Story of the Union League Club of Chicago and Its Times, 1880–1955*. Chicago: Rand McNally, 1955.

Greeley, Andrew M. *Confessions of a Parish Priest: An Autobiography*. New York: Simon and Schuster, 1986.

Green, Paul M., and Melvin G. Holli, eds. *The Mayors: The Chicago Political Tradition*. Rev. ed. Carbondale: Southern Illinois University Press, 1995.

Grimshaw, William J. *Bitter Fruit: Black Politics and the Chicago Machine, 1931–1991*. Chicago: University of Chicago Press, 1992.

Harrison, Carter H. *Stormy Years: The Autobiography of Carter H. Harrison, Five Times Mayor of Chicago*. New York: Bobbs-Merrill, 1935.

Heidenheimer, Arnold J., Michael Johnston, and Victor T. Levine, eds. *Political Corruption: A Handbook*. New Brunswick, NJ: Transaction Publishers, 1989.

Hess, G. Alfred, Jr. *School Restructuring, Chicago Style*. Newbury Park, CA: Corwin Press, 1991.

Hirsch, Susan E., and Robert I. Goler. *A City Comes of Age: Chicago in the 1890s*. Chicago: Chicago Historical Society, 1990.

Hoffman, Dennis E. *Scarface Al and the Crime Crusaders: Chicago's Private War Against Capone*. Carbondale: Southern Illinois University Press, 1993.

Holli, Melvin G., and Paul M. Green, eds. *Bashing Chicago Traditions: Harold Washington's Last Campaign*. Grand Rapids, MI: William B. Eerdmans, 1989.

———. *The Making of a Mayor: Chicago, 1983*. Grand Rapids, MI: William B. Eerdmans, 1984.

Holli, Melvin G., and Peter d'A. Jones. *Ethnic Chicago: A Multi-Cultural Portrait.* 4th ed. Grand Rapids, MI: William B. Eerdmans, 1995.

Hoover, Herbert. *The Memoirs of Herbert Hoover.* Vol. 1. *The Cabinet and the Presidency, 1920–1933.* New York: Macmillan, 1952.

Howard, Robert B. *Mostly Good and Competent Men: Illinois Governors, 1818–1988.* Rev. ed. Springfield: *Illinois Issues,* Sangamon State University, and Illinois Historical Society, 1988.

Ickes, Harold. *The Autobiography of a Curmudgeon.* 1943. Reprint, Westport, CT: Greenwood Press, 1985.

Johnson, Curt, with R. Craig Sautter. *Wicked City: Chicago from Kenna to Capone.* Highland Park, IL: December Press, 1994.

Johnson, Paul. *A History of the American People.* New York: HarperCollins Publishers, 1997.

Kallina, Edmund F., Jr. *Courthouse over White House: Chicago and the Presidential Election of 1960.* Orlando: University of Central Florida Press, 1988.

Kleppner, Paul. *Chicago Divided: The Making of a Black Mayor.* De Kalb: Northern Illinois University Press, 1985.

———. *The Cross of Culture: A Social Analysis of Midwestern Politics, 1850–1900.* 2d ed. New York: Free Press, 1970.

Klitgaard, Robert, Ronald MacLean-Abaroa, and H. Lindsay Parris. *Corrupt Cities: A Practical Guide to Cure and Prevention.* Oakland, CA: ICS Press, 2000.

Kohn, Aaron. *The Kohn Report: Crime and Politics in Chicago.* Chicago: Independent Voters of Illinois, 1953.

Lindberg, Richard C. *Chicago by Gaslight: A History of Chicago's Netherworld, 1880–1920.* Chicago: Academy Chicago Publishers, 1996.

———. *Return to the Scene of the Crime: A Guide to Infamous Places in Chicago.* Nashville: Cumberland House, 1999.

———. *To Serve and Collect: Chicago Politics and Police Corruption from the Lager Beer Riot to the Summerdale Scandal.* 1991. Reprint, Carbondale: Southern Illinois University Press, 1998.

Merriam, Charles E. *Chicago: A More Intimate View of Urban Politics.* New York: Macmillan, 1929.

———. *Report on the Municipal Revenues of Chicago.* Chicago: City Club of Chicago, 1906.

Merriner, James L. *The City Club of Chicago: A Centennial History.* Carbondale: Southern Illinois University Press, forthcoming.

———. *Mr. Chairman: Power in Dan Rostenkowski's America.* Carbondale: Southern Illinois University Press, 1999.

Miller, Donald L. *City of the Century: The Epic of Chicago and the Making of America.* New York: Simon and Schuster, 1996.

Moore, William Howard. *The Kefauver Committee and the Politics of Crime, 1950–1952.* Columbia: University of Missouri Press, 1974.

Morris, Norval, and Gordon Hawkins. *The Honest Politician's Guide to Crime Control.* Chicago: University of Chicago Press, 1970.

Nowlan, James D. *Glory, Darkness, Light: The Union League Club of Chicago.* Evanston, IL: Northwestern University Press, forthcoming.

O'Connor, Len. *Requiem: The Decline and Demise of Mayor Daley and His Era.* Chicago: Contemporary Books, 1977.

Peterson, Virgil W. *Barbarians in Our Midst: A History of Chicago Crime and Politics.* Boston: Little, Brown, 1952.

Pierce, Bessie Louise, ed. *As Others See Chicago: Impressions of Visitors, 1673–1933.* Chicago: University of Chicago Press, 1933.

———. *A History of Chicago.* 3 vols. New York: Alfred A. Knopf, 1937–57.

Piper, Alexander R. *Report on Police Discipline and Administration.* Chicago: City Club of Chicago, 1904.

Rakove, Milton L. *Don't Make No Waves, Don't Back No Losers: An Insider's Analysis of the Daley Machine.* Bloomington: Indiana University Press, 1975.

———. *We Don't Want Nobody Nobody Sent: An Oral History of the Daley Years.* Bloomington: Indiana University Press, 1979.

Rex, Frederick. *The Mayors of Chicago from March 4, 1837, to April 13, 1933.* Chicago: Municipal Reference Library, 1934.

Roemer, William F. *Roemer: How the F.B.I. Cracked the Chicago Mob.* New York: Donald I. Fine, 1989.

Rose-Ackerman, Susan. *Corruption and Government: Causes, Consequences, and Reform.* New York: Cambridge University Press, 1999.

Royko, Mike. *Boss: Richard J. Daley of Chicago.* New York: Signet, 1971.

Russo, Gus. *The Outfit: The Role of Chicago's Underworld in the Shaping of Modern America.* New York: Bloomsbury, 2002.

Sautter, R. Craig, and Edward M. Burke. *Inside the Wigwam: Chicago Presidential Conventions, 1860–1996.* Chicago, Loyola University Press, 1996.

Sawyers, June Skinner. *Chicago Portraits: Biographies of 250 Famous Chicagoans.* Chicago: Loyola University Press, 1991.

Simpson, Dick. *Chicago City Council Reform.* Chicago: City Club of Chicago, 1989.

———. *Rogues, Rebels, and Rubber Stamps: The Politics of the Chicago City Council from 1863 to the Present.* Boulder, CO: Westview Press, 2001.

Smith, Richard Norton. *The Colonel: The Life and Legend of Robert R. McCormick.* Boston: Houghton Mifflin, 1997.

Smith, Zay, and Pamela Zekman. *The Mirage: A Story of Chicago Corruption.* New York: Random House, 1979.

Stead, William T. *If Christ Came to Chicago!* 1894. Reprint, New York: Living Books, 1964.

Steffens, Lincoln. *The Autobiography of Lincoln Steffens.* New York: Harcourt, Brace, 1931.

St. John, Robert. *This Was My World.* Garden City, NY: Doubleday, 1953.

Sullivan, Frank. *Legend: The Only Inside Story about Mayor Richard J. Daley.* Chicago: Bonus Books, 1989.

Sullivan, William L., ed. and comp. *Dunne: Judge, Mayor, Governor.* Chicago: Windemere Press, 1916.

Tarr, Joel Arthur. *A Study of Boss Politics: William Lorimer of Chicago.* Chicago: University of Illinois Press, 1971.

Teaford, Jon C. *The Unheralded Triumph: City Government in America, 1870–1900.* Baltimore: Johns Hopkins University Press, 1984.

Touhy, Roger, with Ray Brennan. *The Stolen Years.* Cleveland: Pennington Press, 1959.

Tuohy, James, and Rob Warden. *Greylord: Justice, Chicago Style.* New York: G. P. Putnam's Sons, 1989.

Wendt, Lloyd. *Chicago Tribune: The Rise of a Great American Newspaper.* Chicago: Rand McNally, 1979.

Werner, M. R. *Julius Rosenwald: The Life of a Practical Humanitarian.* New York: Harper and Brothers, 1939.

Wilkins, Roy, and Ramsey Clark. *Search and Destroy: A Report by the Commission of Inquiry into the Black Panthers and the Police.* New York: Metropolitan Applied Research Center, 1973.

Williams, Elmer Lynn. *The Fix-it Boys: The Inside Story of the New Deal and the Kelly-Nash Machine.* Chicago: Elmer Lynn Williams, 1940.

Articles and Manuscripts

Adler, Jeffrey S. "'Chicago, the Worst City on Earth.'" Paper presented to the Chicago Historical Society Urban History Seminar, 15 November 2001.

Balestier, Joseph N. "The Annals of Chicago: A Lecture Delivered Before the Chicago Lyceum, January 21, 1840." In *Fergus Historical Series.* No. 1. Chicago: Fergus Printing, 1876.

Barra, Allen. "Most Overrated Gangster." *American Heritage,* May-June 1999.

Baylen, Joseph O. "A Victorian's 'Crusade' in Chicago, 1893–1894." *Journal of American History* 51, December 1964.

Bradley, Donald S., and Mayer N. Zald. "From Commercial Elite to Political Administrator: The Recruitment of the Mayors of Chicago." *American Journal of Sociology* 71, September 1965.

Buenker, John D. "Dynamics of Chicago Ethnic Politics, 1900–1930." *Journal of the Illinois State Historical Society* 67, April 1974.

Bukowski, Douglas. "Judge Edmund J. Jarecki: A Rather Regular Independent." *Chicago History* 84, Winter 1979–80.

Burrows, Edwin G. "Corruption in Government." In *Encyclopedia of American Political History,* edited by Jack P. Greene. New York: Charles Scribner's Sons, 1984.

Bushnell, George D. "Buzz Saw Reformer." *Chicago History* 18, Fall 1989.

———. "Chicago's Leading Men's Clubs." *Chicago History* 11, Summer 1982.

Chandler, Christopher. "'Shoot to Kill . . . Shoot to Maim.'" *Chicago Reader,* 5 April 2002.

Clayton, John. "The Scourge of Sinners: Arthur Burrage Farwell." *Chicago History* 3, Fall 1974.

Cleaver, Charles. "Early-Chicago Reminiscences." In *Fergus Historical Series.* No. 19. Chicago: Fergus Printing, 1882.

Clements, Bill. "Uncovering the Cardinal." *Chicago,* December 2002.

Conroy, John. "Town Without Pity: Torture in Chicago's Area 2." *Chicago Reader,* 12 January 1996.

Davis, Allen F. "Jane Addams vs. the Ward Boss." *Journal of the Illinois State Historical Society* 53, Autumn 1960.

Downard, William L. "William Butler Ogden and the Growth of Chicago." *Journal of the Illinois State Historical Society* 75, Spring 1982.

Duis, Perry R., and Glen M. Holt. "The Real Legacy of 'Poor Martin' Kennelly." *Chicago,* July 1978.

Gould, Alan B. "Walter L. Fisher: Profile of an Urban Reformer, 1880–1910." *Mid-America* 57, July 1975.

Green, Paul M. "Making the City Work: Machine Politics and Mayoral Reform." *Chicago History* 14, Fall 1985.

Greene, Lee S., ed. "City Bosses and Political Machines." *Annals of the American Academy of Political and Social Sciences* 353, May 1964.

Griffin, Richard. "Big Jim: Gambler Boss iv th' Yards." *Chicago History* 5, Winter 1976–77.

———. "Sin-Drenched Revels at the Infamous First Ward Ball." *Smithsonian,* November 1976.

Haller, Mark H. "Organized Crime in Urban Society: Chicago in the Twentieth Century." *Journal of Social History* 5, Winter 1971–72.

Holli, Melvin G. "Varieties of Urban Reform." In *American Urban History,* edited by Alexander B. Callow Jr. 3rd ed. New York: Oxford University Press, 1982.

Joravsky, Ben, and Richard C. Lindberg. "Backstabbers." *Chicago Reader,* 13 April 2001.

Keyes, Jonathan A. "The Forgotten Fire." *Chicago History* 26, Fall 1997.

Lindberg, Richard C. "The Evolution of an Evil Business." *Chicago History* 22, July 1993.

———, "No More Greylords?" *Illinois Police and Sheriff's News,* Summer 1994.

Locke, Herbert G. "Ethics in American Government: A Look Backward." *Annals of the American Academy of Political and Social Sciences* January 1995.

Lombardo, Robert M. "The Genesis of Organized Crime in Chicago." *Illinois Police and Sheriff's News,* 19 July 2001.

Lotchkin, Roger W. "Machine Politics." In *Encyclopedia of American Political History,* edited by Jack R. Greene. New York: Charles Scribner's Sons, 1984.

Marks, Donald David. "Polishing the Gem of the Prairie: The Evolution of Civic

Reform Consciousness in Chicago, 1874–1900." PhD diss., University of Wisconsin at Madison, 1974.

McCarthy, Michael P. "Businessmen and Professionals in Municipal Reform: The Chicago Experience, 1887–1920." PhD diss., Northwestern University, 1970.

———. "Prelude to Armageddon: Charles E. Merriam and the Chicago Mayoral Election of 1911." *Journal of the Illinois State Historical Society* 67, 1974.

McKitrick, Eric L. "The Study of Corruption." *Political Science Quarterly* 72, December 1957.

Merriner, James L. "Fathers, Sons, and Unholy Ghosts." *Illinois Issues,* July 1996.

———. "Political Hits." *Illinois Issues,* September 2000.

———. "Richie Romances the 'Burbs." *North Shore,* January 1999.

———. "Running Up the Scores." *Chicago,* December 2001.

———. "The Stealth Boss." *Illinois Issues,* March 1998.

Miller, Joan S. "The Politics of Municipal Reform in Chicago During the Progressive Era: The Municipal Voters' League as a Test Case, 1896–1920." Master's thesis, Roosevelt University, 1980.

Nelli, Humbert S. "John Powers and the Italians: Politics in a Chicago Ward, 1896–1921." *Journal of American History* 57, June 1970.

Nelson, Bruce C. "Revival and Upheaval: Religion, Irreligion, and Chicago's Working Class in 1886." *Journal of Social History* 25, 1991.

O'Rourke, John J. "The Structure of Organized Crime in Chicago." *Illinois Police and Sheriff's News,* 2000.

Porter, Jeremiah. "The Earliest Religious History of Chicago." In *Fergus Historical Series.* No. 13. Chicago: Fergus Printing, 1881.

Renner, R. W. "In a Ferment: Chicago, the Know-Nothings, and the Riot for Lager Beer." *Chicago History* 5, Fall 1976.

Roberts, Sidney I. "Businessmen in Revolt: Chicago, 1874–1900." PhD diss., Northwestern University, 1960.

———. "The Municipal Voters' League and Chicago's Boodlers." *Journal of the Illinois State Historical Society* 53, Summer 1960.

Schottenhamel, George. "How Big Bill Thompson Won Control of Chicago." *Journal of the Illinois State Historical Society* 45, Spring 1952.

Sikes, George C. "What's the Matter with Chicago?" *Christian Century,* 23 March 1922.

Skerrett, Ellen. "The Irish of Chicago's Hull-House Neighborhood." *Chicago History* 30, Summer 2001.

Steffens, Lincoln. "Chicago: Half Free and Fighting On." *McClure's,* 21 October 1903.

Sutherland, Douglas. *50 Years on the Civic Front 1893–1943: A Report on the Achievements of the Civic Federation of Chicago.* Chicago: Civic Federation, 1943.

Tarr, Joel A. "William Kent to Lincoln Steffens: Origins of Progressive Reform in Chicago." *Mid-America* 47, January 1965.

Wade, Richard C. "The Enduring Chicago Machine." *Chicago History* 15, Spring 1986.

Women's Civic Council of the Chicago Area. "Dishonest Elections and Why We Have Them, Edited from the Records of the County Court." No. 1. June 1934. No. 2. March 1938.

Index

Democratic National Convention of 1968, 28, 168, 182–86, 200; and Democratic national conventions of 1972 and 1976, 202; health of, 121, 186, 202; and investigations of his political machine, 191–200; as mayor, first term (1955–59), 169–75; as mayor, second and third terms (1959–67), 173–77, 187; as mayor, fourth and fifth terms (1967–76), 181–202; and mayoral election of 1955, 167–69; and mayoral election of 1963, 178–79; and mayoral election of 1971, 200; and mayoral election of 1975, 200, 229, 249; and organized crime, 161, 174–75, 284; and police, 170–71, 173–75, 181, 182–84, 186–87, 199–200, 215; and political scandals, 256–61; and race, 165, 179–81, 182–84, 186–87; and reform, 2, 140, 169–70, 188–89, 192–93, 241

Daley, Richard M. (son of Richard J.): and Chicago Public Schools, 248–52; and Richard J. Daley, 198, 239, 248–49, 253, 258; as mayor, 5, 173, 237, 241; mayoral campaigns of, 219, 229, 239, 241–43, 247; and organized crime, 243, 253–54, 258–59; and police, 255–56; and political scandals, 256–61; and reform, 243, 247–48, 254–55

Dana, Charles A., 57, 284
D'Arco, John, 175, 245
D'Arco, John A., Jr., 245
Darrow, Clarence J., 83, 103, 104, 108
Dawes, Charles G., 119
Dawson, William L., 159–60, 169, 179, 219
Democratic National Convention: of 1896, 74; of 1932, 128; of 1944, 152; of 1956, 154; of 1968, 168, 182, 184–86, 190; of 1972 and 1976, 202; of 1996, 272n24

Despres, Leon, 3, 6, 181–82, 224
Dever, William, 1, 110–12
Dobry, Alan M., 4
Douglas, Paul H., 3, 137–38, 150
Duff, John, Jr., 258–59
Duff, John, III, 258–59
Dunne, Edward F., 1, 83, 85–86, 104, 110, 216
Dunne, George W., 229–31
Dvorak, James E., 253–54
Dyer, Thomas, 25

Elrod, Richard J., 253
El Rukns, 235–36
Epton, Bernard, 220–21
Evans, Timothy C., 238

Farwell, Arthur Burrage, 57–58, 60, 91–92
Federal Bureau of Investigation, 178, 199, 214–15, 225, 227, 247
Field, Marshall: as businessman, 31, 40, 62, 67, 95, 158, 207, 273n1; and labor, 46, 48, 65; and reform, 37, 64, 71, 146, 158
fires: Great Chicago Fire of 1871, 33–35, 41, 61–62, 68, 96, 119; of 1874, 36–39; Iroquois Theater, 91
First Ward: and organized crime, 168, 169, 243–45, 254; and vice, 41, 59, 67, 91–92
Fisher, Walter L., 73, 75–76, 83, 86, 90, 284
Fort Dearborn, 11, 16
Fort Sheridan, 47, 65
Frost, Wilson, 208, 220, 221

Gage, Lyman J., 34, 64, 67
Gambat, Operation, 243–45, 254
gambling: campaigns against, 12, 14, 56, 58, 82, 147, 159; operations of, 43–44, 84–85, 138, 191–94. *See also* vice raids

James L. Merriner is the author of *Mr. Chairman: Power in Dan Rostenkowski's America* (1999) and *The City Club of Chicago: A Centennial History, 1903–2003* (2003), and is coauthor of *Against Long Odds: Citizens Who Challenge Congressional Incumbents* (1999). He covered local, state, and national politics for thirty years as the political editor of the *Chicago Sun-Times* and the *Atlanta Constitution*. Merriner has served as the James Thurber Writer in Residence at Ohio State University and now is an independent writer and editor and a university instructor.